Always Superb

Recipes for Every Occasion

ALWAYS SUPERB

RECIPES FOR EVERY OCCASION

A collaborative cookbook from the Junior Leagues of Minneapolis and Saint Paul

ALWAYS SUPERB

RECIPES FOR EVERY OCCASION

© Copyright 2003 by
The Junior Leagues of
Minneapolis and Saint Paul, Minnesota
Photographs copyright
© by John Reed Forsman Photography

ISBN: 0-9729882-0-3
Library of Congress Number: 2003104334

Edited, Produced and Manufactured by
Favorite Recipes® Press

P.O. Box 305142
Nashville, Tennessee 37230
800-358-0560

FRP Art Director: Steve Newman
Project Manager: Susan Larson

Manufactured in the United States of America
First Printing: 2003
25,000 copies

Inquiries about this book or orders for
additional copies should be directed to;
JLM & JLSP
6250 Wayzata Blvd.
Minneapolis, Minnesota 55416
763-545-9423

Cover: Many thanks to T.R. Christian for supplying the beautiful props featured in the outdoor ice shots.

Acknowledgments

The Junior Leagues of Minneapolis and Saint Paul wish to thank the following people for devoting their time and talents to the making of this book:

John Forsman, Photographer.

John Reed Forsman is the man and artist behind the photography featured in *Always Superb.* Words cannot describe the aesthetic appeal of the culinary masterpieces in this book; nor can they describe our gratitude to John for showcasing our favorite foods and settings, both table and seasonal. Fortunately we had John's discerning eye and photo lens to capture the images that make this book as appropriate for the coffee table as it is for the kitchen. John's award-winning photography has appeared in *Vogue Entertaining, Departures, Food and Wine,* and *Better Homes and Gardens.* He lives in Minnesota with his wife Diana and their three children.

Megan A. Taylor, Art Director and Designer.

Megan Taylor is founder of MegPie Design Co., a graphic design studio in Minneapolis. A cold-weather girl by birth, Megan is a hot talent in the Twin Cities. Her work has won several AIGA (American Institute of Graphic Arts) awards and has also been featured in *Print* and *How* magazines. Her sophisticated yet eminently approachable design style is the perfect complement to this book, as is her own entertaining style, which is *always superb.*

Debora O'Donnell, Writer and Editor.

Debora O'Donnell is a fashion and events writer for Marshall Field's in Minneapolis. Her work appears in direct mail books, newspaper, radio, and television. Debora has worked on many designer fashion campaigns and nationally publicized events like Glamorama, a benefit for Children's Cancer Research Fund, and though she may not know how to cook, she certainly knows what to wear.

Jennifer Dickie, Photo Stylist.

Jennifer came to the Twin Cities by way of New York, where she was contributing photo stylist for *Food and Wine* magazine and *O, Oprah's* magazine. She has collaborated with *Always Superb* photographer John Forsman on several projects, as is evidenced by the impeccably styled photos that reveal both her talent and her good taste.

Norman Stewart, Food Stylist.

Norman Stewart is on everyone's A-list. Trained in the French Culinary School and famed for his fabulous food styling, Norman has worked with everyone from A to Z, from Andre Agassi and Jennifer Aniston to Billy Zane and Renee Zellweger, and many names in between, including Muhammad Ali, Sir Elton John, Nastassja Kinski, Spike Lee, Sela Ward, Vanessa Williams, Whoopi Goldberg, Steven Tyler, Kate Moss, Mike Meyers, Jimmy Smits, and just about everyone else you've seen in a Got Milk? campaign. He has collaborated with photographers Annie Leibovitz, David LaChappelle, and John Reed Forsman, just to name a few; and his beautiful work has been showcased in the pages of *Food and Wine, Vogue, Australian Vogue, Bon Appétit, People, Shape, Vanity Fair,* and many others. In fact, you can't open a magazine, turn on the television, or even drive down a street without seeing Norman Stewart's art at work.

Junior League Cookbook Committee

Anna Anderson, Dawn Bagaas, Mary Bartlett, Katy Boo-Holmes, Patty Boo-Pryor, Sue Brainer, Dana Bruce, Tory Bunce, Peggy Cummings, Diana Danielson, Polly Dean, Nikki Dobbs, Jayne Dow, Carlon Doyle, Jill Droubie, Janet Eaton, Roxanne Eggen, Amy Fletcher, Sue Ellen Gebert, Christine Gerbig-Lema, Fran Glover, Kristin Morrison Goetze, Claire Harvey, Rachelle Heinen, Laura Hewitt, Jane Hopkins, Samantha Hubbard, Amy Johnson, Karin Johnson, Karen Judge, Mimi Keating, Kelly Kilen, Kathryn Koessel, Genevera Koonce, Shelly Lester, Joan Manolis, Rhonda Miller, Laura Mueller, Joan Musumeci, Sarah Nanzig, Nicole Neighbors, Kris Newcomer, Amy Pearce, Kris Prochniak, Marcia Rehnberg, Terry Reine, Jennifer Risdall, Tina Scheid, Kaija Shaffer, Sandy Shuster, Karen Snedeker, Jennifer Swenson, Megan Taylor, Susan Waldoch, Sue Walker, Jan Witort, Lyn Wojtowicz

MISSION STATEMENT

The Junior Leagues of Minneapolis and Saint Paul are organizations of women committed to promoting voluntarism, developing the potential of women, and improving communities through effective action and leadership of trained volunteers. Its purpose is exclusively educational and charitable.

OUTREACH STATEMENT

The Junior Leagues of Minneapolis and Saint Paul reach out to women of all races, religions, and national origins who demonstrate an interest and commitment to voluntarism.

Dear Friends:

The Junior League of Minneapolis (JLM) has been a vital force in the community for nearly eighty years. Founded in 1923 by a small group of women, the JLM is true to its founders' vision as an organization of women, sharing a common philosophy of community service, who dedicate their resources and efforts to solving some of the immediate needs of their community. This spirit of social concern and community service prevails today; while the issues are different and our society is much changed, the commitment and dedication of the women who volunteer in the JLM have not wavered.

The Junior League of Minneapolis created its first cookbook in 1987, entitled *Celebrated Seasons*. This cookbook has become a well-worn copy in our cookbook collections. We not only showcase these recipes on special occasions for friends and neighbors but also use the cookbook to make everyday meals for our families. We are sure that you will discover the menus and recipes in our new cookbook, *Always Superb*, to be an equally timeless and welcome addition to your cooking repertoire. The wide range of recipes are suitable for an array of occasions and address everyone's desire for convenience combined with a love of food and entertaining.

We are excited to introduce *Always Superb*, a cookbook created by the Junior Leagues of Minneapolis and Saint Paul. The partnership of the two Leagues of the Twin Cities continues the Junior League tradition of gathering our favorite recipes to share with family and friends. But most of all it celebrates the spirit of sharing and collaboration that are the very foundation of our Leagues.

Thank you for supporting the Junior League of Minneapolis. The proceeds from this cookbook will support the projects and services of both Junior Leagues of the Twin Cities. We wish you many warm memories centered around good food and great friends.

Sincerely,

Kim Hunnewell
JLM President 2003-2004

Lisa Warren
JLM President 2002-2003

Always Superb: Recipes for Every Occasion

Dear Friends:

The Junior League of Saint Paul (JLSP) is known for its commitment to bettering the lives of those in our communities. We train volunteers, develop women as leaders, and promote community service. In Saint Paul, we have been building better communities since 1917.

The Junior League of Saint Paul was established by three committed women, initially focused on supporting the war efforts of the Red Cross, Belgium Relief, Armenian Orphans, and the Near East Relief organizations during World War I. The tradition of serving the community continues today as the JLSP reaches out to its community with projects and services such as First Steps, a program for teen parents; Silent Witness Initiative, a project addressing domestic abuse issues; and many other programs designed to improve the lives of those in our community.

To fund worthy programs like these, Junior Leagues throughout the nation participate in a variety of fund-raisers. One of the most popular is the Junior League cookbook. With the collaboration between the Junior Leagues of Saint Paul and Minneapolis, we now can claim a cookbook of our own, one which we hope will put us in a "League" of our own.

In addition to creating theme-oriented menus to keep you entertaining in style year-round, we tested each recipe included in the book. On behalf of the Junior League of Saint Paul, we hope you enjoy these recipes as much as we did. Thank you for supporting our Junior Leagues.

Sincerely,

Barbara Westgard
JLSP President 2003-2004

Judy Nelson
JLSP President 2002-2003

**JUNIOR LEAGUE OF
MINNEAPOLIS**
Women building better communities

**JUNIOR LEAGUE OF
SAINT PAUL**
Women building better communities

Contents

Foreword by Andrew Zimmern

There is no greater treasure, no method of creating deeper bonds, no better way to touch another heart than through food. From community service and fund-raising to deepening family and cultural strength, the Junior Leagues of Minneapolis and Saint Paul reach hearts and touch people's lives through their charitable and social activities.

So when asked to contribute an introduction to *Always Superb: Recipes for Every Occasion*, I rushed to say "yes." Sales of this book support the missions of the Junior Leagues of Minneapolis and Saint Paul. My mission is to support the development of honest and authentic food style. *Always Superb* is the result of that collaboration, a recipe for success I am proud to endorse.

Chef Andrew Zimmern

Chef Andrew Zimmern is currently a featured regular cast member of KMSP Fox 9 Good Day. Channel surfers across the five-state area tune in four times a week to see his irreverent, intelligent, and informative segments on cooking for a modern lifestyle. A proponent of "Natural Cuisine," Andrew adheres to the theory that the freshest foods, simply prepared and presented, are often the healthiest and most delicious.

Andrew is a featured regular on both HGTV's Rebecca's Garden and HGTV's Tip-ical Mary Ellen. Andrew was also the featured chef during the 1997 season of UPN's nationally televised Everyday Living. He has also been featured on The Food Network's Best Of..., CNN's Health, and NBC's The Today Show. Andrew has been profiled in Gourmet, Restaurant Business, Food and Wine, Bon Appétit, and many other magazines.

In 1992, Andrew moved to Minnesota, where he gained wide acclaim as the executive chef of Cafe Un Deux Trois. He is also the founder of Food Works, Inc., a full-service restaurant development and food service consulting company. Food Works' client roster includes Fortune 500 companies such as Pillsbury, Land O' Lakes, Cargill, General Mills, and Schwan's, as well as many of the best-known restaurants in the country.

Introduction

Recipes are meant to be shared. The dog-eared cards, the yellowed newspaper clippings, the notebooks written in a careful hand and passed down from generation to generation reveal a common history, a crossing of paths, a bonding between friends and family.

In that spirit of sharing, the Junior Leagues of Minneapolis and Saint Paul have collaborated to create the first-ever combined League cookbook. The Twin Cities of Minneapolis and Saint Paul share a similar heritage, a love of the outdoors, tolerance for cold weather, and an enviable wealth of cultural attractions. Like twins, the two cities share many outward characteristics yet prize their individuality. But perhaps the most notable characteristic we share is a deep commitment to the communities we serve and the causes we support.

Always Superb: Recipes for Every Occasion is our tribute to those communities and to the many families and friends who have shared their recipes, their homes, and their hearts with us. Whether you are hosting lunch at the cabin or dinner in black tie, these recipes and tips for entertaining will ensure that every meal is always superb and every memory one to be shared.

Minnesota

You know the joke: There are only two seasons in Minnesota: winter and road construction. Despite what seems like a six-month winter—or perhaps because of it—we appreciate the changing of the seasons and celebrate their arrival with our favorite local and family traditions.

Historically, our regional cuisine has been dictated by the weather. Laura Ingalls Wilder, one of Minnesota's most famous residents, recalled the long days spent catching, cooking, curing, and canning food in her *Little House* books. Preparing food stores for winter, planting in the spring, making cheese in the summer, harvesting in the fall—all were community endeavors in which even young children were pressed into service.

With so many hours devoted to the procuring, preparing, or preserving of food, there was little time for recreation or formal entertaining; yet these gatherings of extended families and neighbors provided opportunities for adults and children to work together, play together, and break bread together.

Today we are far removed from life on the prairie. We gather with our friends and families not out of a common need but a common bond formed from generations of seasonal traditions. We may not live in a log house, but we still go to the cabin. Food is abundant year-round, yet we welcome thick soups and hearty meals in the winter. Fall brings us brilliant foliage that we mimic with the brightly colored squashes and vegetables on our table. And spring brings us fragrant pastel blooms to grace our table once again.

In this book we offer you our favorite menus, courtesy of the seasons. The four seasons yield hundreds of tantalizing dishes and dozens of reasons to entertain. Each season brings its own beauty, and each ushers in its favorite foods—sometimes hot, sometimes cold, but always superb.

Chapter One

THEMED MENUS

Marinated Rack of Lamb (*recipe on page 169*)

Splendor IN THE GRASS

Spring is an invitation to open the windows, and our doors, to our friends and neighbors. It's a time of teas and trifles, of Saturday lunches and Sunday brunches. April showers bring May flowers and June brides, and the profusion of lilies, irises, peonies, and lilacs creates the perfect table setting for bridal showers and other special occasions.

Indeed, our menu reflects the changing landscape around us. The warm, comforting meals of winter are replaced by lighter, fresher fare. Green is in abundance, both on the trees and on the table, in the form of salad greens and grilled vegetables. Desserts are lovely, lightweight confections, frothy and pastel-pretty.

One could argue that spring is the perfect season for entertaining. We can dress without fear of wilting in the heat, prepare a meal in cool comfort, and entertain against a backdrop that inspires poets and cooks alike.

spring menus

- Ladies' Night

- Opera Dessert Party

- Brunch

- Spring Dinner

spring menus

LADIES' NIGHT

appetizers
Olive Salsa
Layered Asian Appetizer
Sweet Potato Quesadillas with Cilantro Pesto
Cheese Crisps

soups
Mexican Corn Chowder
Italian Tortellini Soup
Gumbo

salads
Maytag Pasta Salad
Dried Cherries with Greens

main dishes
Chicken Satay with Three Sauces
Spanish Soft Tacos
Lamb Kabobs

desserts
Kahlúa Praline Brownies
Baked Lemon Custard
Heavenly Chocolate Sauce

OPERA DESSERT PARTY

appetizers
Toffee Apple Dip
Sinfully Sweet Pecans
Boursin Cheese
Baked Brie with Habanero Marmalade

soups
Strawberry Soup
Apple Stilton Soup

desserts
Caramel Pecan Turtle Cake
Amish Coconut Cake
Cherries in the Snow
Crustless Italian Cheesecake
Crème de Menthe Bars
Chocolate Cheesecake
English Toffee
Lemon Tart with Strawberries

Always Superb: Recipes for Every Occasion

BRUNCH

breads
Bubbling Blueberry Buckle Coffee Cake
Rhubarb Muffins
Crumb Coffee Cake

salads
Bibb Salad with Lime Soy Vinaigrette
Frisée Salad with Poached Eggs and
Warm Bacon Dressing

sides
Asparagus and New Potatoes
with Toasted Hazelnuts
Fennel Potatoes

main dishes
Frittata
Crustless Quiche
Easiest Eggs Benedict
Minnesota Bed and Breakfast Oven
French Toast
Ginger Pancakes
Poached Salmon with Cucumber Cream Sauce

desserts
Zesty Citrus Bars
Pecan Peach Cake with Caramel Glaze
Pavlova
Almond Strawberry Pain Perdue

SPRING DINNER

appetizers
Salmon Spread
Pea and Shallot Bruschetta
Spring Rolls

soups
Cream of Avocado Soup
Vichyssoise

salads
Pear and Walnut Salad
Grilled Vegetable Salad with
Balsamic Vinaigrette

sides
Roasted Asparagus with
Goat Cheese and Bacon
Balsamic Apricot Glazed Onions
Smashed Red Potatoes with
Gorgonzola Cheese

main dishes
Hawaiian Pork Roast
Marinated Rack of Lamb
Pork Tenderloin with Chinese Five-Spice
Gingered Sea Bass

desserts
Berrimisu
Rhubarb Meringue Tart
Crème Brûlée

Summertime

AND THE LIVING IS EASY

Ease is the operative word for this season. When the heat and humidity become oppressive, we head into the air conditioning or up to the cabin, where a pretty pareo is considered formal attire, and the amount of prep time for a meal is inversely proportionate to the length of the days.

Foods should be a welcome respite from the heat. Salads are crisp, soups are chilled, and drinks are cold. Up at the cabin, the catch of the day is fried that night, and the seating is al fresco. Days are spent swimming and sunning; appetites are big, and worries are small.

If summers at the cabin are a Minnesota tradition, golf in Minnesota is something of a religion. The Land of 10,000 Lakes boasts more than 450 of the finest golf courses, and Minnesota leads the nation in per capita participation. Golf is as much a social event as a sport and, as with any social event, has its own themed cuisine. In this section, you will find menu ideas worthy of Augusta.

A summer spent in Minnesota is a summer worth remembering. These fun, fresh menu ideas will make some of the most memorable meals yet.

summer menus

+ Welcome to the Cabin

+ Golf Dinner

+ Father's Day Dinner

+ Farmer's Market Picnic

summer menus

WELCOME TO THE CABIN

appetizers
Black Beans with Lime Vinaigrette
Venison Sausage with Cranberry Pineapple
Chutney Cream Cheese
Boundary Water Granola

breads
Mixed Berry Coffee Cake
Pecan-Cinnamon Coffee Cake

salads
Smoked Trout and Apple Salad
Gingered Asian Salad

sides
Lemon Oregono Potatoes
Traditional Green Bean Casserole
Orzo and Wild Rice

main dishes
Hawaiian Chicken Barbecue
Pan-Fried Walleye with Tartar Sauce
Marinated Buffalo Ribeyes with Grilled Polenta
Almond-Crusted Trout with Romesco Sauce

desserts
White Chocolate Macadamia Nut Cookies
Blueberries and Cream Pie
Rhubarb Strawberry Crunch

GOLF DINNER

appetizers
Pesto Terrine
Zesty Olive-Topped Appetizers
Goat Cheese and Tomato with Basil

salads
Summer Salad with Walnuts and Raspberries
Twin Cities Marinated Salad
Wild Rice Crab Cakes on Greens

sides
Oriental Green Beans
Carrot Soufflé
Glazed Beets

main dishes
Honey-Glazed Salmon
Halibut Steaks with Mango Salsa
Grilled Tuna with Soy Marinade
Swordfish with Saffron and Caper Sauce
Beef Tenderloin with Green Peppercorn Sauce

desserts
Summer Berry Trifle
Lemon Sorbet with Crème de Cassis
and Raspberries
Tiramisu

FATHER'S DAY DINNER

appetizers
Crab Pizza
Coconut Shrimp with
Tabasco Marmalade Sauce
Petite Pesto Cheesecake

salads
Spinach and Strawberry Salad
Citrus Almond Salad

sides
Lemon Green Beans
Three-Grain Casserole
Roasted Brussels Sprouts with Pancetta
Baunjaun Bouranee

main dishes
Grilled Ginger Lamb Chops
Sweet-and-Sour Pork Tenderloin
Terrific Beef Tenderloin Tureen
Madeira Chicken

desserts
Baklava
Lemon Supreme Cheesecake
Crème à la Orange

FARMER'S MARKET PICNIC

appetizers
Hummus
Mango Salsa
Cactus Dip

salads
Pea, Red Pepper and Pesto Pasta Toss
Summer Salad with Tomatoes, Cucumbers
and Onions
Tabouli
French Tarragon Potato Salad

soups
Chilled Asparagus Soup
Chilled Creamy Cucumber Soup

main dishes
Muffuletta
Ginger-Peanut Chicken Wraps
Mango Chicken Salad

desserts
Fresh Strawberry Pie
Lemon and Spice Sugar Cookies
Upside-Down Plum Cake

Sweater-Weather

GET-TOGETHERS

The Twin Cities fall marathon has been dubbed "the most beautiful urban marathon in America." The superlative is justified. Fall in the Twin Cities makes you catch your breath, and not because you're running. The lakes sparkle under the Indian summer sun. The leaves are riotously colorful. The skies are straight out of a child's drawing: bright yellow sun, Crayola blue skies, white fluffy clouds.

Fall foods are just as colorful. We regale our tables with brilliant orange pumpkins, carrots, and sweet potatoes; warm rich butternut squash; shiny apples in burnished golds and reds. Our taste changes, too, with the season. Fresh fish is replaced by rich game. Green beans and tomatoes are joined by robust squashes. Summer fruits make way for bread puddings and spice cookies.

The bountiful harvest yields an abundance of menu ideas for fall entertaining, many of which may have been found on the tables of those who once harvested the food themselves. Creamy wild rice soup, smoked pheasant, corn cakes—Laura Ingalls Wilder would feel right at home. Of course, she might be surprised—and delighted—to see the sophisticated takes on these classic Minnesota favorites.

autumn menus

- Twin Cities Marathon

- Foliage Picnic

- Harvest Dinner

- Great Pumpkin Halloween Party

24 **Always Superb:** Recipes for Every Occasion

autumn menus

TWIN CITIES MARATHON

appetizers
Sun-dried Tomatoes with Cheese
Rosemary Pine Nut Bruschetta
Roasted Red Pepper Dip

breads
Crunchy Garlic Scones
No-Knead Braided Parmesan Bread

salads
Romaine Salad with Gingered Walnuts and
Blue Cheese
Balsamic Marinated Asparagus on
Baby Field Greens
Caesar Salad

main dishes
Artichoke Cheese Fettucine
Vegetable Lasagna
Paella
Shrimp Linguini with Sun-Dried Tomatoes
Portobello Risotto

desserts
Chocolate Bread Pudding
Almond Sugar Cookies
Rice Pudding

FOLIAGE PICNIC

breads
Grape-Nuts Bread
Whole Wheat Zucchini Bread
Pepperoni Bread
Viennese Banana Nut Bread
Bran Muffins

soups
Tomato Basil Soup
Pumpkin Apple Soup
Carrot Ginger Soup

salads
Wheat Berry Salad
Avocado Corn Confetti Salad
Italian Pasta Salad with Sausage and Artichokes
Antipasto Salad

desserts
Butterscotch Crumble Apple Pie
Ginger Spice Cookies
Pistachio Brittle
Pecan Crunch Cookies

HARVEST DINNER

appetizers
Goat Cheese Crostini
Cranberry Salsa
Country Pork Pâté

soups
Nutty Pumpkin Soup
Minnesota Wild Rice Soup
Harvest Butternut Squash Soup with
Ginger Maple Sauce

salads
Avocado and Roasted Beet Salad
Greens with Garlic Dressing

sides
Brandied Carrots
Baked Butternut Squash with Apples
Asiago au Gratin Potatoes
Mushroom Strudel

main dishes
Tandoori Chicken
Pheasant in Madeira Wine
Moroccan Stew
Venison Stroganoff

GREAT PUMPKIN HALLOWEEN PARTY

appetizers
Cheese Cubes
Hot and Zesty Spinach Dip
Miniature Stuffed Potatoes with
Roasted Garlic

sides
Broccoli Purée
Corn Pudding
Smoky Hot Beans
Artichoke Vegetable Dish

main dishes
Superb Short Ribs
Crispy Sesame Chicken
Barbecue Pork Sandwiches
Chicken Enchiladas
Stromboli Sandwich

desserts
Sautéed Bananas
Homemade Chocolate Peanut Buttter Cups
Chocolate Dessert Wraps

Home FOR THE HOLIDAYS

Minnesotans think they own the winter season, so it's not surprising that we have such delicious cold-weather and holiday recipes. With Thanksgiving begins the most wonderful time of the year, a social whirlwind of friends and families. It is a nostalgic season, filled with memories triggered by the whiff of a familiar spice or a favorite dessert.

Winter entertaining is both practical and aesthetic. The weather is cold, so the food is often hot and hearty. But it is also the season of entertaining, requiring delectable delicacies for the most discriminating palates. Thus these winter menus are filled with everything from warm-welcome chili to chichi cocktails and canapés.

We have many reasons to celebrate this season, and just as many reasons to entertain. Much has been written about the stress of the holidays—perhaps too much. To this we say bah humbug. The holidays are the season of giving, and giving brings great joy. Entertaining is our gift to friends and loved ones. These seasonal menus are our gift to you and yours.

winter menus

- Ice Skating Party

- New Year's Day Buffet

- Progressive Dinner

- Pre-Theater Party

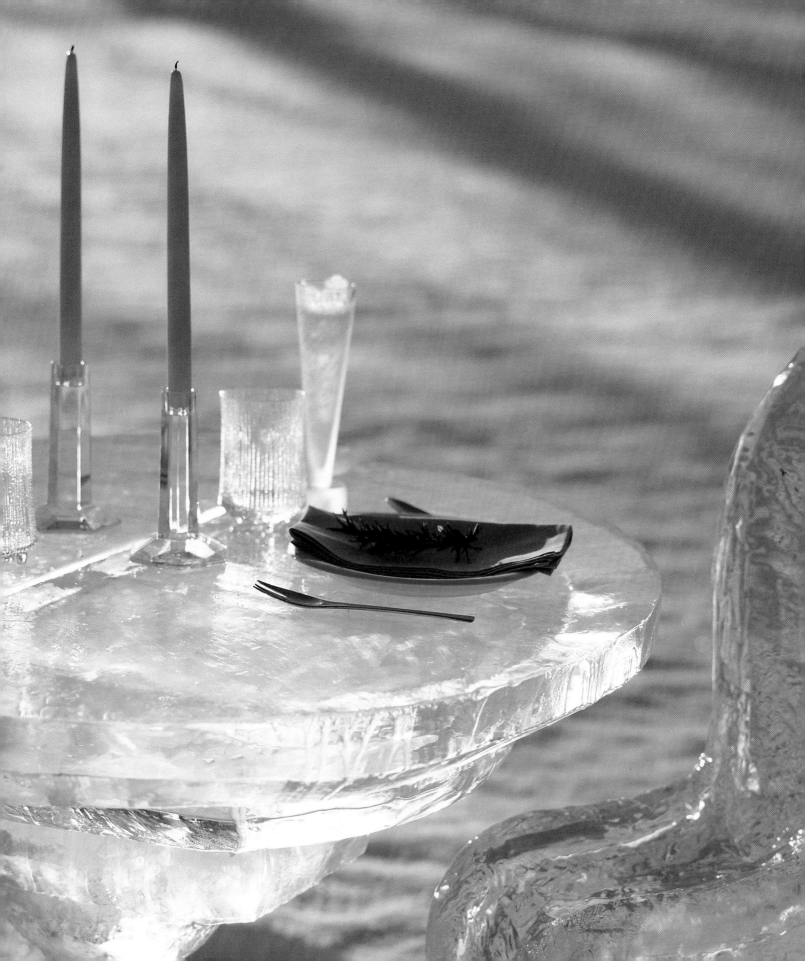

winter menus

ICE SKATING PARTY

appetizers
Artichoke and Goat Cheese Spread
Mushroom Cheesecake with Crab
Swedish Meat Balls

breads
Minnesota Cheese Biscuits
Swedish Corn Bread
Bread Bouquet

salads
Warm Cabbage-Apple Salad
Wilted Spinach Salad

main dishes
Mediterranean Chili
Vegetarian Chili
White Chili with Chicken and Corn
Spicy No-Bean Chili with Turkey

desserts
Indoor S'mores
Crazy Buttermilk Cake
Cranberry Almond Pound Cake
Nutty Good Bars

NEW YEAR'S DAY BUFFET

appetizers
Blue Cheese Cream Puffs
Warm Mushroom Spread
Miniature Crab Cakes with
Red Chili Mayonnaise
Toasted Almond Spread

salads
Winter Salad
Tequila Lime Fruit Salad
Molded Gazpacho Salad

main dishes
Seafood Stew
Ginger Beef Stew
Shrimp Étouffé
Fiesta Stew
Black-Eyed Peas with Ham

desserts
Apple Cake
Cranberry Walnut Pie
Rum Cake

Always Superb: Recipes for Every Occasion

PROGRESSIVE DINNER

appetizers
Mushroom Duxelle with Hearty Brown Bread
Emmentaler and Gruyère Cheese Puffs
Seafood Appetizer Cheesecake

salads
Cranberry Parmesan Salad
Mixed Greens with Gorgonzola and
Caramelized Pecans
Minnesota Salad: Wild Rice and Soybeans

sides
Broccoli with Lemon Cream Sauce
Baked Goat Cheese Potatoes
Gingered Carrots
Sweet Potato Soufflé

main dishes
Pesto-Packed Pork Chops
Lamb Shanks with White Beans
Orange Black Pepper-Glazed Filets Mignons
Individual Salmon Wellingtons with
White Dill Sauce

desserts
Pear Tart
Black Russian Bundt Cake
Cranberry Holiday Cake

PRE-THEATER PARTY

appetizers
Grape Leaves Stuffed with Wild Rice and
Yogurt Mint Sauce
Martini Dip
Pecan Cheese Stuffed Mushrooms
Chutney Glazed Lobster with
Chipotle Mayonnaise
Brie and Sun-Dried Tomato Pesto Torta
Asparagus Risotto with
Parmesan Cheese Cups
Roast Beef Grissini with Remoulade
Crunchy Olive Bites
Rosemary Walnuts
Cajun Spice Shrimp
Black Magic Caviar Dip

desserts
Scandinavian Tea Cakes
Chocolate Truffle Bars
Cranberry Caramel Cake
Date Bars

Chapter Two

APPETIZERS

Miniature Crab Cakes with Red Chili Mayonnaise (*recipe on page 73*)

ENTERTAINING

HISTORY OF HORS D'OEUVRE

"Little dishes outside the work meal" is the literal French translation for the pre-meal, bite-size food we know as hors d'oeuvre. In Spain, these "little dishes" are referred to as tapas. The appetizer is generally accompanied by cocktails or aperitifs and can be served hot or cold. Two common pre-meal bites are canapés (toasted breads or crackers topped with garnishes, including caviar, anchovies, or cheese) and crudités (raw vegetables), often accompanied by a chilled dip.

BLACK BEANS WITH LIME VINAIGRETTE

YIELD: 10 TO 12 SERVINGS

BEANS
4 (15-ounce) cans black beans, drained
2 cups frozen corn kernels, thawed
2 cups chopped fresh tomatoes
3/4 cup sliced scallions
1/2 cup chopped cilantro

VINAIGRETTE
1/3 cup olive oil
1/2 cup lime juice
2 teaspoons salt
1 teaspoon cumin

GARNISH
Cilantro sprigs
Lime slices

FOR THE BEANS, combine the beans, corn, tomatoes, scallions and cilantro in a bowl and mix well.

FOR THE VINAIGRETTE, whisk the olive oil, lime juice, salt and cumin in a small bowl.

TO ASSEMBLE, pour the vinaigrette over the bean mixture and toss to combine. Garnish with cilantro sprigs and lime slices. Serve at room temperature or slightly chilled.

Always Superb: Recipes for Every Occasion

HUMMUS

YIELD: 6 SERVINGS

2 or 3 garlic cloves
1 (15-ounce) can garbanzo beans, rinsed
  and drained
1/4 cup tahini
Juice of 1 lemon
1 1/2 teaspoons cumin
1/4 cup (about) water

GARNISH
Paprika
Parsley sprigs

Chop the garlic in a food processor. Add the beans and process. Add the tahini, lemon juice and cumin and process. Add the water in a fine stream, processing constantly until the hummus is smooth and of the desired consistency. Pour into a serving bowl. Shake the paprika over the top and arrange the parsley sprigs as garnish. You may refrigerate this until ready to serve. Serve with fresh veggies or pita triangles.

NOTE: Garbanzo beans are also referred to as chick-peas and tahini is also referred to as sesame seed paste.

CACTUS DIP

YIELD: 8 SERVINGS

1 cup mayonnaise
1 1/2 cups cactus salsa
1 (4-ounce) can chopped green chiles
1/2 cup chopped scallions
1/2 cup (2 ounces) shredded mild
  Cheddar cheese
1/2 cup (2 ounces) grated Parmesan cheese

Combine the mayonnaise, salsa, green chiles, scallions, Cheddar cheese and Parmesan cheese in a bowl and mix well. Spoon into a 9x13-inch baking dish.

Bake at 325 degrees for 20 minutes or until bubbly. Serve with corn chips.

PARTY PERFECT BAR

As you prepare for a party or gathering, it is always important to have enough drinks and ice on hand. In general, use the following guidelines to create a well-stocked bar:

Ice = 2 to 3 pounds per person
    (not worth running out!)
Glasses = 2 to 3 per person
Wine = 4 to 5 servings
    per bottle
Champagne (750 ml) =
    5 to 6 servings per bottle
Liquor = 17 servings
    per bottle
Appetizers = 8 single-serving
    items per person per hour

For a cocktail party, generally assume that people will drink two drinks per hour. To keep the drinks fresh, fill glasses ²/₃ full with ice.

MARTINI DIP

YIELD: 8 SERVINGS

8 ounces cream cheese, softened
1 teaspoon Worcestershire sauce
¹/₂ cup mayonnaise
12 ounces vermouth-marinated chopped
    olives, drained

Combine the cream cheese, Worcestershire sauce and mayonnaise in a bowl and mix until smooth. Stir in the olives.

Chill, covered, in the refrigerator until serving time. Excellent served with crackers or vegetables.

ROASTED RED PEPPER DIP

YIELD: 6 TO 8 SERVINGS

2 red bell peppers
2 garlic cloves
3 ounces cream cheese, softened
¹/₂ cup sour cream
2 tablespoons chopped basil
1 tablespoon chopped parsley
Salt to taste
Pepper to taste

Place the bell peppers on a broiling pan. Broil until blackened on all sides. Place in a sealable plastic bag. Seal and let stand for 10 minutes. Remove the skin, seeds and stems.

Combine the roasted bell peppers, garlic, cream cheese, sour cream, basil and parsley in a food processor with a steel blade. Process until smooth. Season with salt and pepper. Serve with crudités.

NOTE: You may grill the bell peppers instead of broiling.

HOT AND ZESTY SPINACH DIP

YIELD: 10 TO 12 SERVINGS

2 tablespoons vegetable oil
1 onion, chopped
2 tomatoes (about 12 ounces), peeled,
   seeded and chopped
1 (4-ounce) can chopped green chiles
1 (10-ounce) package frozen spinach, thawed
2 cups (8 ounces) shredded Monterey
   Jack cheese
8 ounces cream cheese, cut into $^1/_2$-inch
   pieces, softened
1 cup half-and-half
2 (2-ounce) cans sliced black olives, drained
1 tablespoon red wine vinegar
$^1/_2$ teaspoon garlic powder
1 teaspoon cumin
Salt to taste
Freshly ground pepper to taste
Tortilla chips

Heat the oil in a heavy medium skillet over medium heat. Add the onion and sauté for 4 minutes or until softened, stirring occasionally. Stir in the tomatoes and green chiles. Cook for 2 minutes.

Press the excess moisture from the spinach. Combine the cooked vegetables, spinach, Monterey Jack cheese, cream cheese, half-and-half, olives and vinegar in a large bowl and mix well. Stir in the garlic powder and cumin. Season with salt and pepper. Spoon into a shallow ovenproof baking dish. You may cover and refrigerate for up to 2 days at this point.

Bake at 400 degrees for 35 minutes or until bubbly and top is browned. Serve with the tortilla chips.

EAT YOUR VEGGIES

Enhance any tray of crudités with a warm, spicy dip.

For Quick Vegetable Dip, combine $^1/_2$ cup mayonnaise, $^1/_2$ cup sour cream and $1^1/_2$ tablespoons curry in a bowl and mix well. For a variation, substitute 1 to 2 tablespoons dill weed for the curry and add grated lemon zest and mustard to taste.

CRANBERRY SALSA

YIELD: 6 TO 8 SERVINGS

1 (12-ounce) package fresh cranberries
1 jalapeño chile
Grated zest of 1 orange
    (about 4 teaspoons)
Grated zest of 1 lemon
    (about 1 teaspoon)
Juice of $1/2$ orange
Juice of $1/2$ lime
$1/2$ cup sugar
$1/2$ cup chopped red onion
Dash of salt

Rinse the cranberries, discarding any soft or bruised berries. Seed and chop the jalapeño chile.

Combine the cranberries, jalapeño chile, orange zest, lemon zest, orange juice, lime juice, sugar, onion and salt in a food processor. Process until of the desired consistency. Prepare this 1 to 2 days in advance for enhanced flavor and softer cranberries. Serve with blue tortilla chips or other chips.

MANGO SALSA

YIELD: 4 TO 6 SERVINGS

1 mango, peeled and chopped
1 jalapeño chile, seeded and finely chopped
Juice of 1 lime
1 red onion, chopped
1 teaspoon coarse salt
$1/4$ cup chopped cilantro
1 can black beans, rinsed and drained
    (optional)

Combine the mango, jalapeño chile, lime juice, onion, salt, cilantro and beans in a bowl and mix well. Serve with tortilla chips.

NOTE: This salsa is also good served over grilled salmon.

OLIVE SALSA

YIELD: 6 TO 8 SERVINGS

1 (7-ounce) jar pitted green olives
1 (3-ounce) can pitted black olives
3 garlic cloves, crushed
2 jalapeño chiles, seeded
$1/3$ cup chopped red onion
1 red bell pepper, seeded
1 yellow bell pepper, seeded
$1/2$ cup pine nuts, toasted
2 tablespoons olive oil
1 tablespoon red wine vinegar

Combine the green olives, black olives, garlic cloves, jalapeño chiles, onion, bell peppers and pine nuts in a food processor. Process until all ingredients are coarsely chopped. Spoon into a bowl. Add the olive oil and vinegar and mix well. Serve with crackers or blue tortilla chips.

TOFFEE APPLE DIP

YIELD: 10 TO 12 SERVINGS

$3/4$ cup packed brown sugar
$1/2$ cup confectioners' sugar
1 teaspoon vanilla extract
8 ounces cream cheese, softened
$3/4$ cup toffee bits
1 cup pineapple juice
Apple wedges

Beat the brown sugar, confectioners' sugar, vanilla and cream cheese in a mixing bowl at medium speed until smooth. Stir in the toffee bits. Chill, covered, in the refrigerator.

Combine the pineapple juice and apples in a bowl. Toss to coat the apples; drain. Place the apples in an airtight container; seal. Chill until ready to serve.

Spoon the dip into a serving bowl. Serve with the apples.

PEARLS OF THE SEA

Whether accompanied simply by iced vodka or served on toast points with chopped egg and capers, the best (and most expensive) caviar is harvested from the beluga sturgeon of the Caspian Sea. The beluga caviar ranges in color from pale gray to dark black, and the eggs are pea-size. There are over twenty species of sturgeon that produce roe. Two other popular caviars are osetra, a medium-size egg of gray or brownish color, and sevruga, a smaller and grayish-colored roe. Red caviar is obtained from salmon, while golden caviar comes from the whitefish of the Great Lakes. While high in salt and cholesterol, a spoonful of caviar provides the daily requirement of vitamin B12.

CHUTNEY GLAZED LOBSTER WITH CHIPOTLE MAYONNAISE

YIELD: 4 TO 6 SERVINGS

CHIPOTLE MAYONNAISE
2 cups mayonnaise
1/2 cup canned chipotle peppers, chopped
2 garlic cloves, crushed and finely chopped
Grated zest of 1 orange
Juice of 1 orange
Grated zest of 1 lime
Juice of 1 lime

LOBSTER
4 (6-ounce) lobster tails, shells removed
3/4 cup Major Grey–style chutney
1 tablespoon Dijon mustard
Juice of 1 lemon
1 tablespoon butter
1 1/2 ounces vodka

FOR THE MAYONNAISE, combine the mayonnaise, chipotle peppers, garlic, orange zest, orange juice, lime zest and lime juice in a bowl and mix well. Chill, covered, in the refrigerator.

FOR THE LOBSTER, cut the lobster meat into bite-size pieces. Purée the chutney in a blender. Combine the puréed chutney, mustard and lemon juice in a small bowl and mix well. Heat the butter in a skillet until melted. Add the lobster and cook over medium-high heat for 1 minute. Add the vodka. Add the chutney mixture and cook for 3 to 6 minutes or until the lobster meat is opaque, stirring frequently. Spoon into a small serving dish. Serve with the mayonnaise on the side.

BLACK MAGIC CAVIAR DIP

YIELD: 6 TO 8 SERVINGS

1 envelope unflavored gelatin
1/2 cup boiling water
8 ounces black caviar
8 hard-cooked eggs, chopped
1 onion, chopped
1/4 cup Durkee sauce
1/4 cup mayonnaise
1/2 cup chopped parsley
1/4 cup chopped chives (optional)
Salt to taste
Pepper to taste
Bibb lettuce leaves
2 cups sour cream

Dissolve the gelatin in the boiling water in a heatproof bowl.

Combine 1/4 cup of the gelatin mixture with the caviar in a separate bowl and mix well. Spoon evenly over the bottom of a 1-quart ring mold. Chill until set.

Combine the remaining 1/4 cup gelatin mixture, eggs, onion, Durkee sauce, mayonnaise, parsley, chives, salt and pepper in a bowl and mix well. Spoon evenly over the caviar layer in the ring mold. Chill until set.

Arrange lettuce leaves on a serving platter. Unmold the caviar ring onto the leaves. Spoon the sour cream into the center. Serve with toast rounds.

TOASTED ALMOND SPREAD

YIELD: 6 TO 8 SERVINGS

8 ounces cream cheese, softened
1 1/2 cups (6 ounces) shredded Swiss cheese
1/3 cup mayonnaise
2 tablespoons chopped green onions
1/8 to 1/4 teaspoon nutmeg
1/3 cup sliced almonds, toasted

GARNISH
Sliced almonds, toasted

Combine the cream cheese, Swiss cheese, mayonnaise, green onions, nutmeg and almonds in a bowl and mix well. Spread evenly in a 9-inch quiche dish. Bake at 350 degrees for 20 minutes. Garnish with almonds. Serve with water crackers.

BOURSIN CHEESE

YIELD: 6 TO 8 SERVINGS

1/2 cup (1 stick) unsalted butter, softened
16 ounces cream cheese, softened
1/2 teaspoon salt
2 garlic cloves, minced
1/4 teaspoon marjoram
1/4 teaspoon thyme
1/4 teaspoon oregano
1/4 teaspoon dill weed
1/4 teaspoon basil
1/4 teaspoon white pepper

Cream the butter, cream cheese, salt, garlic, marjoram, thyme, oregano, dill weed, basil and white pepper in a bowl. Chill, covered, until ready to serve. Prepare this one day in advance for enhanced flavor.

The arrival of summer in Minnesota gives us reason to celebrate. Two classic Twin Cities traditions mirror the culture and historical roots of each city. Saint Paul's Grand Old Days, a tribute to summer, began in 1973 and now draws over 200,000 visitors per year. The event takes place along historic Grand Avenue the first Sunday of June. The Minneapolis Aquatennial, a week-long event during the third week of July, features many water-related activities, including milk-carton boat races, sand sculpture contests, a sailing regatta, and the Torchlight Parade.

ARTICHOKE AND GOAT CHEESE SPREAD

YIELD: 8 TO 10 SERVINGS

3 (6-ounce) jars marinated artichoke
   hearts, drained
1 tablespoon olive oil
1/2 teaspoon finely grated lemon zest
1 pound goat cheese
1 tablespoon finely chopped parsley
1 3/4 teaspoons coarsely ground black pepper
1 teaspoon minced garlic
1/2 teaspoon salt
Dash of cayenne pepper
1 tablespoon lemon juice

Pulse the artichoke hearts in a food processor until coarsely chopped. Combine in a bowl with the olive oil and lemon zest and toss to combine.

Process the goat cheese in a food processor until smooth. Fold the goat cheese, parsley, black pepper, garlic, salt and cayenne pepper into the artichoke mixture. Stir in the lemon juice. Chill, covered, for up to 2 days. Bring to room temperature. Serve with crostini and fresh vegetables.

NOTE: For a main dish, toss the spread with angel hair pasta.

GOAT CHEESE AND TOMATO WITH BASIL

YIELD: 4 TO 6 SERVINGS

8 ounces fresh goat cheese or fresh
  mozzarella cheese
2 ripe tomatoes
1 tablespoon (or more) balsamic vinegar
1 tablespoon chopped fresh basil
1 package wheat crackers

Crumble the goat cheese evenly into a small dish or bowl with edges. Cut the tomatoes into small chunks and sprinkle over the cheese. Drizzle with balsamic vinegar. Sprinkle with basil. Serve with the wheat crackers.

WARM MUSHROOM SPREAD

YIELD: 10 TO 12 SERVINGS

4 slices bacon
1 onion, finely chopped
12 ounces fresh mushrooms, chopped
$1/8$ teaspoon garlic powder
2 tablespoons flour
$1/4$ teaspoon salt
Dash of pepper
8 ounces cream cheese, softened and
  cut into cubes
$1 1/8$ teaspoons soy sauce
2 teaspoons Worcestershire sauce
$1/2$ cup sour cream
Rye bread rounds

GARNISH
Parsley

Cook the bacon in a large skillet until crisp. Remove the bacon and set on paper towels. Discard the drippings, reserving 2 tablespoons.

Sauté the onion and mushrooms in the reserved bacon drippings until tender and most of the liquid has evaporated. Stir in the garlic powder, flour, salt and pepper. Add the cream cheese, soy sauce and Worcestershire sauce. Cook until the cream cheese melts, stirring frequently.

Stir the sour cream into the mushroom mixture. Crumble the bacon and stir in. Cook until heated through; do not boil. Spoon into a serving bowl. Garnish with parsley and serve with rye bread rounds.

Minnesotans pride themselves on their ability to withstand the long, harsh winters. One of the ways they cope with the long, dark winters is to celebrate with festivals of lights and ice. The Saint Paul Winter Carnival originated in 1886 and honors the mythical King Boreas, "King of the Winds." The highlight is an elaborate ice castle created from the ice on Minnesota lakes. Another perennial favorite is the Holidazzle Parade on Nicollet Mall in Downtown Minneapolis, a fanciful procession of storybook characters, whimsical creatures, and, of course, Santa Claus.

SALMON SPREAD

YIELD: 6 TO 8 SERVINGS

2 cups skinned smoked salmon pieces
8 ounces cream cheese, softened
2 tablespoons chopped green onions
1 tablespoon lemon juice
$1/4$ cup sour cream
$1/4$ cup mayonnaise
$1/8$ teaspoon dill weed
$1/4$ teaspoon Worcestershire sauce
2 tablespoons capers

Process the salmon, cream cheese, green onions, lemon juice, sour cream, mayonnaise, dill weed and Worcestershire sauce in a food processor until well mixed. Spoon into a serving bowl. Stir in the capers. Chill, covered, for 1 hour. Serve with crackers.

LAYERED ASIAN APPETIZER

YIELD: 10 TO 12 SERVINGS

ZIPPY SWEET-AND-SOUR SAUCE
1/4 cup packed brown sugar
2 teaspoons cornstarch
1 cup water
1/4 cup ketchup
2 tablespoons vinegar
1 tablespoon Worcestershire sauce
3 drops of hot red pepper sauce

TOPPING
3/4 cup chopped cooked chicken
1/2 cup finely shredded carrot
1/4 cup chopped unsalted peanuts
3 tablespoons sliced scallions
1 tablespoon chopped fresh parsley
2 teaspoons soy sauce
1/4 teaspoon ground ginger, or
   1 teaspoon grated gingerroot
1 garlic clove, minced

BASE
8 ounces cream cheese, softened
1 tablespoon milk

FOR THE SAUCE, combine the brown sugar and cornstarch in a small saucepan and mix well. Stir in the water, ketchup, vinegar, Worcestershire sauce and hot sauce gradually. Cook over medium heat for 5 minutes or until the mixture thickens slightly, stirring frequently. Let stand until cool. Chill, covered, until ready to use; this will thicken in the refrigerator.

FOR THE TOPPING, combine the chicken, carrot, peanuts, scallions, parsley, soy sauce, ginger and garlic in a bowl and mix well. Chill, covered, for 8 to 12 hours.

FOR THE BASE, combine the cream cheese and milk in a mixing bowl. Beat until smooth and fluffy.

TO ASSEMBLE, spread the base mixture over the bottom of a 10-inch round serving dish. Spoon the topping evenly over the base. Drizzle with 1/2 cup of the sauce, reserving the remaining sauce for another use. Serve with table water crackers and other assorted crackers.

NOTE: You may double the base and topping recipes and use a larger dish.

While hockey purists will tell you hockey originated in Nova Scotia, a visit here in the winter might make you think otherwise. After all, with 10,000 lakes you're going to get a lot of ice time. And if you run out of daylight, between October and May you can play hockey twenty-four hours a day at indoor rinks. No wonder so many players on both the Men's and Women's U.S. Olympic Hockey Teams hail from Minnesota.

BRIE AND SUN-DRIED TOMATO PESTO TORTA

YIELD: 10 TO 12 SERVINGS

1 (16-ounce) round of Brie
^{1}/2 cup oil-pack sun-dried tomatoes,
    chopped, oil reserved
^{1}/2 cup chopped fresh basil leaves
^{1}/2 cup pine nuts
2 garlic cloves, minced

GARNISH
Fresh basil leaves

Cut the top rind off the Brie in a circle, leaving a ^{1}/2-inch rim of the rind around the edge. Cut the Brie into halves horizontally, making the top portion slightly thicker than the bottom. Place the bottom portion on a parchment-lined baking sheet.

Combine the sun-dried tomatoes, basil, 2 tablespoons of the reserved oil, pine nuts and garlic in a bowl and mix well. Spoon ^{2}/3 cup over the bottom round of Brie. Place the Brie top over the sun-dried tomato mixture. Spoon the remaining sun-dried tomato mixture over the top of the Brie; press gently.

Bake at 325 degrees for 12 to 15 minutes or until the Brie is softened; do not melt. Place on a serving platter. Garnish with basil leaves. Serve warm with baguette toasts or melba rounds.

BAKED BRIE WITH HABANERO MARMALADE

MARMALADE
1³/4 ounces (4 or 5) fresh habanero chiles
1¹/2 pounds red bell peppers
1¹/2 cups distilled white vinegar
6¹/2 cups sugar
2 (3-ounce) packages liquid pectin

BRIE
1 (6-inch) wheel of Brie

FOR THE MARMALADE, wash seven 1-cup canning jars, rings and lids in hot sudsy water. Rinse them well and place in a 6- to 8-quart pan. Add enough water to cover. Bring the water to a boil over high heat. Remove the pan from the heat, leaving the jars, rings and lids in the water.

Remove and discard the stems and seeds from the habanero chiles, using rubber gloves. Remove and discard the stems from the bell peppers. Cut off the curved sections and set aside. Remove and discard the membranes, reserving the seeds. Cut the sides into ¹/8x2¹/2-inch strips.

Purée the habanero chiles, reserved bell pepper sections and ¹/2 cup of the vinegar in a blender. Combine the purée, bell pepper strips, bell pepper seeds, remaining 1 cup vinegar and sugar in an 8- to 10-quart pan. Bring to a full boil over high heat, stirring constantly. Boil for 3 minutes. Add the pectin. Bring to a full boil over high heat, stirring constantly. Boil for 1 minute.

Remove the jars, rings and lids from the water and place them on paper toweling or a clean cloth. Ladle the marmalade into the jars, leaving ¹/8 inch headroom. Wipe the tops and outside rims of the jars with a clean cloth. Place the domed lids on top and screw on the metal rings tightly; do not use force. Bring any remaining marmalade to room temperature, place in an airtight container and store in the refrigerator for up to 2 weeks.

Invert the filled jars on a clean towel for 5 minutes and turn every 5 minutes for 45 to 60 minutes or until the marmalade has set and seeds are evenly distributed. Let stand for 2 additional hours. Serve or store for up to 2 years.

FOR THE BRIE, place the Brie on a baking sheet. Bake at 350 degrees for 10 minutes or until warm. Place on a serving plate. Pour one or more jars of the marmalade over the Brie, reserving the remaining jars of marmalade for another use.

SWEET POTATO QUESADILLAS WITH CILANTRO PESTO

YIELD: 8 SERVINGS

CILANTRO PESTO
2 cups cilantro leaves
3/4 cup extra-virgin olive oil
1/4 cup pine nuts, toasted
6 garlic cloves
1 cup (4 ounces) grated asiago cheese

SWEET POTATO QUESADILLAS
1 pound sweet potatoes, cut into
   1/4-inch-thick slices
1/2 teaspoon cinnamon
1/2 teaspoon cumin
1/2 teaspoon coriander
1/2 teaspoon star anise
1/2 teaspoon salt
1 tablespoon butter, melted
1 teaspoon butter
4 ounces onion, julienned
3 cups (12 ounces) shredded Monterey
   Jack cheese
4 (10-inch) flour tortillas

FOR THE PESTO, combine the cilantro, olive oil, pine nuts, garlic and asiago cheese in a blender. Process until smooth.

FOR THE QUESADILLAS, combine the sweet potato slices, cinnamon, cumin, coriander, star anise, salt and melted butter in a large bowl and toss to coat the sweet potatoes. Arrange the sweet potato slices in a single layer on a baking sheet. Bake at 375 degrees for 8 minutes. Chill in the refrigerator until cool.

Heat the butter in a skillet over medium heat until melted. Add the onion and sauté until tender. Combine the baked sweet potatoes, onion and Monterey Jack cheese in a bowl and mix well. Spoon the sweet potato mixture evenly over half of each tortilla. Fold each tortilla in half and place on a baking sheet. Bake at 375 degrees until heated through and cheese is melted.

Place the quesadillas on a serving plate. Cut into wedges. Serve with the cilantro pesto.

PESTO TERRINE

YIELD: 24 SERVINGS

^{1}/2 cup sun-dried tomatoes
1 garlic clove
^{1}/2 cup unsalted or raw pistachio nuts
16 ounces cream cheese, softened
^{3}/4 cup (3 ounces) grated Parmesan cheese
^{1}/2 teaspoon pepper
1 tablespoon Worcestershire sauce
1 cup (4 ounces) grated Parmesan cheese
4 garlic cloves
1^1/2 cups basil leaves
^{1}/2 cup olive oil
16 ounces provolone cheese

Chop the sun-dried tomatoes in a food processor. Remove and set aside. Chop 1 garlic clove and pistachio nuts in the food processor. Remove and set aside. Process the cream cheese in the food processor until smooth. Add the sun-dried tomatoes, nut mixture, ^{3}/4 cup Parmesan cheese, pepper and Worcestershire sauce. Process until blended. Remove and set aside.

Process 1 cup Parmesan cheese, 4 garlic cloves, basil leaves and olive oil in the food processor until mixed well.

Cut the provolone cheese into large thin slices. Line a 2^1/2-quart loaf pan with plastic wrap, leaving a long edge over each side. Line the pan with provolone cheese slices. Layer the cream cheese mixture, basil mixture and remaining provolone cheese slices ^{1}/2 at a time in the pan. Fold the plastic wrap edges over the top. Chill for 2 to 12 hours. Invert onto a serving dish. Serve with a variety of crackers.

NOTE: You may substitute sun-dried tomato bits for the sun-dried tomatoes and omit the chopping of the tomatoes.

The softer a cheese, the more perishable it is. *Firm, semi-firm, and semi-soft cheese* are best stored wrapped tightly in plastic wrap and stored in a refrigerator's cheese compartment (or warmest location) for up to several weeks. Such cheeses can be frozen, but likely will undergo a textural change. *Fresh and soft-ripened cheeses* should be tightly wrapped and stored in the coldest part of the refrigerator, generally for no more than two weeks. While mold is ugly, it does not mean the cheese is inedible. Simply remove the offending moldy portion (plus a little extra) and discard. In any case, cheese generally should be served at room temperature to deepen its flavor.

SEAFOOD APPETIZER CHEESECAKE

YIELD: 10 TO 12 SERVINGS

1 1/4 cups crushed butter crackers
3 tablespoons butter, melted
1 (12-ounce) package small frozen
    shrimp, thawed
16 ounces cream cheese, softened
1/4 cup sour cream
1 teaspoon lemon juice
1/2 teaspoon white pepper
3 eggs
1 teaspoon onion powder
1/2 cup sour cream
2 teaspoons dill weed

Combine the cracker crumbs and butter in a bowl and mix well. Press over the bottom of a 9-inch springform pan. Bake at 350 degrees for 10 minutes.

Coarsely chop the shrimp in a food processor. Set aside. Combine the cream cheese and 1/4 cup sour cream in the food processor and process at medium speed. Stir in the shrimp, lemon juice, white pepper, eggs and onion powder. Pour over the crust.

Bake at 325 degrees for 45 minutes. Place on a wire rack. Loosen the cheesecake from the side of the pan. Let stand until cool. Remove the side of the pan. Spread 1/2 cup sour cream over the top. Sprinkle with the dill weed. Serve with crackers.

PETITE PESTO CHEESECAKE

YIELD: 8 TO 10 SERVINGS

1 tablespoon butter, softened
^{1}/4 cup fine dry Italian-seasoned
   bread crumbs
^{1}/4 cup plus 2 tablespoons (1^1/2 ounces)
   grated Parmesan cheese
8 ounces cream cheese, softened
^{1}/2 cup ricotta cheese
^{1}/4 teaspoon salt
^{1}/8 teaspoon cayenne pepper
2 eggs
^{1}/4 cup pesto sauce
^{1}/4 cup pine nuts
Crackers

GARNISH
Fresh basil sprigs

Rub the butter over the bottoms and up the sides of two 1^3/4-inch deep 4-inch springform pans. Combine the bread crumbs and 2 tablespoons of the Parmesan cheese in a bowl and mix well. Sprinkle over the bottoms and up the sides of the pans.

Beat the remaining ^{1}/4 cup Parmesan cheese, cream cheese, ricotta cheese, salt and cayenne pepper in a mixing bowl until light and fluffy. Add the eggs one at a time, mixing well after each addition. Pour half the cheese mixture into a separate bowl. Stir the pesto sauce into the remaining half. Pour half the pesto mixture into each of the prepared pans, smoothing the tops. Spoon half the remaining cheese mixture over the pesto mixture in each of the pans, smoothing the tops gently. Sprinkle half the pine nuts over the tops of each.

Bake at 325 degrees for 30 minutes or until the center is firm. Place on a wire rack to cool. Chill, tightly covered with plastic wrap, for 8 to 12 hours. Run a small knife around the sides of the pans to loosen the cheesecakes. Place each on a platter. Circle with crackers. Garnish with basil sprigs.

MUSHROOM CHEESECAKE WITH CRAB

YIELD: 16 SERVINGS

CRUST

1³/4 cups bread crumbs
1 cup (4 ounces) grated Parmesan cheese
6 tablespoons butter, melted

FILLING

1 tablespoon olive oil
1 cup chopped onion
1 cup chopped red bell pepper
4 cups coarsely chopped assorted fresh
    wild mushrooms such as crimini, oyster
    and shiitake
28 ounces cream cheese, softened
2 teaspoons salt
1 teaspoon pepper
4 eggs
¹/2 cup heavy cream
2 cups crab meat, well-drained
1 cup (4 ounces) shredded smoked
    Gouda cheese
¹/2 cup chopped fresh parsley

TOPPING

¹/4 cup sliced mushrooms
¹/4 cup chopped red bell pepper
Butter
French baguette, sliced and toasted

FOR THE CRUST, combine the bread crumbs, Parmesan cheese and butter in a bowl and mix well. Press over the bottom of a 9-inch springform pan. Bake at 350 degrees for 10 minutes or until golden brown.

FOR THE FILLING, heat the olive oil in a skillet over medium heat. Add the onion and bell pepper. Sauté for 2 minutes. Add the mushrooms. Sauté for 10 minutes or until the liquid evaporates and the mushrooms begin to brown. Remove from the heat.

Beat the cream cheese, salt and pepper in a mixing bowl until light and fluffy. Beat in the eggs one at a time, mixing well after each addition. Whip in the cream. Stir in the mushroom mixture, crab meat, Gouda cheese and parsley. Pour over the crust.

Place the springform pan on a baking sheet. Bake for 1¹/2 hours or until the cheesecake puffs and browns on the top and the center is almost firm. Place on a wire rack to cool. Run a small sharp knife around the edge and remove the side of the pan. Place the cheesecake on a platter.

CRAB PIZZA

YIELD: 8 SERVINGS

FOR THE TOPPING, sauté the mushrooms and bell pepper in a small amount of butter in a skillet until tender. Sprinkle over the top of the cheesecake. Serve immediately with toasted baguette slices. You may prepare this up to 1 day in advance and store, covered, in the refrigerator, preparing the topping and sprinkling on just before serving.

NOTE: For a low-fat version, substitute 1/3-less-fat cream cheese for the cream cheese, egg substitute for the eggs and fat-free half-and-half for the heavy cream.

1/2 cup mayonnaise
1 tablespoon lemon juice
1/4 teaspoon salt
6 ounces crab meat
1 cup (4 ounces) shredded Swiss cheese
1 tablespoon chopped green onions
1 (12-inch) pizza crust
2 tablespoons chopped green onions

Combine the mayonnaise, lemon juice, salt, crab meat, Swiss cheese and 1 tablespoon green onions in a bowl and mix well. Spread over the pizza crust. Sprinkle 2 tablespoons green onions over the top. Place on a greased baking sheet. Bake at 450 degrees for 10 minutes. Cut into wedges or small bite-size squares.

COUNTRY PORK PÂTÉ

YIELD: 24 SERVINGS

$^1/_2$ cup minced onion

I tablespoon butter

I garlic clove, minced

$^1/_2$ cup dry white wine

I Cornish game hen (optional)

2 tablespoons flour

I teaspoon coriander

$^1/_2$ teaspoon thyme

$^1/_2$ teaspoon freshly ground black pepper

$^1/_4$ teaspoon curing salt

$^3/_4$ teaspoon fine salt

$^1/_4$ teaspoon allspice

8 ounces salt pork

I pound ground pork

I egg

Sauté the onion in the butter in a 10-inch skillet over medium heat for 6 minutes or until translucent. Add the garlic and cook for I to 2 minutes; do not brown the onion or garlic. Add the wine and simmer until reduced by two-thirds. Remove from the heat and let stand until room temperature.

Skin and debone the Cornish game hen, cutting the breast meat into $^1/_2$-inch strips.

Mix the flour, coriander, thyme, pepper, curing salt, fine salt and allspice in a small bowl.

Remove the rind from the salt pork and discard. Cut the salt pork into $^1/_4$-inch cubes. Place in a food processor and process until smooth or finely mince with a sharp knife. Combine the salt pork, ground pork, onion mixture and egg in a 4-quart mixing bowl and mix well. Add the flour mixture and mix well.

Spread a half-inch layer of the pork mixture over the bottom of a terrine mold or 9-inch loaf pan. Arrange half the game hen meat over the pork mixture. Spread a half-inch layer of the pork mixture over the game hen meat. Arrange the remaining game hen meat over the pork mixture. Spread the remaining pork mixture over the game hen meat. Pat the layers gently to remove any air pockets. Cover the terrine mold tightly with foil and place in a larger baking pan. Add water to the larger pan until the water is halfway up the sides of the terrine mold. Bake at 350 degrees for 1 hour and 50 minutes or until the internal temperature measures 160 degrees on a meat thermometer.

Remove from the oven. Let stand in the water bath until room temperature. Remove from the water bath and pour off any excess juices. Cover with plastic wrap and place a loaf pan on top of the pâté. Weight the loaf pan with 1 to 2 pounds of cans to firm the texture, securing the cans with rubber bands or masking tape. Chill for 24 hours.

Remove the weights and remove the pâté from the mold. Rinse the pâté quickly to remove any congealed juices and pat dry with paper towels. Cut into slices and arrange on a serving plate. Let stand at room temperature for 30 minutes to enhance the flavor.

BLUE CHEESE CREAM PUFFS

YIELD: 12 SERVINGS

1/2 cup water
1/4 cup (1/2 stick) butter or margarine
1/2 cup flour
1/4 teaspoon salt
3/4 teaspoon chopped fresh parsley leaves
1/8 teaspoon coarsely ground pepper
2 eggs
1 cup (4 ounces) crumbled blue cheese
2 tablespoons chopped walnuts

Spray a large baking sheet with nonstick cooking spray.

Bring the water and butter to a boil in a 3-quart saucepan over medium heat. Add the flour, salt, parsley and pepper all at once. Cook for 30 to 60 seconds or until the mixture forms a ball, stirring constantly. Remove from the heat.

Add the eggs one at a time and beat at medium speed, mixing well after each addition. Drop the dough by heaping teaspoonfuls 2 inches apart onto the prepared baking sheet.

Bake at 425 degrees for 15 to 20 minutes or until golden brown. Cool on the baking sheet for 5 minutes. Press the center of each puff gently with the tip of a spoon, making a slight indentation. Sprinkle with the blue cheese and walnuts. Bake for an additional 2 to 4 minutes or until the cheese is melted. Serve warm.

GOAT CHEESE CROSTINI

YIELD: 8 TO 10 SERVINGS

ROASTED GARLIC
1 head garlic
1 teaspoon olive oil

TOMATO SAUCE
1 tablespoon olive oil
1/4 cup minced white onion
1/2 teaspoon minced shallots
1 (14-ounce) can diced tomatoes
1/4 teaspoon salt
1/4 teaspoon freshly ground pepper
1 teaspoon chopped fresh basil
1 bay leaf

GARLIC CROSTINI
1 baguette
1/3 cup olive oil
2 teaspoons minced garlic
1/4 teaspoon freshly ground black pepper
1/4 teaspoon salt
1/8 teaspoon cayenne pepper

GOAT CHEESE GRATIN
12 ounces goat cheese
2 teaspoons chopped fresh rosemary
1 teaspoon snipped fresh chives
2 teaspoons fresh thyme
1/4 teaspoon freshly ground pepper
1 tablespoon freshly grated Parmesan cheese

FOR THE ROASTED GARLIC, cut the top quarter off the head of garlic, exposing the cloves. Place on a piece of foil. Drizzle the exposed cloves with the olive oil. Wrap tightly in the foil. Bake at 350 degrees for 30 to 45 minutes or until the cloves are soft and begin to turn golden brown. Let stand until room temperature. Squeeze the cloves from the garlic head, discarding the peel.

FOR THE TOMATO SAUCE, heat the olive oil in a small saucepan over medium heat. Add the onion and cook for 2 to 3 minutes or until tender, stirring frequently. Add the shallots and cook for 1 minute. Add the tomatoes, salt, pepper, basil and bay leaf. Bring to a simmer. Reduce the heat to low. Simmer for 20 minutes, stirring occasionally. Adjust the seasonings as desired. Remove and discard the bay leaf.

FOR THE CROSTINI, cut the baguette into
1/4-inch-thick round slices. Whisk the olive oil,
garlic, black pepper, salt and cayenne pepper
in a bowl. Brush each side of the bread
rounds with the olive oil mixture. Arrange
in a single layer on a baking sheet. Bake at
350 degrees for 20 minutes or until the
crostini are crisp and begin to turn golden
brown. Cool on a wire rack. Store in an
airtight container at room temperature.

FOR THE GRATIN, lightly oil the bottom of
a 9-inch gratin dish. Preheat the broiler.
Crumble the goat cheese over the bottom
of the gratin dish. Combine the rosemary,
chives, thyme and pepper in a bowl and mix
well. Sprinkle half the herb mixture over the
goat cheese. Sprinkle the Parmesan cheese
over the herbs. Pour the tomato
sauce over the layers. Scatter the roasted
garlic cloves over the tomato sauce. Sprinkle
with the remaining herb mixture. Broil until
the cheese melts and the top begins to
brown. Serve immediately with garlic crostini.

NOTE: You may make the tomato sauce,
roasted garlic and crostini up to 3 days
in advance.

CHEESE 101

Cheese is made in all parts
of the Western world, and,
like wine, it takes on unique
flavors, textures, and tastes
depending on its origin and
the period of time it has aged.

Fresh cheese, such as ricotta,
cream cheese, and cottage
cheese, has not aged.

Ripened cheese must be cured
using heat, soaking, etc., and
then allowed to age. *Ripened*
cheeses are further classified
as either hard, semi-firm,
semi-soft, or soft-ripened.

A *hard* cheese, such as
pecorino or Parmesan, is
aged for an extended time.

Semi-firm cheeses, including
Cheddar, Edam, and Jarlsburg,
are aged less and usually are
firm but not crumbly.

Semi-soft cheeses, such as Gouda,
can be sliced but are soft.

Soft-ripened cheese, including
Brie and Camembert, develop
a generally edible soft rind.

EMMENTALER AND GRUYÈRE CHEESE PUFFS

YIELD: 22 SERVINGS

1 cup flour
1 teaspoon dry mustard
1/4 teaspoon cayenne pepper
1 cup hot water
1/2 cup (1 stick) unsalted butter
1/4 teaspoon salt
1/4 cup sugar
3 eggs
1/2 cup (2 ounces) shredded
   Emmentaler cheese
1/2 cup (2 ounces) shredded Gruyère cheese

Combine the flour, dry mustard and cayenne pepper in a bowl and mix well. Combine the hot water, butter, salt and sugar in a small saucepan. Cook until the butter melts and the mixture comes to a full boil, stirring constantly. Stir in the flour mixture vigorously. Cook over medium heat until the mixture leaves the side of the pan, stirring constantly. Remove from the heat.

Stir the eggs one at a time into the dough, mixing well after each addition. Stir in the Emmentaler and Gruyère cheeses. Drop by teaspoonfuls onto a greased baking sheet. Bake at 450 degrees for 10 minutes. Reduce the oven temperature to 375 degrees. Bake for an additional 15 minutes or until puffed and golden brown. Turn off the oven and let the puffs stand for 3 minutes.

ROSEMARY PINE NUT BRUSCHETTA

YIELD: 24 SERVINGS

1 package Italian herb bread machine mix
1 (6-ounce) can tomato paste
3 tablespoons pesto
Grated mozzarella cheese
Fresh rosemary leaves
Pine nuts

Prepare the bread mix according to directions for making pizza dough in a bread machine. After the first rising of the dough, roll dough out on a lightly floured surface. Cut with a 2-inch round cutter. Place rounds on an oiled baking sheet.

Combine the tomato paste and pesto in a bowl and mix well. Spread over the dough rounds. Sprinkle with mozzarella cheese, rosemary and pine nuts. You may prepare the bruschetta up to this point and store in the freezer.

Bake at 400 degrees for 12 to 15 minutes.

ZESTY OLIVE-TOPPED APPETIZERS

YIELD: 10 TO 12 SERVINGS

1 baguette, cut into $1/4$-inch-thick slices
1 garlic clove
1 (3-ounce) container onion and chive
  cream cheese spread
$1/2$ cup chopped green olives
$1/2$ cup chopped black olives
1 or 2 garlic cloves, minced

Rub the bread slices with the garlic clove and place on a baking sheet. Broil until toasted. Spread with the cream cheese spread. Combine the olives and minced garlic in a bowl and mix well. Spread over the cream cheese. Chill, covered, until ready to serve.

NOTE: Use pimento-stuffed green olives if desired.

SUN-DRIED TOMATOES WITH CHEESE

YIELD: 10 SERVINGS

6 ounces (about) marinated oil-pack
  sun-dried tomatoes
1 large loaf French bread, cut into
  $1/4$-inch-thick slices
$1/3$ cup Alouette spread with herbs
1 cup ricotta cheese
1 cup (4 ounces) shredded
  mozzarella cheese
$1/4$ cup (1 ounce) grated Parmesan cheese
2 garlic cloves, minced

Drain the tomatoes, reserving the marinade. Cut the tomatoes into halves. Brush the bread slices with the reserved marinade and arrange on a baking sheet. Combine the spread, ricotta cheese, mozzarella cheese, Parmesan cheese and garlic in a bowl and mix well. Place about 2 teaspoons of the mixture on each bread slice. Arrange 2 or 3 tomato halves on top. Bake at 350 degrees for 10 minutes or until bubbly.

ICE LUMINARIA

Ice not only keeps the drinks cold but can add glamour and glitz to any party. Frozen luminarias make lovely decorations on the front walk during the winter, centerpieces, or wine coolers. Create wonderful winter luminaries using frozen water, cranberries, evergreens, marbles, or other colorful items that can withstand the cold.

Spread a thin layer of cooking oil over the inside of a medium-size bucket (e.g., plastic ice cream pails work well) and place a layer of greens, trinkets, etc., on the bottom of the bucket. Invert a smaller, lightly greased can or empty wine bottle (filled with beans) into the larger bucket. Fill the larger bucket with water. Place in the freezer, or outside if it is cold enough. Once the ice is frozen, remove the inverted can or bottle and gently remove the ice from the larger container. Place a small candle in the indentation to create a stunning winter luminary!

PEA AND SHALLOT BRUSCHETTA

YIELD: 25 APPETIZERS

BRUSCHETTA
1 large baguette
2 tablespoons olive oil
1 large garlic clove

TOPPING
1 tablespoon butter
4 shallots, minced
1 cup fresh spring baby peas
1/4 cup chopped mint leaves
Salt to taste
Pepper to taste

FOR THE BRUSCHETTA, cut the baguette into 25 rounds. Brush each round lightly with olive oil and place on a broiler pan. Broil until toasted. Rub each round with the garlic clove.

FOR THE TOPPING, heat the butter in a skillet until melted. Add the shallots and peas. Cook until the shallots are tender and the peas are cooked through. Stir in the mint. Season with salt and pepper. Spoon the mixture into a food processor and coarsely chop. Spoon evenly over the bruschetta. Serve warm.

Always Superb: Recipes for Every Occasion

MUSHROOM DUXELLE WITH HEARTY BROWN BREAD

YIELD: 2 SERVINGS

HEARTY BROWN BREAD
3 cups whole wheat flour
1/2 cup cornmeal
1/2 cup wheat germ
1 3/4 teaspoons baking soda
1 teaspoon salt
1/4 cup vegetable oil
2 tablespoons honey
1 1/2 cups buttermilk
Melted butter

MUSHROOM DUXELLE
1 teaspoon butter
2 tablespoons minced shallots
5 ounces mushrooms, chopped
2 tablespoons heavy whipping cream
Salt to taste
White pepper to taste

FOR THE BREAD, combine the wheat flour, cornmeal, wheat germ, baking soda and salt in a bowl and mix well. Combine the oil, honey and buttermilk in a separate bowl and mix well. Add the dry ingredients and mix well. Knead on a floured surface until smooth. Divide the dough into 2 equal portions and shape into balls. Place on a baking sheet. Cut an X across the top of each loaf. Bake at 350 degrees for 30 minutes. Brush the tops with melted butter.

FOR THE DUXELLE, heat a 10-inch skillet over medium-high heat. Add the butter and swirl to coat the bottom of the pan. Reduce the heat to medium. Add the shallots and sauté until translucent.

Arrange the mushrooms evenly over the shallots. Cook over medium-high heat until the liquid has evaporated and a brown glaze begins to form on the bottom of the pan. Stir in the cream. Season with salt and white pepper. Cook until the mixture thickens. Remove from the heat and spoon into a bowl. Let stand until cooled. Chill, covered, until ready to serve.

Cut the bread into slices. Serve the duxelle with the bread.

BAKED CHEESE DELIGHTS

YIELD: 15 SERVINGS

8 ounces cream cheese
1/2 cup (1 stick) unsalted butter
2 cups (8 ounces) shredded sharp
    Cheddar cheese
1/8 teaspoon garlic powder
2 egg whites, beaten
1 loaf French or Italian bread, cut into
    1-inch cubes

Combine the cream cheese, butter, Cheddar
cheese and garlic powder in a medium
saucepan. Cook over low heat until the cream
cheese, butter and Cheddar cheese are
melted and the ingredients are combined,
stirring constantly. Remove from the heat and
let stand until cool.

Fold the beaten egg whites into the
cheese mixture. Dip the bread cubes in
the cheese mixture, turning to coat all sides
and spreading the mixture on the bread
cubes with a knife if needed.

Place the cheese-covered cubes on a baking
sheet lined with waxed paper. Freeze for 1 to
2 hours. Place the frozen cubes on a separate
baking sheet. Bake at 400 degrees for
10 minutes or until brown; do not burn.

CHEESE CRISPS

YIELD: ABOUT 95 CRACKERS

$^{1}/_{2}$ cup (1 stick) butter, softened
8 ounces (or more) Pepper Jack, Colby or
   sharp Cheddar cheese, shredded
1 egg yolk
1 teaspoon salt, or to taste
2 teaspoons Cajun Seasoning
1 cup flour
1 egg white
Pinch of salt

Line 2 baking sheets with parchment paper.

Process the butter and 8 ounces Pepper Jack cheese in a food processor until smooth, increasing the amount of cheese for a stronger cheese flavor. Add the egg yolk, 1 teaspoon salt and cayenne pepper and process until combined. Add the flour and process until a dough forms.

Spoon the dough a portion at a time into a pastry bag or dough press fitted with a $^{7}/_{8}$-inch ribbon tip. Form the dough in long strips 2 inches apart on the prepared baking sheets; dough strips may break but do not need to be repaired.

Whisk the egg white and pinch of salt in a bowl. Brush over each dough strip. Bake dough strips at 375 degrees for 10 to 15 minutes or until golden brown. Slice diagonally into 1$^{1}/_{2}$-inch crackers while hot. Remove to a wire rack to cool completely. Store in an airtight container for up to 1 week. You may bake the crackers on a baking sheet at 300 degrees for 5 minutes if they become soft to make them crisp again.

NOTE: Pepper Jack cheese will make the crackers extra spicy, Colby provides a nice texture and moderate cheese flavor, and sharp Cheddar gives a rich orange color and full cheese flavor. You may substitute other spices for the cayenne pepper or use a variety of flavors such as chives and dill, Italian seasoning, finely chopped pecans, or thyme and marjoram. You may also sprinkle the crackers with toasted sesame seeds, poppy seeds, fennel seeds or caraway seeds before baking.

NOTE: You may shape the dough into a log, wrap in plastic wrap, chill for 8 to 12 hours or until dough is firm, and cut into $^{1}/_{8}$-inch-thick slices if you do not have a pastry bag or dough press.

PECAN CHEESE STUFFED MUSHROOMS

YIELD: 30 APPETIZERS

3 slices bacon
30 large fresh mushrooms, stems removed
  and discarded
1/2 cup (1 stick) butter, melted
1 cup chopped pecans
3 tablespoons chopped green onions
1 tablespoon dry white wine
3/4 cup Italian bread crumbs
8 ounces cream cheese, softened

GARNISH
Chopped parsley

Cook the bacon in a small skillet until crisp.
Place on paper towels to drain. Let stand
until cool; crumble.

Brush the mushroom caps with the
melted butter.

Preheat the broiler. Combine the pecans,
green onions, wine, bacon, bread crumbs and
cream cheese in a medium bowl and mix
well. Fill the mushroom caps with the cream
cheese mixture. Place the mushrooms filled
side up on a baking sheet. Broil for 3 to
5 minutes. Place on a serving platter. Serve
hot, garnished with chopped parsley.

You may stuff the mushrooms ahead of time
and chill in the refrigerator. Bring to room
temperature before broiling.

CRUNCHY OLIVE BITES

YIELD: 40 TO 60 APPETIZERS

1 cup (4 ounces) shredded sharp
  Cheddar cheese
1/2 cup flour
1/4 cup (1/2 stick) butter, cut into 1-inch pats
3 dashes of Tabasco sauce
40 to 60 small stuffed green olives

Process the Cheddar cheese, flour, butter and
Tabasco sauce in a food processor until a
smooth ball is formed. Scoop out a small
amount and shape into a ball. Flatten the ball
and place an olive in the center. Seal the
edges around the olive and roll until the olive
is completely covered by the dough; the
dough covering should be thin enough that
the olive color can be seen. Place on a baking
sheet. Repeat the process with the remaining
dough and olives. Bake at 425 degrees for 12
to 18 minutes or until golden brown.

NOTE: You may prepare the dough in advance
and chill, covered, in the refrigerator until
ready to assemble the olive bites.

MINIATURE STUFFED POTATOES WITH ROASTED GARLIC

YIELD: 24 APPETIZERS

2 heads garlic
Olive oil for drizzling
24 small red potatoes
Salt
1 1/2 cups (6 ounces) shredded
    Cheddar cheese
3/4 cup cooked spinach (optional)
4 teaspoons parsley
1 tablespoon salt
1 tablespoon pepper
1 grilled large portobello mushroom,
    finely chopped
1/2 cup (or more) sour cream

Cut the top quarter off each head of garlic, exposing the cloves. Place on a piece of foil. Drizzle the exposed cloves with olive oil. Wrap tightly in the foil. Bake at 375 degrees for 30 minutes or until the cloves are soft. Squeeze the cloves from the garlic heads into a small bowl, discarding the peel. Mash the garlic cloves.

Scrub the potatoes and place in a saucepan with enough water to cover and a small amount of salt. Bring to a boil. Boil for 25 minutes or until tender; drain. Let stand until slightly cooled.

Cut the bottom off each cooked potato so that it will stand upright. Scoop the potato pulp into a bowl, leaving the shells intact; reserve the shells. Mash the potato pulp. Add the Cheddar cheese, spinach, parsley, 1 tablespoon salt, pepper, mushroom and enough sour cream to make of the desired consistency and mix well. Spoon into each of the reserved potato shells, mounding the mixture over the top. Reserve any remaining potato mixture to serve at another time. Spread the roasted garlic over the tops of the filled potato shells.

Place the stuffed potatoes on a baking sheet. Bake at 350 degrees for 25 minutes or until heated through.

ASPARAGUS RISOTTO WITH PARMESAN CHEESE CUPS

YIELD: 8 SERVINGS

CHEESE CUPS

2 cups (8 ounces) freshly grated
    Parmesan cheese

RISOTTO

5 cups water
Salt
1 pound asparagus, trimmed
2 cups chicken stock
2 tablespoons olive oil
1 shallot, chopped
1^1/2 cups arborio rice
^{1}/4 cup (1 ounce) freshly grated
    Parmesan cheese
^{1}/2 teaspoon salt
^{1}/4 teaspoon white pepper

FOR THE CHEESE CUPS, heat a 7-inch nonstick skillet over medium-low heat. Sprinkle ^{1}/4 cup of the Parmesan cheese over the bottom of the skillet. Cook until golden brown on both sides, turning once. Remove from the skillet and place over an inverted bowl, shaping into a cup. Repeat the process with the remaining cheese.

FOR THE RISOTTO, bring the water and a small amount of salt to a boil in a saucepan. Add the asparagus and cook for 2 to 3 minutes or until tender-crisp and bright green. Remove the asparagus and plunge into an ice bath, reserving the water. Let stand until completely cool. Drain 8 to 10 spears and set aside. Remove the tips from the asparagus and set aside. Chop the remaining stalks into ^{1}/2-inch pieces.

Add the chicken stock to the reserved water and bring to a boil. Reduce the heat to low.

Heat the olive oil in a large deep skillet. Add the shallot and sauté. Add the rice and cook for 1 minute, stirring constantly. Stir in 1 cup of the stock mixture. Cook until all of the liquid is absorbed, stirring frequently.

Add $^1/_2$ cup of the remaining stock mixture to the rice. Cook until all of the liquid is absorbed, stirring frequently. Repeat the process with $3^1/_2$ cups of the remaining stock mixture. Add the chopped asparagus stalks.

Add $^1/_2$ cup of the remaining stock mixture to the rice. Cook until all of the liquid is absorbed, stirring frequently. Repeat the process with the remaining stock mixture until all is used or the rice is tender to the bite, stirring in the asparagus tips before the last addition of the stock mixture. Remove the risotto from the heat and stir in the Parmesan cheese, $^1/_2$ teaspoon salt and white pepper.

Spoon the risotto into the cheese cups. Garnish with the reserved asparagus spears and additional Parmesan cheese.

NOTE: You may substitute a blend of Parmesan and Romano cheeses for the Parmesan cheese. You may add 8 ounces sautéed mushrooms to the risotto. You may make the cheese cups smaller and top with a sweet and spicy salsa or chutney. You may prepare the cheese cups 1 day ahead and store in an airtight container after cooling completely.

GRAPE LEAVES STUFFED WITH WILD RICE AND YOGURT MINT SAUCE

YIELD: 30 APPETIZERS

STUFFED GRAPE LEAVES

2 tablespoons olive oil
1 onion, chopped
$1/3$ cup long grain rice
$1/3$ cup wild rice
$1/2$ teaspoon allspice
$1/2$ teaspoon mint
$1 1/2$ cups water
$1/4$ cup dried currants
2 tablespoons olive oil
$1/2$ cup pine nuts
$1/2$ teaspoon salt
$1/2$ teaspoon white pepper
1 (8-ounce) jar grape leaves
1 onion, thinly sliced
3 tablespoons olive oil
$1/2$ cup freshly squeezed lemon juice
$1/4$ cup water

YOGURT MINT SAUCE

2 cups yogurt
$1/4$ cup chopped fresh mint leaves
3 garlic cloves, minced
Pinch of salt

GARNISH

Lemon wedges
Chopped fresh parsley

FOR THE GRAPE LEAVES, heat 2 tablespoons olive oil in a medium saucepan. Add the chopped onion. Sauté for 5 minutes or until tender. Stir in the long grain rice, wild rice, allspice and mint. Cook for 30 seconds, stirring constantly. Add $1 1/2$ cups water and currants. Bring to a boil. Reduce the heat. Simmer for 20 minutes or until the water is absorbed and the rice is tender. Remove from the heat.

Heat 2 tablespoons olive oil in a small heavy skillet over medium-low heat. Add the pine nuts and cook for 6 minutes or until brown, stirring frequently. Stir into the rice mixture. Stir the salt and white pepper into the rice mixture.

Bring a large pot of water to a boil. Add the grape leaves, stirring to separate. Turn off the heat and let stand for 1 minute; drain. Rinse with cold water to cool the leaves; drain. Cover the bottom of a large skillet with the sliced onion. Arrange 10 grape leaves over the onion and 1 inch up the side, pressing to adhere.

Place a leaf vein side up on a plate. Spoon 1 tablespoon of the rice mixture near the stem. Fold in the sides and roll to enclose the filling. Place seam side down in the prepared skillet. Repeat the process with the remaining grape leaves.

Drizzle 3 tablespoons olive oil over the stuffed grape leaves. Pour the lemon juice and 1/4 cup water over the stuffed grape leaves. Bring to a boil. Reduce the heat and simmer for 50 minutes. Let stand to cool completely.

FOR THE SAUCE, combine the yogurt, mint, garlic and salt in a bowl and mix well.

Arrange the stuffed grape leaves on a platter. Drizzle with the sauce. Garnish with lemon wedges and parsley.

SWEDISH MEATBALLS

2 cups soft bread crumbs
   (about 3 slices dried bread)
2/3 cup milk
1/4 cup (1/2 stick) butter
1/2 cup minced onion
1 1/2 pounds ground beef or veal
3 eggs, lightly beaten
2 teaspoons salt
1/2 teaspoon pepper
1 teaspoon nutmeg
1 teaspoon paprika
1 tablespoon beef base
3 tablespoons flour
1 cup water
Pepper to taste
1 cup sour cream
2 tablespoons minced parsley

Soak the bread crumbs in the milk in a bowl until softened. Melt 1 tablespoon of the butter in a small saucepan over low heat. Add the onion and cook for 3 minutes, stirring occasionally. Combine the softened bread, cooked onion and beef in a bowl and mix well. Add the eggs, salt, 1/2 teaspoon pepper, nutmeg and paprika and mix until smooth and light.

Shape beef mixture into small balls, dusting your hands with flour while shaping. Melt the remaining 3 tablespoons butter in a large skillet. Add the meatballs and cook until golden brown on all sides.

Remove the meatballs and set aside. Add the beef base and flour to the skillet, stirring to combine. Add the water and pepper to taste. Cook until thickened, stirring constantly. Reduce the heat to low. Cook for 5 minutes, stirring occasionally. Stir in the sour cream 1 rounded tablespoon at a time, mixing well after each addition. Return the meatballs to the skillet. Simmer, covered, for 10 minutes. Sprinkle with parsley.

ROAST BEEF GRISSINI WITH REMOULADE

YIELD: 24 APPETIZERS

REMOULADE SAUCE
$^1/_2$ cup mayonnaise
1 hard-cooked egg, finely chopped
2 tablespoons minced gherkins
1 tablespoon plus 1 teaspoon Dijon mustard
1 tablespoon drained finely chopped capers
1 tablespoon finely chopped flat-leaf parsley
1 tablespoon finely chopped dill
2 teaspoons finely chopped chives
1 teaspoon minced garlic
Freshly ground pepper

GRISSINI
2 garlic cloves, thinly sliced
2 tablespoons olive oil
8 ounces roast beef, thinly sliced
Salt to taste
Freshly ground pepper to taste
24 arugula leaves, stemmed
8 to 10 grissini, broken into 4-inch pieces

FOR THE SAUCE, combine the mayonnaise, egg, gherkins, mustard, capers, parsley, dill, chives, garlic and pepper in a bowl and mix well. Chill, covered, for up to 12 hours.

FOR THE GRISSINI, combine the garlic and olive oil in a skillet. Cook over medium heat until garlic is golden brown. Remove the garlic and discard. Let the garlic oil stand until completely cool.

Cut the beef slices into twenty-four 1$^1/_2$x6-inch strips. Spread on a work surface. Brush each strip with the garlic oil. Sprinkle with salt and pepper. Cover each with an arugula leaf slightly larger than the strip. Roll each strip and leaf around one end of a grissino piece. You may prepare to this point and refrigerate for up to 1 hour in advance.

Arrange the grissini on a platter and serve with the sauce.

NOTE: Other bread or breadsticks may be substituted for the grissini.

VENISON SAUSAGE WITH CRANBERRY PINEAPPLE CHUTNEY CREAM CHEESE

YIELD: VARIABLE

BRUSCHETTA
1 baguette
Butter

CRANBERRY PINEAPPLE CHUTNEY
1 pineapple, peeled and chopped, or
   1 (20-ounce) can chopped pineapple
1 small sweet onion, finely chopped
1 small green bell pepper, finely chopped
$1/2$ cup sugar
$1/2$ cup cider vinegar
12 cardamom seeds, crushed
2 tablespoons finely chopped
   crystallized ginger
1 cup whole cranberries
Salt to taste

ASSEMBLY
8 ounces cream cheese, softened
Venison or beef summer sausage, sliced

FOR THE BRUSCHETTA, cut the baguette into thin slices. Butter one side of each bread slice. Arrange in a single layer on a baking sheet. Bake at 250 degrees for 25 minutes or until golden brown.

FOR THE CHUTNEY, combine the pineapple, onion, bell pepper, sugar, vinegar, cardamom seeds and ginger in a saucepan. Let stand for 1 hour. Bring mixture to a boil. Stir in the cranberries. Reduce the heat. Simmer for 40 minutes, stirring occasionally. Season with salt. Let stand until completely cool.

TO ASSEMBLE, combine $1/2$ cup of the chutney with the cream cheese in a bowl and mix well, reserving the remaining chutney for another use. Spread over one side of each toast. Top with a slice of venison sausage.

MINIATURE CRAB CAKES WITH
RED CHILI MAYONNAISE

YIELD: 24 APPETIZERS

CRAB CAKES

1 pound fresh or thawed frozen crab meat,
  shells removed and flaked
3/4 cup fresh bread crumbs
1/4 cup chopped fresh parsley
2 tablespoons finely chopped scallions
2 tablespoons chopped celery
3 tablespoons freshly squeezed lime juice
1/2 teaspoon Worcestershire sauce
1 tablespoon mayonnaise
1 egg
3 tablespoons butter

RED CHILI MAYONNAISE

1 cup mayonnaise
4 teaspoons chili-garlic sauce
3 1/2 teaspoons lemon juice

GARNISH

Lime slices

FOR THE CRAB CAKES, combine the crab meat, bread crumbs, parsley, scallions, celery, lime juice, Worcestershire sauce, mayonnaise and egg in a bowl and mix well. Shape into small cakes. Heat the butter in a large skillet until melted. Add the crab cakes. Cook over medium heat for 2 to 3 minutes per side. Remove to paper towels to drain.

FOR THE MAYONNAISE, combine the mayonnaise, chili-garlic sauce and lemon juice in a bowl and mix well. Chill, covered, until ready to use.

Arrange the crab cakes on a platter. Garnish with lime slices and serve with the mayonnaise.

NOTE: The crab cakes can be made larger and served over greens for a great lunch.

COCONUT SHRIMP WITH TABASCO MARMALADE SAUCE

YIELD: 24 APPETIZERS

TABASCO MARMALADE SAUCE
2 cups orange marmalade
Tabasco sauce to taste

SHRIMP
24 large shrimp with tails
Tempura mix
2 cups (or more) unsweetened
    shredded coconut
3 eggs, beaten
Vegetable oil for frying

FOR THE SAUCE, combine the marmalade and Tabasco sauce in a bowl and mix well.

FOR THE SHRIMP, peel, devein and butterfly the shrimp, leaving the tails on. Prepare the tempura batter using the package directions. Stir in 2 cups coconut. Dip each shrimp in the beaten eggs and then in the tempura mixture, pressing additional coconut onto the shrimp if desired. Place on a baking sheet lined with waxed paper. Freeze for 1 hour.

Heat the oil in a deep fryer or skillet to 350 degrees. Add 6 to 8 shrimp. Cook for 3 minutes or until golden brown. Place on paper towels to drain. Repeat the process with the remaining shrimp.

Arrange the shrimp on a serving plate. Serve with the sauce.

SPRING ROLLS

YIELD: 8 TO 12 APPETIZERS

DIPPING SAUCE
1 cup fish sauce
2 tablespoons minced garlic
2 tablespoons chili-garlic sauce
1 cup sugar
1/3 cup lemon juice
1/2 cup rice vinegar
1/2 cup water

SPRING ROLLS
8 ounces rice noodles
1 teaspoon sesame oil
1 teaspoon fish sauce
1 tablespoon soy sauce
1 head lettuce, torn into bite-size pieces
8 ounces carrots, shredded
1/2 cup minced cilantro
1/2 cup bean sprouts
2 tablespoons chopped jalapeño chiles
8 to 12 spring roll wrappers
8 ounces cooked small shrimp

GARNISH
Lemon wedges
Lime wedges
Cilantro sprigs
Bean sprouts
Jalapeño chiles

FOR THE DIPPING SAUCE, combine the fish sauce, garlic, chili-garlic sauce, sugar, lemon juice, vinegar and water in a bowl and mix well.

FOR THE SPRING ROLLS, combine the rice noodles with enough cold water to cover in a bowl. Let stand for 15 minutes; drain. Combine the noodles, sesame oil, fish sauce and soy sauce in a bowl and toss to combine. Add the lettuce, carrots, cilantro, bean sprouts and jalapeño chiles to the noodle mixture.

Place the wrappers in warm water in a bowl and let stand until soft. Drain and place on a towel. Place a shrimp and a small amount of the noodle mixture on one of the wrappers; do not overfill or wrapper will rip. Fold the edges toward the center and roll tightly to enclose the filling. Cover with a damp towel. Repeat the process with the remaining ingredients.

Arrange the spring rolls on a serving plate. Garnish with lemon wedges, lime wedges, cilantro, bean sprouts and jalapeño chiles. Serve with the dipping sauce.

EDAMAME

A quick and healthy appetizer with Japanese origins, edamame is the Japanese name for green soybeans. Because of their fresh, bright green color, they make an eye-pleasing addition on any buffet or for a cocktail party. And, they're low fat and loaded with protein!

Place frozen or fresh soybean pods (available at most grocery stores, co-ops and farmers' markets) in briskly boiling water with a dash of salt. Boil for 2 to 5 minutes or until tender; do not overcook. Drain the water, rinse with a cool bath, and let cool for about 5 minutes or until warm to the touch. Pat dry and sprinkle liberally with sea salt. Generally, you do not eat the pod but rather extract the soybeans from the pod and enjoy this protein-rich, salty snack.

CAJUN SPICE SHRIMP

YIELD: 6 TO 8 SERVINGS

1 pound medium shrimp
1 to 2 tablespoons vegetable oil
1 teaspoon tomato paste
1 teaspoon garlic paste
1 tablespoon Cajun spice

Peel and devein the shrimp. Heat the oil in a large cast-iron skillet until the oil begins to smoke. Add the shrimp. Sear on high for 3 to 4 minutes. Add the tomato paste, garlic paste and Cajun spice and stir to combine. Cook until the shrimp turn pink; do not overcook. Serve immediately.

BOUNDARY WATER GRANOLA

YIELD: 4 SERVINGS

$1/4$ cup canola oil
$1/4$ cup honey
2 teaspoons cinnamon
$1/4$ cup raw hulled sesame seeds
$1/4$ cup raw hulled sunflower seeds
$1/4$ cup sliced almonds
$1/2$ cup raw wheat germ
3 cups rolled oats

Heat the canola oil, honey and cinnamon in a saucepan, stirring frequently. Remove from the heat. Stir in the sesame seeds, sunflower seeds, almonds, wheat germ and oats one at a time, mixing well after each addition. Spread evenly on a baking sheet. Bake at 350 degrees for 15 to 20 minutes or until golden brown, stirring after the first 10 minutes and then every 5 minutes.

SINFULLY SWEET PECANS

YIELD: 6 TO 8 SERVINGS

1 1/2 cups pecans
1 cup sugar
1/4 cup water
1 teaspoon cinnamon
Dash of salt

Combine the pecans, sugar, water, cinnamon and salt in a saucepan. Cook over medium heat until sugar crystals begin to form on the side of the pan, stirring frequently; the mixture will be thick. Remove from the heat. Stir quickly to coat the pecans completely. Spread on waxed paper to cool.

NOTE: You may store these pecans in an airtight container for up to 1 week or freeze for up to 2 months. They are a festive, sweet addition to the end of a meal or served in a crystal bowl on the coffee table. They are also a great holiday gift idea!

ROSEMARY WALNUTS

YIELD: 8 SERVINGS

2 teaspoons dried rosemary
2 1/2 tablespoons butter, melted
1/2 to 1 teaspoon salt
1/2 teaspoon cayenne pepper
2 cups walnut halves

Crush the rosemary using a mortar and pestle. Combine the rosemary, butter, salt and cayenne pepper in a bowl and mix well. Add the walnuts and toss to coat. Spread on a baking sheet. Bake at 350 degrees for 10 minutes. Let stand until cool; serve.

Chapter Three

Soups and Breads

Apple Stilton Soup (*recipe on page 85*)

As one of the fifteen largest metropolitan communities in the United States, the Twin Cities is home to four major league teams, including the Minnesota Vikings football team, the Minnesota Wild hockey team, the Minnesota Timberwolves basketball team, and two-time World Series champions Minnesota Twins.

CHILLED ASPARAGUS SOUP

YIELD: 4 SERVINGS

1 bunch fresh asparagus
2 (14-ounce) cans chicken stock
1/2 onion, chopped
1/2 cup uncooked rice
1 teaspoon salt
1 teaspoon pepper
2 cups cream
Juice of 1 lemon

Cut the asparagus into 2-inch pieces, reserving the tips. Combine the asparagus pieces, chicken stock, onion, rice, salt and pepper in a saucepan. Bring to a boil. Reduce the heat. Simmer for 30 to 40 minutes or until the asparagus pieces are very soft.

Purée the asparagus mixture in a blender. Pour through a mesh sieve into a bowl to remove the strings. Refrigerate, covered, until chilled.

Bring enough water to cover the reserved asparagus tips to a simmer in a saucepan. Add the reserved asparagus tips and simmer for 5 minutes; drain. Refrigerate until chilled.

Stir the cream and lemon juice into the puréed asparagus mixture. Adjust the seasonings as desired. Ladle into soup bowls. Sprinkle with the chilled asparagus tips.

NOTE: You may use evaporated skim milk instead of the cream for a low-fat version.

CHILLED CREAMY CUCUMBER SOUP

YIELD: 4 TO 6 SERVINGS

2 tablespoons unsalted butter
1 onion, chopped
2 large cucumbers, peeled, seeded and
   coarsely chopped
2 tablespoons flour
1 cup chicken stock or broth
$1/2$ teaspoon salt
$1/4$ teaspoon white pepper
$1/4$ cup finely chopped parsley
Dash of garlic powder
1 cup sour cream

GARNISH
Dill weed or cucumber slices

Heat the butter in a saucepan until melted.
Add the onion and cook until tender. Add the
cucumbers, flour, chicken stock, salt, white
pepper, parsley and garlic powder. Bring to a
simmer. Simmer for 10 minutes, stirring
frequently. Let stand until cool.

Purée the cucumber mixture in a blender.
Add the sour cream and mix well. Pour into
a bowl. Chill, covered, in the refrigerator.

Ladle into soup bowls. Sprinkle with dill weed
or place a cucumber slice on top.

GOLF

According to recent statistics, there are more golfers per capita in the state of Minnesota than in any other state in the union. There are over five hundred golf courses in the state and nearly one hundred and fifty within the Twin Cities metropolitan area. While the summer season is short—or maybe because of it—golfers can be found on the course anytime there's not snow covering the hole.

STRAWBERRY SOUP

YIELD: 8 TO 10 SERVINGS

1 quart strawberries, hulled
1 cup buttermilk
3/4 cup sugar
3 cups buttermilk
2/3 cup sour cream
1 tablespoon kirsch

GARNISH
Fresh mint sprigs

Process the strawberries, 1 cup buttermilk and sugar in a food processor.

Combine 3 cups buttermilk, sour cream and kirsch in a large bowl and mix well. Pour the strawberry mixture into the sour cream mixture and stir to combine. Chill, covered, in the refrigerator.

Ladle into soup bowls. Garnish with mint sprigs.

VICHYSSOISE

YIELD: 6 SERVINGS

3 cups potatoes, peeled and cubed
  (about 6 medium)
3 cups sliced leeks (white and tender green
  parts only)
4 cups chicken broth
Salt to taste
White pepper to taste
2 cups heavy cream

GARNISH
Snipped chives
Chive flowers

Combine the potatoes, leeks and chicken broth in a large saucepan. Bring to a boil. Reduce the heat. Simmer, covered, for 30 to 40 minutes or until the vegetables are very tender. Purée the mixture with an immersion blender, blender or food processor. Season with salt and white pepper. Pour into a large bowl. Chill, covered, in the refrigerator.

Stir the cream into the chilled soup. Season with salt and white pepper. Ladle into soup bowls. Garnish with snipped chives and chive flowers.

The Twin Cities has a rich history of live theater, second only to New York City in the number of theater seats per capita. Theatergoers can enjoy Broadway shows at large venues such as the Ordway Center for the Performing Arts in St. Paul or the State or Orpheum Theater in Minneapolis. The famed Guthrie Theater, a seven-sided asymmetrical stage theater, features stage classics as well as new works. Local productions, off-Broadway, and off-off Broadway productions, including many original works, are previewed regularly across the Twin Cities in over thirty live theater settings, featuring an ever-changing landscape of well-known and up-and-coming theater companies and troupes. Children can enjoy productions at Children's Theater Company, the largest children's theater in the nation.

CREAM OF AVOCADO SOUP

YIELD: 6 SERVINGS

2 large avocados
1 cup cream
1 tablespoon lime juice
1/4 teaspoon salt
2 cups chicken broth
1/4 cup dry sherry (optional)

GARNISH
Lime slices

Purée the avocados, cream and lime juice in a blender or food processor. Pour into a large bowl. Stir in the salt. Add the chicken broth and mix well. Stir in the sherry. Ladle into soup bowls. Garnish with lime slices.

NOTE: You may add warm chicken broth for a warm soup or cold chicken broth for a cold soup.

APPLE STILTON SOUP

YIELD: 6 SERVINGS

3 Granny Smith apples
2 tablespoons unsalted butter
I yellow onion, thinly sliced
3 shallots, thinly sliced
3 garlic cloves, pressed
Salt to taste
Pepper to taste
2 sprigs of thyme
2 sprigs of basil
2 bay leaves
6 cups chicken stock
$1/4$ to $1/2$ cup (I to 2 ounces) crumbled
    Stilton cheese
$1/2$ cup cream
I tablespoon freshly squeezed lemon juice

GARNISH
Lightly whipped whipping cream
Crumbled Stilton cheese
Freshly cracked pepper

Peel and chop the apples. Heat the butter in a saucepan over medium heat until melted. Add the apples, onion, shallots and garlic and sauté until tender. Season with salt and pepper.

Wrap the thyme, basil and bay leaves in cheesecloth and tie closed. Add to the apple mixture. Pour in the chicken stock. Bring to a boil. Reduce the heat and simmer until the apples and vegetables are cooked through. Remove the herbs.

Stir $1/4$ cup Stilton cheese and cream into the apple mixture. Purée in batches in a blender or food processor. Stir in the lemon juice. Season with salt and pepper, adding additional Stilton cheese if desired. Strain through a chinois. Reheat in a saucepan.

Ladle into soup bowls. Drizzle with whipped cream and garnish with crumbled Stilton cheese and freshly cracked pepper.

Bouquet Garni

Whether as a starter or as a main course, soups and stews can be the star of the show. To intensify the flavor without leaving behind sprigs of herbs, create a bouquet garni using cheesecloth and fresh herbs. Spread out the cheesecloth, and lay upon it bay leaves, sprigs of thyme, rosemary, cloves, peppercorns, and other herbs. Gather the cloth, tie it into a little bundle with kitchen string, and drop the bouquet into the cooking pot. If you are serving a chilled soup, don't be afraid to use a heavy hand with the seasonings, as cold numbs the palate.

CARROT GINGER SOUP

YIELD: 10 TO 14 SERVINGS

1/4 cup (1/2 stick) butter
2 pounds carrots, peeled and sliced
2 large onions, chopped
1 1/2 teaspoons ground ginger
1 tablespoon grated orange zest
1/2 teaspoon coriander
5 cups chicken broth
1/2 cup milk
1/2 cup half-and-half
Salt to taste
Pepper to taste

GARNISH
1/2 cup (2 ounces) grated Parmesan cheese
1/2 cup fresh parsley sprigs or
    chopped parsley

Heat the butter in a large saucepan until melted. Add the carrots and onions. Cook for 15 minutes or until tender, stirring frequently. Stir in the ginger, orange zest, coriander and 2 cups of the chicken broth. Simmer for 30 minutes.

Purée the carrot mixture in a blender or food processor. Return to the saucepan. Stir in the remaining 3 cups chicken broth, milk and half-and-half. Season with salt and pepper. Cook over medium heat until heated through.

Ladle into soup bowls. Garnish with Parmesan cheese and parsley.

NUTTY PUMPKIN SOUP

YIELD: 6 SERVINGS

3 tablespoons butter
1 large onion, chopped
1^1/2 cups vegetable stock
2 (8-ounce) cans pumpkin pie filling
1 teaspoon nutmeg
1 teaspoon thyme
1^1/2 cups heavy cream
^{1}/4 cup peanut sauce
1 tablespoon flour

Heat the butter in a large saucepan until
melted. Add the onion and sauté until tender.
Pour in the bouillion and bring to a boil. Stir
in the pumpkin pie filling. Reduce the heat
to low. Add the nutmeg and thyme and stir
to combine.

Pour the heavy cream into the pumpkin
mixture and stir to combine. Add the peanut
sauce. Increase the heat to medium-high.
Whisk in the flour; the soup will be lumpy.

Cook the soup for 15 to 20 minutes or until
the flour is dissolved, whisking constantly.
Reduce the heat to low. Cook for 10 minutes.
Ladle into soup bowls.

NOTE: You may substitute 2 vegetable bouillon
cubes dissolved in 1^1/2 cups water for the
vegetable stock.

PUMPKIN APPLE SOUP

YIELD: 6 SERVINGS

2 teaspoons butter
1 onion, chopped (about $1/2$ cup)
1 garlic clove, minced
3 cups chicken stock or broth
1 (16-ounce) can pumpkin
1 tablespoon sugar
$1/4$ teaspoon cinnamon
2 tart baking apples such as Granny Smith,
    coarsely chopped
1 cup heavy cream
Salt to taste
Freshly ground pepper to taste

GARNISH
Crème fraîche
Thin apple slices

Heat the butter in a heavy saucepan until melted. Add the onion and garlic. Cook for 3 to 4 minutes or until tender; do not brown. Stir in the chicken stock, pumpkin, sugar and cinnamon. Add the apples. Bring to a boil. Reduce the heat. Simmer, covered, for 10 minutes. Stir in the cream. Purée in batches in a blender or food processor.

Return the puréed soup to the saucepan. Cook until heated through. Season with salt and pepper. Ladle into soup bowls. Drizzle the soup with crème fraîche and arrange a few apple slices on top.

HARVEST BUTTERNUT SQUASH SOUP WITH GINGER MAPLE SAUCE

YIELD: 8 TO 10 SERVINGS

SOUP
2 pounds butternut squash
$^1/2$ cup chopped onion
$^1/4$ cup chopped celery
$^1/4$ cup chopped parsnip
$^1/2$ cup chopped carrots
4 cups chicken stock
2 cups half-and-half
1 teaspoon cinnamon
$^1/2$ teaspoon nutmeg
Salt to taste
Pepper to taste

GINGER MAPLE SYRUP
3 ounces pure maple syrup
1 teaspoon grated gingerroot

FOR THE SOUP, split, seed and peel the squash. Place on a baking sheet. Bake at 375 degrees for 30 minutes or until tender.

Place the onion, celery, parsnip and carrots in a large heavy stockpot. Cook, covered, over low heat until the vegetables are tender. Pour in the chicken stock. Simmer for 5 minutes. Add the baked squash. Return to a simmer and simmer for 5 minutes. Stir in the half-and-half.

Purée the soup in batches in a food processor, pouring the soup into a large bowl after each batch. Stir in the cinnamon and nutmeg. Season with salt and pepper.

FOR THE SYRUP, purée the maple syrup and gingerroot in a food processor.

Ladle the soup into soup bowls. Drizzle with the syrup.

Despite being landlocked and far from the bright lights of Hollywood or Broadway, the arts are alive and well in the Twin Cities. Minneapolis and St. Paul are home to numerous museums, nearly twenty musical organizations, and many art galleries and studio groups. The Minneapolis Sculpture Center at the Walker Art Gallery features one of the Twin Cities' most recognized pieces of public art, the *Spoonbridge and Cherry,* a giant fountain-sculpture designed by Claes Oldenburg and Coosje van Bruggen. Visitors can view whimsical expressions of artistic thought, both professional and amateur, in office buildings, on front yards, and in galleries across the Twin Cities.

TOMATO BASIL SOUP

YIELD: 4 SERVINGS

10 to 12 Roma tomatoes, peeled and seeded
3 cups tomato juice or purée
2 cups vegetable or other stock
10 to 15 fresh basil leaves
1^1/2 cups heavy cream
^{3}/4 cup (1^1/2 sticks) butter, cut into
    small pieces
^{1}/2 teaspoon salt
^{1}/2 teaspoon pepper

Combine the tomatoes, tomato juice and stock in a saucepan. Bring to a simmer and simmer for 30 minutes. Add the basil leaves. Purée in batches in a food processor.

Pour the puréed tomato mixture into a saucepan and place over low heat. Whisk in the cream and butter. Cook until heated through. Season with salt and pepper. Ladle into soup bowls.

GUMBO

1 pound andouille or smoked
   sausage, chopped
3 ribs celery, chopped
1 bell pepper, chopped
1 small onion, chopped
1 tablespoon chopped garlic
$^1/_2$ cup vegetable oil
$^1/_2$ cup flour
8 cups hot water
1 tablespoon salt
1 teaspoon freshly ground black pepper
Cayenne pepper to taste
Tabasco sauce to taste
4 cups chicken broth
1 pound chopped cooked chicken
20 pods fresh or frozen okra,
   sliced (optional)
1 tablespoon gumbo filé powder (optional)

Cook the sausage in a skillet until brown, stirring frequently. Remove the sausage to a bowl, reserving the drippings in the skillet. Cook the celery, bell pepper, onion and garlic in the reserved drippings in the skillet until the vegetables are tender, stirring occasionally. Remove from the heat and set aside.

Cook the oil and flour in a Dutch oven for 20 to 30 minutes or until the roux turns a dark chestnut brown and begins to smell nutty, stirring constantly; do not burn. Add the water and stir to incorporate the roux. Add the salt, black pepper, cayenne pepper and Tabasco sauce. Bring to a boil. Stir in the chicken broth, chicken and cooked sausage. Cook over medium heat for 1 hour.

Add the okra and cooked vegetables to the gumbo. Return to a boil. Cook over medium heat for 30 minutes. Adjust the seasonings as desired. Turn off the heat. Stir in the filé powder. Let stand for 30 minutes. Serve over hot rice.

ITALIAN TORTELLINI SOUP

YIELD: 8 SERVINGS

1 pound Italian sausage
1 cup coarsely chopped onion
2 garlic cloves, sliced
5 cups beef broth
$^1/_2$ cup water
$^1/_2$ cup dry red wine or water
2 cups chopped peeled tomatoes
   (about 4 medium tomatoes)
2 cups thinly sliced carrots
$^1/_2$ teaspoon oregano leaves
$^1/_2$ teaspoon basil leaves
1 (8-ounce) can tomato sauce
1$^1/_2$ cups sliced zucchini
8 ounces frozen meat- or cheese-filled
   tortellini (about 2 cups)
3 tablespoons chopped fresh parsley
1 green bell pepper, cut into $^1/_2$-inch pieces
Grated Parmesan cheese

Remove the casing from the sausage. Brown the sausage in a 5-quart Dutch oven, stirring until crumbly. Remove the sausage and set aside. Discard the drippings, reserving 1 tablespoon.

Sauté the onion and garlic in the reserved drippings in the Dutch oven until the onion is tender. Add the beef broth, water, wine, tomatoes, carrots, oregano, basil, tomato sauce and cooked sausage and stir to combine. Bring to a boil. Reduce the heat. Simmer for 30 minutes, skimming any fat from the surface.

Stir the zucchini, tortellini, parsley and bell pepper into the soup. Simmer, covered, for 35 to 40 minutes or until the vegetables are tender. Ladle into soup bowls. Sprinkle the soup with Parmesan cheese.

Always Superb: Recipes for Every Occasion

MEXICAN CORN CHOWDER

YIELD: 8 TO 10 SERVINGS

1 pound fresh chorizo in casing
2 garlic cloves, minced
1 cup chopped onion
1/2 cup chopped celery
1 red or yellow bell pepper, chopped
1 green bell pepper, chopped
1 1/2 tablespoons flour
4 cups fresh or frozen corn
1 bay leaf
1 teaspoon thyme, crumbled
6 cups chicken broth
2 boiling potatoes, peeled and cut into
    1/2-inch cubes
3/4 cup half-and-half
2 scallions, cut into 1/4-inch slices
Salt to taste
Pepper to taste

GARNISH
2 tablespoons cilantro

Brown the sausage in a stockpot over medium heat. Remove the sausage and cut into bite-size pieces. Set aside. Discard the drippings, reserving 1 to 2 tablespoons.

Cook the garlic, onion, celery and bell peppers in the reserved drippings in the stockpot until the vegetables are tender, stirring occasionally. Add the flour. Cook for 5 minutes, stirring constantly. Add the corn, bay leaf, thyme and chicken broth. Cook for 1 minute, stirring constantly.

Add the potatoes and half-and-half to the corn mixture. Bring to a simmer and simmer for 20 minutes or until the potatoes are tender, stirring occasionally. Stir in the cooked sausage. Add the scallions. Cook for 5 minutes.

Remove and discard the bay leaf from the chowder. Season with salt and pepper. Ladle into soup bowls and garnish with cilantro.

If you need to thicken the soup and don't want to add flour or eggs, purée a portion of the soup and then stir it back into the pot. Finely chopped onions will also help thicken a soup or stew. If you need to remove the fat but can't wait for it to chill, draw a slice of bread across the soup's surface to soak up the excess fat. Too salty? Add a potato to the soup or stew while it cooks to draw out the excess salt. To ensure that the soup's ingredients cook evenly, chop all vegetables into small bite-size pieces with many angles, to increase the cooking surface area.

MINNESOTA WILD RICE SOUP

YIELD: 8 TO 10 SERVINGS

$^1/_2$ cup (1 stick) butter
1 small onion, finely chopped
$^1/_2$ cup chopped celery
$^1/_2$ cup shredded carrots
8 ounces wild mushrooms, sliced (optional)
$^1/_2$ cup flour
6 cups chicken broth
3 cups cooked wild rice
1 cup chopped cooked ham
$^1/_4$ cup slivered almonds, chopped
$^1/_2$ cup sherry (optional)
2 cups half-and-half
$^1/_2$ teaspoon salt
1 teaspoon freshly ground pepper

GARNISH
Chopped parsley or chives

Heat the butter in a stockpot until melted.
Add the onion, celery, carrots and mushrooms.
Sauté until the onion is tender; do not brown.
Add the flour. Cook for 2 minutes, stirring
constantly. Whisk in the chicken broth gradually.
Bring to a boil, stirring occasionally. Turn off
the heat.

Add the wild rice, ham, almonds, sherry and
half-and-half to the vegetable mixture and mix
well. Stir in the salt and pepper. Adjust the
seasonings as desired.

Cook the soup until of the desired
temperature. Ladle into soup bowls. Garnish
with chopped parsley.

NO-KNEAD BRAIDED PARMESAN BREAD

YIELD: 8 TO 10 SERVINGS

PARMESAN GARLIC FILLING
1/2 cup (2 ounces) grated Parmesan cheese
1/2 cup (1 stick) butter, softened
3 tablespoons snipped parsley
1/2 teaspoon garlic powder

BREAD
1 envelope dry yeast
1/4 cup warm (105- to 115-degree) water
1 cup lukewarm scalded milk
1/4 cup (1/2 stick) butter, softened
1/4 cup sugar
2 eggs
1 1/2 teaspoons salt
4 to 4 1/2 cups flour
1 egg yolk
1 tablespoon water
Sesame seeds

FOR THE FILLING, combine the Parmesan cheese, butter, parsley and garlic powder in a bowl and mix well.

FOR THE BREAD, dissolve the yeast in 1/4 cup warm water in a large bowl. Stir in the milk, butter, sugar, eggs and salt. Stir in 1 cup of the flour. Stir in enough of the remaining flour to form a soft sticky dough, scraping down the side of the bowl occasionally. Let rise, covered, in a warm place for 1 hour or until doubled in bulk.

Deflate the risen dough by stirring 25 times. Roll or pat into a 12×18-inch rectangle on a lightly floured surface. Spread the filling evenly over the dough. Cut the dough into three 4×18-inch strips. Roll each strip into a rope, sealing the ends.

Place the dough ropes diagonally close together on a lightly greased baking sheet. Braid the ropes gently and loosely; do not stretch. Seal the ends and tuck under securely. Let rise for 30 minutes or until doubled in bulk.

Combine the egg yolk and 1 tablespoon water in a small bowl and mix well. Brush over the dough braid. Sprinkle with sesame seeds. Place on the lower oven rack.

Bake at 350 degrees for 25 to 30 minutes or until golden brown and the bread sounds hollow when tapped.

VIENNESE BANANA NUT BREAD

YIELD: 5 MINIATURE LOAVES

2 small bananas
3/4 cup milk
2 teaspoons vinegar
2 cups flour
1 teaspoon baking powder
1/2 teaspoon salt
1 teaspoon baking soda
1/2 cup (1 stick) butter, softened
1 1/2 cups sugar
2 eggs
1 tablespoon vanilla extract
1/2 cup chopped pecans

Mash the bananas in a small bowl. Add the milk and vinegar and mix well. Combine the flour, baking powder, salt and baking soda in a separate bowl and mix well.

Cream the butter and sugar in a mixing bowl until light and fluffy. Beat in the eggs. Add the flour mixture alternately with the banana mixture, beating at low speed for 2 to 3 minutes or until blended after each addition. Stir in the vanilla and pecans.

Spoon the batter evenly into 5 miniature loaf pans sprayed with nonstick cooking spray. Bake at 350 degrees for 25 to 30 minutes or until a wooden pick inserted in the center comes out clean. Cool in the pan for 5 minutes. Invert onto a wire rack to cool completely.

NOTE: You may freeze the loaves.

GRAPE-NUTS BREAD

YIELD: 2 LOAVES

1 cup Grape-Nuts cereal
2 cups buttermilk
1 1/2 cups sugar
4 cups flour
1 teaspoon baking soda
2 teaspoons baking powder
2 eggs

Soak the cereal in the buttermilk in a large
bowl for 3 or more minutes or until soft. Sift
the sugar, flour, baking soda and baking powder
together. Beat the eggs in a small bowl.

Add the sifted dry ingredients and the eggs
to the cereal mixture and mix well. Pour into
2 greased 5×9-inch loaf pans. Bake at 350
degrees for 1 hour or until a wooden pick
inserted in the center comes out clean.

ORANGE BUTTER

Fruit butter is a delicious
addition to any brunch or
breakfast. It can be prepared
ahead of time, frozen and
then thawed as needed. Zest
an orange or lemon and mix
approximately 1 teaspoon of
the zest with 1 to 2 teaspoons
of orange or lemon juice in
a bowl. Add 1/2 cup (1 stick)
softened butter and a dash of
salt and blend until smooth.
Form the butter mixture into
a roll and chill. When firm,
slice into appropriate-sized
servings, wrap tightly and
freeze. Prior to serving,
thaw the orange butter in
the refrigerator.

Instead of citrus zest, use
1 to 2 tablespoons of fresh
preserves, marmalade or
honey to create a sweeter,
fruitier butter.

FLOUR PERFECT

Always sift flour before measuring. Don't pack the flour into the cup or spoon as that will "unsift" it. Instead, heap the cup or spoon to overflowing and then level the surface with the back of a knife blade. Use the following guidelines to measure flour.

1 cup all-purpose flour =
    5 ounces unsifted or
    $4^{1}/_{2}$ ounces sifted
1 cup cake flour =
    4 ounces unsifted or
    $3^{1}/_{2}$ ounces sifted

If you do a fair amount of baking, keep two kinds of white flour on hand: one with high-gluten content for bread and one with low-gluten content for cakes, cookies, and quick breads.

WHOLE WHEAT ZUCCHINI BREAD

YIELD: 2 LOAVES

3 cups shredded zucchini
$1^{2}/_{3}$ cups sugar
$^{2}/_{3}$ cup olive oil
1 tablespoon vanilla extract
4 eggs, or an equivalent amount of
    egg substitute
3 cups whole wheat flour
2 teaspoons baking soda
1 teaspoon cinnamon
$^{1}/_{2}$ teaspoon ground cloves
$^{1}/_{2}$ teaspoon baking powder

Grease the bottoms of two 4x8-inch loaf pans with shortening.

Combine the zucchini, sugar, olive oil, vanilla and eggs in a large bowl and mix well. Add the whole wheat flour, baking soda, cinnamon, cloves and baking powder and mix well. Pour into the prepared pans.

Bake at 350 degrees on the lowest oven rack for 50 to 60 minutes or until a wooden pick inserted in the center comes out clean. Cool in the pans for 10 minutes. Loosen the loaves from the sides of the pans. Invert onto wire racks to cool completely before slicing.

NOTE: You may use one 5x9 inch loaf pan and bake for 70 to 80 minutes.

BREAD BOUQUET

YIELD: 8 TO 10 SERVINGS

1 round loaf sourdough bread
$1/2$ cup (1 stick) butter or margarine, melted
1 tablespoon chopped fresh oregano
1 tablespoon chopped fresh basil
$1/2$ tablespoon fresh rosemary
1 tablespoon chopped garlic
$1/2$ cup (2 ounces) grated Parmesan cheese

Cut the bread into 1-inch slices stopping 1-inch from the bottom of the loaf. Turn the bread and repeat, forming a criss-cross pattern. Place on a large sheet of foil.

Combine the butter, oregano, basil, rosemary and garlic in a small bowl and mix well. Pour over the loaf in between the breadsticks. Sprinkle with the Parmesan cheese. Wrap in the foil.

Bake at 350 degrees for 10 to 15 minutes or until golden brown.

SWEDISH CORN BREAD

YIELD: 15 SERVINGS

$1/2$ cup (1 stick) unsalted butter, softened
$1^1/2$ cups sugar
3 eggs
2 cups water
2 cups yellow cornmeal
2 cups flour
1 tablespoon baking powder
1 teaspoon salt

Cream the butter and sugar in a mixing bowl until light and fluffy. Beat in the eggs. Add the water and cornmeal and mix well. Stir in the flour, baking powder and salt just until mixed. Pour into a buttered 9x13-inch baking dish. Bake at 400 degrees for 35 minutes or until golden brown.

PEPPERONI BREAD

YIELD: 2 LARGE LOAVES

3 eggs
3 tablespoons grated Parmesan cheese
1 teaspoon Italian seasoning
2 (16-ounce) loaves frozen bread dough,
    thawed
1 (8-ounce) package sliced pepperoni
1 pound provolone cheese, shredded

Combine the eggs, Parmesan cheese, and Italian seasoning in a bowl and mix well.

Roll each bread dough loaf into an 8×14-inch rectangle on a lightly floured surface. Brush the egg mixture evenly over the rectangles, reserving 3 tablespoons. Arrange the pepperoni slices over the rectangles. Sprinkle with the provolone cheese. Roll as for a jelly roll, sealing the edges and ends. Place seam side down on a large baking sheet. Brush with the reserved egg mixture.

Bake at 350 degrees for 20 to 30 minutes or until golden brown.

NOTE: You may make four small bread loaves by cutting the bread dough loaves into halves and rolling into 7×8-inch rectangles.

MINNESOTA CHEESE BISCUITS

YIELD: 8 TO 10 BISCUITS

2 cups flour
1 tablespoon baking powder
2 teaspoons sugar
$^1/_2$ teaspoon cream of tartar
$^1/_4$ teaspoon salt
$^1/_2$ cup (1 stick) butter
1 cup buttermilk
$^3/_4$ cup (3 ounces) shredded Cheddar cheese

Combine the flour, baking powder, sugar, cream of tartar and salt in a bowl and mix well. Cut in the butter until crumbly. Add the buttermilk and mix well. Stir in the Cheddar cheese.

Drop large spoonfuls of the batter onto a greased baking sheet. Bake at 450 degrees for 12 to 15 minutes or until golden brown.

BRAN MUFFINS

YIELD: 6 DOZEN

$2^1/_2$ cups sugar
5 cups flour
8 teaspoons baking soda
5 cups buttermilk
2 cups chopped dates (optional)
3 cups bran flakes
2 cups All-Bran
4 eggs
$1^1/_2$ cups canola oil

Combine the sugar, flour, baking soda, buttermilk, dates, bran flakes, All-Bran, eggs and canola oil in a bowl and mix well. Place muffin cup liners in the muffin cups and fill $^2/_3$ full. Bake at 375 degrees for 15 minutes.

NOTE: You may substitute an equivalent amount of pasteurized egg substitute for the eggs and store the batter, covered, in the refrigerator for 6 to 8 weeks.

HERB BUTTER

Herb butter can be prepared when the fresh herbs are harvested and then frozen for use throughout the year. Chop a cup or more of fresh herbs and blend with $^1/_2$ cup (1 stick) softened butter and a dash of lemon juice until smooth. Form the butter mixture into a roll and chill. When firm, slice into appropriate-sized servings, wrap tightly and freeze. Prior to serving, thaw the herb butter in the refrigerator.

While most flour is made of wheat, it may be milled from rye, oats, or even corn. When flour is milled, the outer coating, known as bran, is stripped from the wheat kernel as is the sprouting portion, known as the germ. Gluten is the protein within the flour that forms the elastic network of gases that are created as the bread rises during baking.

Bread flour is generally unbleached and contains higher levels of gluten, malted barley flour, and vitamin C or potassium bromate, which results in better yeast activity and dough elasticity.

Cake flour generally has a higher starch content and is finer in texture.

Self-rising flour is multi-purpose, and generally salt and baking powder have been added.

Continued on next page

102

RHUBARB MUFFINS

YIELD: 18 MUFFINS

2^1/2 cups flour
1 teaspoon baking soda
1 teaspoon salt
1^1/2 cups packed brown sugar
^{2}/3 cup vegetable oil
1 cup buttermilk
1 egg, lightly beaten
1 teaspoon vanilla extract
1^1/2 cups chopped rhubarb
^{1}/2 cup packed brown sugar
1 teaspoon butter, melted

Grease muffin cups or line with muffin cup liners.

Mix the flour, baking soda and salt together in a bowl. Combine 1^1/2 cups brown sugar, oil, buttermilk, egg and vanilla in a separate bowl and mix well. Stir in the flour mixture just until moistened. Fold in the rhubarb. Fill prepared muffin cups ^{3}/4 full.

Combine ^{1}/2 cup brown sugar and the butter in a bowl and mix well. Sprinkle over the tops of the muffin batter. Bake at 325 degrees for 35 minutes or until a wooden pick inserted in the center comes out clean. Remove from the pans.

CRUNCHY GARLIC SCONES

YIELD: 16 SCONES

3 cups flour
1 tablespoon sugar
2 1/2 teaspoons baking powder
1/2 teaspoon baking soda
1/4 teaspoon salt
6 tablespoons cold unsalted butter, sliced
7 large heads roasted garlic, or 1 cup (about)
    packaged minced roasted garlic
1/2 to 1 cup buttermilk
2 tablespoons butter, melted
1 tablespoon (about) coarse sea salt
1 tablespoon (about) freshly ground pepper

Combine the flour, sugar, baking powder, baking soda and salt in a bowl and mix well. Cut in 6 tablespoons butter with a pastry blender until mixture resembles coarse crumbs. Add the roasted garlic and mix well. Sprinkle 1/2 cup of the buttermilk over the mixture. Stir with a fork until dough begins to form; dough should be soft but rough. Add enough of the remaining buttermilk 1 tablespoon at a time until the dough is firm but soft, stirring constantly with a fork. Knead the dough on a lightly floured surface until it holds together; the dough will be sticky.

Divide the dough into 2 equal portions. Pat each portion into a circle 1/2 inch thick. Brush with 1 teaspoon melted butter. Mix the sea salt and pepper together in a small bowl. Sprinkle over the dough.

Cut each circle into 8 triangles. Place 1 inch apart on a lightly greased baking sheet. Bake at 425 degrees for 10 to 12 minutes or until the scones are light brown on top.

NOTE: You may stir the sea salt and pepper into the dough, knead the dough in the bowl, and drop by heaping teaspoonfuls onto a lightly greased baking sheet to reduce the preparation time. You may freeze the scones, thaw and reheat, covered in foil, at 350 degrees for 5 to 8 minutes. You may make the dough and chill, covered, for 1 to 3 days before baking.

Flour may be stored in an airtight container for up to six months at room temperature. However, whole wheat flours contain part of the grain's germ and thus have a high oil content. As a result, wheat flours may turn rancid if not stored in a cool place, such as the freezer.

BUBBLING BLUEBERRY BUCKLE COFFEE CAKE

YIELD: 12 TO 14 SERVINGS

CAKE
$^1/_2$ cup (1 stick) butter, softened
1$^1/_2$ cups sugar
2 eggs
1 cup milk
4 cups flour
4 teaspoons baking powder
1 teaspoon salt
4 cups fresh blueberries, rinsed and
    stemmed, or 4 cups frozen blueberries

TOPPING
1 cup sugar
1 teaspoon cinnamon
1 cup flour
1 cup (2 sticks) butter

FOR THE CAKE, cream the butter and sugar in a mixing bowl until light and fluffy. Add the eggs and milk and mix well. Beat in the flour, baking powder and salt. Pour into a greased and floured 9×13-inch baking dish. Sprinkle the blueberries over the batter.

FOR THE TOPPING, mix the sugar, cinnamon and flour in a bowl. Cut in the butter until crumbly. Sprinkle over the blueberries.

Bake at 350 degrees for 45 to 55 minutes or until a wooden pick inserted in the center comes out clean. Serve warm or cold.

MIXED BERRY COFFEE CAKE

YIELD: 12 SERVINGS

TOPPING
3/4 cup packed brown sugar
1/2 cup quick-cooking oats
1/3 cup flour
1 teaspoon cinnamon
1/4 cup (1/2 stick) cold butter

CAKE
2 cups flour
1 teaspoon baking soda
1/2 teaspoon salt
1 cup packed brown sugar
1/2 cup (1 stick) butter, softened
2 eggs
1 tablespoon grated orange zest
1 teaspoon vanilla extract
1 cup orange yogurt
1 cup blueberries
1/2 cup raspberries
1/2 cup blackberries

GLAZE
1/3 cup confectioners' sugar
1 tablespoon orange juice

FOR THE TOPPING, combine the brown sugar, oats, flour and cinnamon in a small bowl and mix well. Cut in the butter until crumbly.

FOR THE CAKE, grease and flour a 10-inch tube or bundt pan. Combine the flour, baking soda and salt in a bowl and mix well. Cream the brown sugar and butter in a mixing bowl until light and fluffy. Add the eggs one at a time, mixing well after each addition. Beat in the orange zest and vanilla. Add 1/2 of the dry ingredients and mix well. Add the yogurt and mix well. Add the remaining dry ingredients and mix well.

Pour 1/2 of the cake batter evenly into the prepared pan. Sprinkle the blueberries, raspberries and blackberries evenly over the batter. Sprinkle 1/2 of the topping over the berries. Repeat with the remaining batter, berries and topping.

Bake at 350 degrees for 50 to 60 minutes or until a wooden pick inserted in the center comes out clean. Cool in the pan for 15 minutes. Invert onto a serving plate.

FOR THE GLAZE, combine the confectioners' sugar and orange juice in a small bowl and mix well. Drizzle over the cake.

CRUMB COFFEE CAKE

YIELD: 12 TO 16 SERVINGS

Grated zest of 1 lemon
2 cups packed brown sugar
2 cups flour
1 teaspoon cinnamon
1 teaspoon salt
$1/2$ cup (1 stick) butter
1 cup buttermilk
1 teaspoon baking soda
$1/2$ teaspoon baking powder
1 egg
$1/4$ teaspoon ground cloves
$1/8$ teaspoon nutmeg

Combine the lemon zest, brown sugar, flour, cinnamon and salt in a bowl and stir to mix well. Cut in the butter until crumbly. Reserve 1 cup of the crumb mixture.

Add the buttermilk, baking soda, baking powder, egg, cloves and nutmeg to the remaining crumb mixture and mix well. Pour into a buttered shallow 8x12-inch baking dish. Sprinkle the reserved crumb mixture over the top.

Bake at 350 degrees for 35 to 40 minutes or until a wooden pick inserted in the center comes out clean.

PECAN-CINNAMON COFFEE CAKE

YIELD: 12 SERVINGS

FILLING
1½ cups packed brown sugar
½ cup sugar
2 teaspoons cinnamon
½ cup (1 stick) butter
1½ cups chopped pecans

CAKE
1 cup (2 sticks) butter, softened
½ cup sugar
3 eggs
2½ cups flour
2 teaspoons baking powder
½ teaspoon salt
1½ cups sour cream
1 teaspoon vanilla extract

FOR THE FILLING, combine the brown sugar, sugar and cinnamon in a bowl and stir to mix well. Cut in the butter until crumbly. Stir in the pecans.

FOR THE CAKE, grease and flour a 9x13-inch cake pan. Cream the butter and sugar in a mixing bowl until light and fluffy. Add the eggs and mix well. Add the flour, baking powder and salt and mix well. Stir in the sour cream and vanilla; the batter will be stiff.

Spoon ½ of the cake batter evenly into the prepared pan. Sprinkle ½ of the filling over the batter. Repeat with the remaining batter and filling.

Bake at 350 degrees for 45 minutes or until a wooden pick inserted in the center comes out clean.

Chapter Four

SALADS AND SIDE DISHES

Mango Chicken Salad (*recipe on page 190*)

PLAN AHEAD—SALAD PREPARATION

Save last-minute preparation time by plating the salad without dressing and storing in the refrigerator, draped with a damp paper towel, until the salad is ready to be served. If you are serving the salad in a large bowl, mix the dressing in the bottom of the salad bowl and then invert a saucer in the bottom of the bowl over the dressing. Next, add the salad greens. When you are ready to serve, gently remove the saucer and toss the salad. Voilà, a perfect salad with no last-minute hassle!

BIBB SALAD WITH LIME SOY VINAIGRETTE

YIELD: 4 SERVINGS

LIME SOY VINAIGRETTE
1 tablespoon red wine vinegar
1 tablespoon rice vinegar
1 tablespoon soy sauce
1 tablespoon lime juice
1/4 teaspoon pepper
1/4 cup olive oil

BIBB SALAD
6 tablespoons pecan halves
1 tablespoon butter
2 dashes of cayenne pepper
1 head Bibb lettuce
1/3 cup crumbled Gorgonzola cheese

FOR THE VINAIGRETTE, combine the red wine vinegar, rice vinegar, soy sauce, lime juice and pepper in a bowl and mix well. Whisk in the olive oil.

FOR THE SALAD, sauté the pecans in the butter in a skillet. Sprinkle with the cayenne pepper. Remove from the heat.

Rinse the lettuce and tear into bite-size pieces. Place in a bowl. Add the vinaigrette and toss to coat. Divide evenly among 4 salad plates. Sprinkle the Gorgonzola cheese over the lettuce. Sprinkle with the sautéed pecans.

BALSAMIC MARINATED ASPARAGUS ON BABY FIELD GREENS

YIELD: SERVES 4 TO 6

DRESSING
1 garlic clove, chopped
1 tablespoon Dijon mustard
3 tablespoons balsamic vinegar
Salt to taste
Pepper to taste
1 cup olive oil

SALAD
Salt to taste
1 pound asparagus, trimmed
1 red onion
1 pound baby field greens, rinsed

FOR THE DRESSING, whisk the garlic, mustard and vinegar together in a bowl. Season with salt and pepper. Drizzle the olive oil into the bowl, whisking constantly. Whisk until the olive oil is incorporated and the dressing is thick.

FOR THE SALAD, bring enough water to cover the asparagus to a boil in a saucepan. Add a small amount of salt. Add the asparagus and cook until tender-crisp. Drain and immediately plunge into a bowl of ice water to stop the cooking process.

Peel the onion and cut into thin strips. Drain the asparagus. Place the asparagus, onion and dressing in a sealable plastic bag. Seal the bag. Marinate in the refrigerator for 2 to 24 hours.

Divide the greens evenly among 4 to 6 salad plates. Drain the asparagus and onion, reserving the dressing. Arrange the asparagus and onion over the field greens. Drizzle the reserved dressing over the top.

The Twin Cities is home to the Twin Cities campus of the University of Minnesota, a land-grant university. The University of Minnesota, the cornerstone of public education in the Upper Midwest, also has campuses in Duluth, Crookston, and Morris. The Minnesota College and University System also calls the Twin Cities home, with thirty-four state-supported technical colleges, community colleges, and state universities located on fifty-three campuses in forty-six communities across the state. In addition, the Twin Cities is the home to fifteen private colleges, universities, and technical schools. Based on recent data, nearly 30 percent of citizens over the age of twenty-five have completed at least four years of college, compared with a national average that hovers closer to 20 percent.

CAESAR SALAD

YIELD: 6 SERVINGS

1 egg
1 1/2 heads romaine lettuce, rinsed and torn into bite-size pieces
3/4 cup olive oil
1 teaspoon anchovy paste
1 teaspoon Worcestershire sauce
1/2 teaspoon dry mustard
2 garlic cloves, minced
Juice of 1/2 lemon or more
Salt to taste
Freshly ground pepper to taste
1/2 cup (2 ounces) freshly grated Pecorino Romano cheese
Croutons

Bring enough water to cover the egg to a boil in a saucepan. Place the egg in the boiling water and turn off the heat. Let stand for 1 minute. Remove the egg and set aside.

Place the lettuce in a salad bowl. Combine the olive oil, anchovy paste, Worcestershire sauce, mustard and garlic in a bowl and mix well. Pour over the lettuce and toss to combine. Break the egg and add to the salad. Squeeze the lemon juice over the egg. Season with salt and pepper. Toss to combine. Adjust the seasonings and lemon juice as desired.

Sprinkle the Pecorino Romano cheese over the salad. Add the croutons and toss to combine.

CRANBERRY PARMESAN SALAD

YIELD: 6 TO 8 SERVINGS

10 cups torn mixed salad greens
$1/2$ cup dried cranberries
$1/2$ cup (2 ounces) grated Parmesan cheese
$1/2$ cup pine nuts, toasted
1 tablespoon Dijon mustard
3 tablespoons balsamic vinegar
Salt to taste
Pepper to taste
1 cup olive oil

Combine the greens, cranberries, Parmesan cheese and pine nuts in a salad bowl and toss to mix well.

Process the mustard, vinegar, salt, pepper and olive oil in a blender. Pour over the salad and toss to combine.

GREENS WITH GARLIC DRESSING

YIELD: 10 SERVINGS

GARLIC DRESSING
$1/2$ cup sour cream
$1/3$ cup mayonnaise
$1/2$ cup half-and-half
2 large garlic cloves, chopped
2 tablespoons white wine vinegar
2 tablespoons vegetable oil
$1 1/2$ teaspoons sugar
$1/2$ teaspoon salt
Freshly ground pepper

SALAD
12 cups salad greens

Process the sour cream, mayonnaise, half-and-half, garlic, vinegar, oil, sugar, salt and pepper in a food processor. Pour into a container. Chill, covered, for 1 hour or longer. Adjust the seasonings if desired.

Divide the greens among 10 salad plates. Pour the dressing over the greens.

SALAD GREENS

Try a variation of salad greens to create a more interesting salad, including any of the following:

Arugula: bunches of crisp, dark green, oak-shaped leaves with a peppery taste

Belgian endive: white with a crisp texture and a strong, almost bitter taste

Bibb: deep rich color, buttery flavor

Boston: light in color, subtle, soft and tender, mild flavor

Chicory: curly-edged with a bitter but pleasing taste

Radicchio: purple-red variety of endive with a slightly bitter taste

Watercress: small flat leaves with a peppery flavor

MIXED GREENS WITH GORGONZOLA AND CARAMELIZED PECANS

YIELD: 4 TO 6 SERVINGS

BALSAMIC VINAIGRETTE
2 tablespoons balsamic vinegar
1 1/2 teaspoons Dijon mustard
1 minced shallot or garlic clove (optional)
1/3 cup olive oil
Freshly ground pepper to taste

SALAD
1/3 cup chopped pecans
3 tablespoons sugar
1 (10-ounce) package mixed greens
1/3 cup dried cranberries
10 grape tomatoes, cut into halves
1/2 red bell pepper, cut into bite-size pieces
1/2 cup (2 ounces) crumbled Gorgonzola cheese
Garlic croutons (optional)

FOR THE VINAIGRETTE, combine the vinegar, mustard and shallot in a bowl and mix well. Pour in the olive oil slowly, whisking constantly. Season with pepper.

FOR THE SALAD, place the pecans in a small skillet. Sprinkle with the sugar. Cook over medium-low heat until the sugar melts and completely coats the pecans, stirring frequently. Place on waxed paper to cool.

Place the greens in a salad bowl. Add the cooled pecans, cranberries, tomatoes, bell pepper, Gorgonzola cheese and croutons and toss to combine. Pour the vinaigrette over the salad and toss to coat.

114

ROMAINE SALAD WITH GINGERED WALNUTS AND BLUE CHEESE

YIELD: 6 SERVINGS

GINGERED WALNUTS
1 tablespoon vegetable oil
1 teaspoon soy sauce
1/4 teaspoon ginger
1/4 teaspoon salt
1/8 teaspoon garlic powder
1 cup walnut halves

SALAD
1/2 head romaine lettuce
1/2 head iceberg lettuce
2 tart green apples
1/4 cup walnut oil
1/4 cup vegetable oil
2 tablespoons white wine vinegar
2 tablespoons lemon juice
2 teaspoons Dijon mustard
1/8 teaspoon salt
1/2 cup dried cranberries
2/3 cup (3 ounces) crumbled blue cheese

FOR THE WALNUTS, pour the oil into an 8-inch square baking pan. Place in the oven. Heat at 250 degrees until the oil is hot. Stir in the soy sauce, ginger, salt and garlic powder. Add the walnut halves and stir to coat. Bake for 30 minutes or until the walnuts are crisp and brown. Let stand until cool. You may store the walnuts in a tightly covered container for up to 1 week.

FOR THE SALAD, tear the lettuces into bite-size pieces and place in a salad bowl. Cut the apples into thin slices and place in the salad bowl. Combine the walnut oil, vegetable oil, vinegar, lemon juice, mustard and salt in a separate bowl and mix well. Pour over the salad and toss to combine. Divide evenly among 6 salad plates. Sprinkle with the cranberries, blue cheese and walnuts.

**CRISP GREENS
EVERY TIME!**

Use very cold water to wash greens. Immediately dry the greens using a salad spinner or wrap the leaves in a dish towel and shake vigorously. Once washed, dry greens can be stored in the crisper for at least a day, wrapped in loose paper toweling or a tea towel.

WINTER SALAD

YIELD: 4 TO 6 SERVINGS

DRESSING
$1/2$ cup sugar
$1/3$ cup lemon juice
$2/3$ cup vegetable oil or olive oil
1 teaspoon Dijon mustard
$1/2$ teaspoon salt
1 tablespoon poppy seeds

SALAD
10 ounces romaine lettuce or spinach,
    torn into bite-size pieces
1 cup (4 ounces) shredded Swiss cheese
2 teaspoons chopped green onions
1 cup cashews
1 (6-ounce) package dried cranberries
1 or 2 pears or apples, chopped

FOR THE DRESSING, whisk the sugar, lemon juice, oil, mustard, salt and poppy seeds together in a bowl.

FOR THE SALAD, combine the lettuce, Swiss cheese, green onions, cashews, cranberries and pears in a salad bowl and toss to mix. Divide evenly among 4 to 6 salad plates. Drizzle with the desired amount of dressing.

CITRUS ALMOND SALAD

YIELD: 6 SERVINGS

1 egg white
1/4 cup sugar
1 cup sliced almonds
2 tablespoons butter, melted
1 head Bibb lettuce, torn into
    bite-size pieces
1 head leaf lettuce, torn into bite-size pieces
1 (11-ounce) can mandarin oranges, drained
10 fresh strawberries, thinly sliced
1 green onion, chopped
3/4 cup olive oil
1/4 cup red wine vinegar
1 tablespoon orange juice
1 teaspoon grated orange zest
1/2 teaspoon poppy seeds
1/8 teaspoon salt
1/8 teaspoon pepper

Beat the egg white at high speed in a mixing bowl until foamy. Add the sugar gradually, beating until stiff peaks form. Fold in the almonds. Pour the butter into a 9-inch square baking dish, tilting to coat the bottom. Spread the coated almonds over the bottom of the pan. Bake at 325 degrees for 20 to 25 minutes or until the almonds are dry, stirring every 5 minutes. Let stand until cool.

Combine the Bibb lettuce, leaf lettuce, oranges, strawberries and green onion in a salad bowl and toss to mix. Whisk the olive oil, vinegar, orange juice, orange zest, poppy seeds, salt and pepper together in a separate bowl. Pour over the salad and toss gently to coat.

Divide the salad evenly among 6 salad plates. Sprinkle with the almonds.

The Twin Cities has a very diversified business base. Rising from its roots in lumber and river trade in St. Paul and milling and financial services in Minneapolis, the Twin Cities now boasts corporate headquarters and/or regional locations for companies involved in financial services, consumer electronics, computer technology and manufacturing, electronics, medical instruments, milling, machine manufacturing, food processing, and graphic arts, including General Mills, Pillbury, Toro, Land o' Lakes, Honeywell, and many more. Fourteen Minnesota-based companies are listed on the FORTUNE 500 list of the largest U.S. corporations. In addition, the Twin Cities is host to the world headquarters for multiple large privately held corporations.

SUMMER SALAD WITH WALNUTS AND RASPBERRIES

YIELD: 4 SERVINGS

1/4 cup walnuts, toasted
1 1/2 cups bite-size pieces Bibb lettuce
1 1/2 cups bite-size pieces red leaf lettuce
1/2 pint red raspberries
1/4 cup olive oil
3 tablespoons honey
1 tablespoon sour cream
1/2 teaspoon mustard

Toss the walnuts and lettuces together in a salad bowl. Arrange the raspberries over the salad. Combine the olive oil, honey, sour cream and mustard in a separate bowl and mix well. Pour over the salad just before serving.

DRIED CHERRIES WITH GREENS

YIELD: VARIABLE

DRESSING
1/3 cup cherry vinegar
1/3 cup vegetable oil
1/3 cup sugar
1 tablespoon dried parsley
2 tablespoons sesame seeds
1/2 teaspoon salt
1/2 teaspoon Worcestershire sauce

SALAD
Romaine or leaf lettuce, torn into
    bite-size pieces
Feta cheese, crumbled
Dried cherries
Slivered almonds

FOR THE DRESSING, whisk the vinegar, oil, sugar, parsley, sesame seeds, salt and Worcestershire sauce together in a bowl.

FOR THE SALAD, toss the lettuce, feta cheese, cherries and almonds together in a salad bowl. Drizzle the desired amount of dressing over the salad.

PEAR AND WALNUT SALAD

YIELD: 4 TO 6 SERVINGS

1/3 cup apricot nectar
1/4 cup olive oil
2 tablespoons cider vinegar
1 tablespoon Dijon mustard
1/8 teaspoon salt
1/8 teaspoon pepper
3 pears, thinly sliced
10 cups bite-size pieces Bibb lettuce
1/2 cup chopped walnuts, toasted
1/2 cup (2 ounces) crumbled blue cheese

Combine the apricot nectar, olive oil, vinegar, mustard, salt and pepper in a bowl and mix well. Add the pears and toss gently to coat. Chill, covered, in the refrigerator.

Add the lettuce to the pear mixture and toss to combine. Sprinkle with the walnuts and blue cheese.

SPINACH AND STRAWBERRY SALAD

YIELD: 6 SERVINGS

8 cups rinsed torn fresh spinach
2 cups fresh strawberries, sliced
8 ounces Brie cheese, cut into cubes
2 tablespoons vegetable oil
1/4 cup vinegar
3 tablespoons honey
1/2 teaspoon poppy seeds
1/4 teaspoon almond extract

Combine the spinach, strawberries and Brie cheese in a salad bowl. Whisk the oil, vinegar, honey, poppy seeds and almond extract together in a separate bowl. Pour over the salad and toss to combine.

TEQUILA LIME FRUIT SALAD

YIELD: 28 SERVINGS

3/4 cup sugar
1/4 cup water
1/4 cup fresh or bottled Key lime juice
2 to 3 tablespoons tequila
1 teaspoon grated Key lime zest or regular lime zest
14 cups cut up fresh fruit, such as pineapple, strawberries, kiwifruit and grapes
Spinach leaves (optional)

Combine the sugar and water in a 1 1/2-quart saucepan and bring to a boil. Reduce the heat and simmer for 2 minutes or until the sugar is dissolved, stirring constantly. Remove from the heat. Stir in the lime juice and tequila. Let stand until room temperature. Chill, covered, for 2 hours or until cooled completely. Stir in the lime zest.

Combine the fruit and lime mixture in a large bowl and toss to coat. Serve immediately over spinach leaves.

NOTE: You may reduce the amount of fruit and store any remaining lime dressing in the refrigerator for up to a week.

Always Superb: Recipes for Every Occasion

AVOCADO CORN CONFETTI SALAD

YIELD: 6 TO 8 SERVINGS

3 avocados
3 (11-ounce) cans Shoe Peg white
   corn, drained
1 red bell pepper, chopped
1 red onion, chopped, or 6 green
   onions, chopped
1/4 cup olive oil
2/3 cup red wine vinegar
2 teaspoons red pepper
2 teaspoons oregano
Juice of 3 or 4 limes

Peel and chop the avocados. Combine with
the corn, bell pepper and onion in a bowl and
mix well.

Combine the olive oil, vinegar, red pepper,
oregano and lime juice in a separate bowl and
mix well. Pour over the salad.

NOTE: You may serve this as an appetizer with
corn chips.

MOVIES/TV

Many visitors to the Twin
Cities still search for Mary
Richards, the mythical news
editor of *Mary Tyler Moore Show*
fame. While her likeness is
bronzed in perpetuity, tossing
her hat on Nicollet Mall in
Downtown Minneapolis, the
Twin Cities and the state
of Minnesota have been
showcased in Prince's *Purple
Moon*, the *Mighty Ducks*, and
Grumpy Old Men. In addition,
Minnesota has played host to
Arnold Schwarzenegger and
the cast of *Jingle All the Way* and
to Tim Allen in *Joe Somebody*.
The distinctiveness of the
four seasons and the state's
reputation as an arts center
make Minnesota an attractive
place to film.

FRENCH TARRAGON POTATO SALAD

YIELD: 6 TO 8 SERVINGS

2 pounds red or other waxy potatoes
2 tablespoons minced shallots
2 tablespoons capers
$1/4$ cup white wine vinegar
1 tablespoon whole-grain mustard
2 tablespoons chopped fresh tarragon
6 tablespoons olive oil

GARNISH
Fresh tarragon
Hard-cooked egg slices

Combine the potatoes with enough water to cover in a saucepan. Bring to a boil. Boil until tender; drain. Peel and cut into slices.

Whisk the shallots, capers, vinegar, mustard and tarragon together in a bowl. Drizzle the olive oil into the bowl, whisking constantly. Whisk until the olive oil is incorporated and the dressing is thick.

Add the warm potato slices to the dressing and toss gently to coat. Garnish with tarragon and egg slices. Serve warm or chilled.

AVOCADO AND ROASTED BEET SALAD

YIELD: 4 TO 6 SERVINGS

SALAD
3 red beets
3 gold beets
Salt to taste
Freshly ground pepper to taste
2 tablespoons extra-virgin olive oil
2 tablespoons raspberry vinegar

VINAIGRETTE
$1/4$ cup white wine vinegar
2 tablespoons lemon juice
2 tablespoons orange juice
Pinch of salt
2 shallots, finely chopped
1 cup extra-virgin olive oil
$1/2$ teaspoon grated orange zest
$1/2$ teaspoon grated lemon zest
2 tablespoons chopped parsley

ASSEMBLY
2 avocados
Large kale leaves
Salt to taste
Pepper to taste

GARNISH
Parsley sprigs

FOR THE SALAD, trim and rinse the red beets. Place the beets in a baking pan. Add enough water to measure $1/2$-inch deep. Cover tightly. Repeat with the gold beets using a separate pan. Bake at 400 degrees for 1 hour or until cooked through. Rub off the skins with paper towels. Let stand until cool. Cut into wedges and place in a large bowl. Sprinkle generously with salt and pepper. Add the olive oil and vinegar and toss to coat.

FOR THE VINAIGRETTE, combine the vinegar, lemon juice, orange juice, salt and shallots in a bowl and mix well. Let stand for 15 minutes. Whisk in the olive oil. Stir in the orange zest, lemon zest and parsley. Adjust the seasonings as desired.

TO ASSEMBLE, peel the avocados and cut each into 6 wedges. Arrange with the kale on the salad plates. Sprinkle with salt and pepper. Arrange the beets over the avocadoes and kale. Drizzle with the vinaigrette. Garnish with parsley sprigs.

TWIN CITIES MARINATED SALAD

YIELD: 8 SERVINGS

1 (6-ounce) jar marinated artichoke hearts
$^1/_2$ cup cherry tomatoes, cut into halves
$^1/_2$ cup pitted black olives
$^1/_3$ cup (1-inch) pieces green onions
8 ounces fresh mushrooms, cut into quarters
$^1/_3$ cup vegetable oil
$^1/_4$ cup lemon juice
$^1/_4$ teaspoon salt
$^1/_4$ teaspoon pepper
1 teaspoon sugar
1 teaspoon tarragon
$^1/_2$ teaspoon thyme
2 fresh peaches or nectarines

Drain the artichoke hearts, reserving the marinade. Cut into quarters. Combine with the tomatoes, olives, green onions and mushrooms in a large bowl.

Combine the reserved marinade, oil, lemon juice, salt, pepper, sugar, tarragon and thyme in a separate bowl and mix well. Pour over the vegetable mixture. Marinate, covered, in the refrigerator for 8 to 12 hours.

Peel the peaches and cut into slices. Add to the vegetable salad and toss gently to combine. Serve immediately.

GRILLED VEGETABLE SALAD WITH BALSAMIC VINAIGRETTE

YIELD: 4 TO 6 SERVINGS

VEGETABLES

8 scallions

4 large portobello mushrooms

1 large red bell pepper, cut into
    1/2-inch strips

1 bunch asparagus, trimmed

2 red onions, cut into quarters

2 summer squash, cut into 1-inch strips

1/4 cup olive oil

Kosher salt

Freshly ground pepper

BALSAMIC VINAIGRETTE

3 tablespoons balsamic vinegar

2 teaspoons Dijon mustard

1 small garlic clove, minced

1/2 teaspoon kosher salt

5 or 6 grinds pepper

3/4 cup olive oil

ASSEMBLY

8 cups lightly packed mixed greens

6 ounces crumbled feta cheese, or fresh
    mozzarella cheese, cut into 1/2-inch pieces

2 tomatoes, cut into chunks

12 or more kalamata olives

FOR THE VEGETABLES, trim the roots from the scallions. Trim the tops leaving 3 inches of the green portion. Remove the stems from the mushrooms. Combine the scallions, mushrooms, bell pepper, asparagus, onions and squash in a bowl. Add the olive oil and toss to coat. Sprinkle with kosher salt and pepper. Place on a grill rack over medium-hot coals. Grill until the vegetables are tender, turning once; the scallions, bell pepper, asparagus and squash will cook in about 5 minutes and the mushrooms and onions will cook in 8 to 10 minutes. Place on a cutting board and cover loosely with foil.

FOR THE VINAIGRETTE, whisk the vinegar, mustard, garlic, kosher salt and pepper together in a small bowl. Drizzle the olive oil into the bowl, whisking constantly. Whisk until the olive oil is incorporated and the vinaigrette is thick.

TO ASSEMBLE, place the greens in a salad bowl. Cut the mushrooms into 1/2-inch slices. Cut the asparagus into 1/2-inch pieces. Arrange the mushrooms, asparagus, onions and squash over the greens. Sprinkle with the feta cheese, scallions, bell pepper, tomatoes and olives. Toss with enough of the vinaigrette to lightly coat the greens and vegetables.

SUMMER SALAD WITH TOMATOES, CUCUMBERS AND ONIONS

YIELD: 6 SERVINGS

1 small yellow onion, thinly sliced
Salt to taste
$^1/_2$ cup milk
$^1/_2$ cup plain yogurt
1 to 2 tablespoons freshly squeezed
    lemon juice
1 garlic clove, minced
1 tablespoon chopped fresh oregano, or
    1 teaspoon dried oregano
1$^1/_2$ tablespoons chopped fresh basil, or
    1$^1/_2$ teaspoons dried basil
2 teaspoons extra-virgin olive oil
Freshly ground pepper
1 English cucumber
6 tomatoes in a variety of colors,
    thinly sliced
$^1/_2$ cup (2 ounces) feta cheese
$^1/_4$ cup pine nuts, toasted
Fresh basil leaves
Cherry tomatoes

Place the onion slices in a bowl and sprinkle with salt. Pour the milk over the onion. Let stand for 30 minutes.

Whisk the yogurt, lemon juice, garlic, oregano, basil, olive oil, salt and pepper together in a small bowl. Chill, covered, in the refrigerator.

Peel the cucumber and cut crosswise into thin slices. Arrange the cucumber and tomato slices on a plate. Drain the onion slices and pat dry with paper towels. Scatter the onion slices over the cucumber and tomato slices. Drizzle with the dressing. Sprinkle with the feta cheese, pine nuts, basil leaves and cherry tomatoes.

WHEAT BERRY SALAD

YIELD: 4 TO 6 SERVINGS

SALAD
2/3 cup wheat berries
1/2 teaspoon lemon juice
1/2 teaspoon salt
1/4 cup barley
1 pint cherry tomatoes, cut into halves
6 ounces smoked mozzarella cheese, cut
    into cubes
1/4 cup chopped chives
2 cups frozen corn kernels, thawed

DRESSING
1/4 cup vegetable oil
2 tablespoons balsamic vinegar
1 garlic clove, minced
Salt to taste
Pepper to taste

FOR THE SALAD, combine the wheat berries with enough water to cover in a bowl. Stir in the lemon juice and salt. Let stand for 8 to 12 hours; drain. Combine the soaked wheat berries with enough water to cover in a saucepan. Bring to a boil. Reduce the heat. Simmer for 20 minutes or until tender and firm; drain.

Prepare the barley using the package directions.

Combine the cooked wheat berries, prepared barley, tomatoes, mozzarella cheese, chives and corn in a large bowl and mix well.

FOR THE DRESSING, whisk the oil, vinegar and garlic together in a bowl. Season with salt and pepper.

Drizzle the dressing over the salad and toss to combine.

WARM CABBAGE-APPLE SALAD

YIELD: 6 SERVINGS

2 tablespoons extra-virgin olive oil
2 large shallots, minced
2 to 3 pounds assorted cabbage, such as red,
    green, napa and savoy, finely shredded
1 teaspoon caraway seeds
2 tart green apples, thinly sliced
3 tablespoons white wine vinegar
Salt to taste
Pepper to taste
1/4 cup fresh Italian parsley

Heat the olive oil in a large skillet over
medium heat. Add the shallots. Sauté until
tender. Add the cabbage and caraway seeds.
Cook, partially covered, for 10 minutes or
until the cabbage begins to soften, stirring
occasionally. Stir in the apples and vinegar.
Cook until the apples are heated through,
stirring occasionally. Season with salt and pepper.

Warm a serving bowl. Stir the parsley into the
cabbage mixture. Spoon into the warmed
serving bowl. Serve immediately.

GINGERED ASIAN SALAD

1/4 cup lime juice

1/4 cup minced shallots

1 tablespoon soy sauce

1 1/2 tablespoons minced gingerroot

1/2 to 1 tablespoon seeded minced
    jalapeño chile

2 teaspoons minced garlic

1 tablespoon honey

2 teaspoons Thai red curry paste

1 tablespoon dark sesame oil

1/2 cup peanut, soy or canola oil

5 cups finely sliced napa cabbage

1 1/2 cups julienned carrots

1 large red bell pepper, thinly sliced

1 large yellow bell pepper, thinly sliced

1/2 cup sliced scallions

1/4 cup chopped cilantro leaves

2 tablespoons unsalted roasted skinned
    peanuts, coarsely chopped

1 tablespoon sesame seeds, toasted

2 teaspoons kosher salt

1/8 teaspoon freshly ground pepper

Combine the lime juice, shallots, soy sauce, gingerroot, jalapeño chile, garlic, honey, curry paste, sesame oil and peanut oil in a large glass jar. Cover tightly and shake vigorously until blended.

Combine the cabbage, carrots, bell peppers, scallions, cilantro, peanuts and sesame seeds in a large bowl and toss to mix. Sprinkle with kosher salt and pepper. Pour the dressing over the salad and toss to coat. Let stand for 10 minutes.

SOYBEANS, THE WONDER PROTEIN

Soybeans, one of Minnesota's major exports, represent over 15 percent of the state's total farm receipts. Minnesota ranks third in soybean production in the United States, representing over 10 percent of the country's total soybean production. In addition to their commercial use in ethanol fuel, soybeans are also transformed into cooking oil, soy milk, and other high-protein, low-cholesterol food products. Soybeans are a wonderful substitute for most legumes, and soy products have also been found to have many health benefits.

MINNESOTA SALAD: WILD RICE AND SOYBEANS

YIELD: 6 TO 8 SERVINGS

SALAD
1/2 cup frozen soybeans
Salt to taste
1 cup wild rice
2 tablespoons chopped celery
2 tablespoons chopped apple
2 tablespoons chopped onion
2 tablespoons chopped carrots
1/4 cup chopped parsley
1 cup craisins

DRESSING
1/2 cup olive oil
1/3 cup red wine vinegar
1/2 cup orange juice
2 teaspoons honey
1 tablespoon grated orange zest
1 teaspoon salt

FOR THE SALAD, cook the soybeans using the package directions; drain. Rinse under cold running water; drain. Bring a large pot of water to a boil. Sprinkle with a small amount of salt. Add the rice. Simmer for 30 to 35 minutes or until tender; drain. Rinse under cold running water; drain. Combine the cooked soybeans, cooked rice, celery, apple, onion, carrots, parsley and craisins in a large bowl.

FOR THE DRESSING, whisk the olive oil, vinegar, orange juice, honey, orange zest and salt together in a small bowl.

Pour the dressing over the rice salad and mix well. Chill the salad, covered, for 2 hours or longer. Serve cold.

TABOULI

YIELD: 8 SERVINGS

SALAD
1 cup fine burghul (cracked wheat)
3 cups finely chopped tomatoes
1 cup finely chopped onion
1 cup finely chopped peeled cucumber
1 to 2 cups finely chopped parsley
1 bunch fresh mint, finely chopped (optional)

DRESSING
$1/2$ cup olive oil
$1/2$ cup freshly squeezed lemon juice, or
   to taste
Salt to taste
Pepper to taste

ASSEMBLY
Romaine lettuce leaves

FOR THE SALAD, rinse the burghul and drain.
Place in a bowl with enough water to cover.
Let stand for 1 hour; drain. Combine the
burghul, tomatoes, onion, cucumber, parsley
and mint in a bowl and mix well. You may
make the salad up to this point and chill,
covered, for 1 day.

FOR THE DRESSING, whisk the olive oil, lemon
juice, salt and pepper together in a bowl.

TO ASSEMBLE, pour the dressing over the salad
and mix well. Arrange the lettuce leaves over
a plate. Spoon the salad over the leaves.
Serve immediately.

OILS AND VINEGARS

Making a delicious salad not only requires a mix of interesting and fresh greens, but also delicious dressings. Two of the most common ingredients of any salad dressing are oil and vinegar. Oils from different sources have different flavors.

Walnut: Full-flavored, nutty oil used in salads; very delicate and should be refrigerated.

Sesame: Strong flavor; use a few drops for flavor.

Canola/Corn/Peanut: High burning temperature with little flavor; good for frying; peanut oil is best for fondue.

Extra-Virgin Olive: The first press of the olives; used mostly in salads; has a very low burning temperature; is very flavorful.

Light Olive: The last press of the olive with hot water; higher burning temperature; very light flavor.

Continued on next page

MAYTAG PASTA SALAD

YIELD: 8 SERVINGS

SALAD
16 ounces spiral pasta
2 cups chopped cooked chicken
10 ounces bacon, crisp-cooked and crumbled
2 cups fresh spinach
1 cup pitted black olives
2 tomatoes, chopped
1 avocado, chopped
8 ounces Maytag blue cheese, crumbled

DRESSING
1 teaspoon coarse grain mustard
1/4 cup red wine vinegar
1 cup olive oil
1 garlic clove, minced
1 teaspoon sugar
Salt to taste
Pepper to taste

FOR THE SALAD, cook the pasta using the package directions until al dente; drain. Rinse and drain again. Combine the cooked pasta, chicken, bacon, spinach, olives, tomatoes, avocado and blue cheese in a bowl and toss to mix.

FOR THE DRESSING, whisk the mustard, vinegar, olive oil, garlic, sugar, salt and pepper together in a bowl. Pour over the salad and toss to coat.

PEA, RED PEPPER AND PESTO PASTA TOSS

YIELD: 12 SERVINGS

24 ounces penne or other similar size pasta
    such as bow tie
1/4 cup olive oil
1 1/2 cups pesto
1 (10-ounce) package frozen chopped
    spinach, thawed and drained
3 tablespoons freshly squeezed lemon juice
1 1/4 cups mayonnaise
1/2 cup (2 ounces) grated Parmesan cheese
1 1/2 cups frozen petite peas, thawed
1 1/2 cups chopped red bell pepper
1/3 cup pine nuts, toasted
3/4 teaspoon kosher salt
3/4 teaspoon freshly ground pepper
1 cup cherry tomatoes, cut into halves

Cook the pasta using the package directions
until al dente; drain. Combine the pasta and
olive oil in a large bowl and toss to coat. Let
stand until room temperature.

Purée the pesto, spinach and lemon juice in
a food processor. Add the mayonnaise and
process until mixed. Stir into the cooled pasta.

Add the Parmesan cheese, peas, bell pepper,
pine nuts, kosher salt and pepper to the pasta
mixture and mix well. Adjust the seasonings
if desired. Sprinkle the tomatoes over the
top. Serve at room temperature.

Even olive oils can have
different flavors depending
on the location of the olive
tree. Oil derived from olives
grown in Italy tends to have
a nutty undertone. Spanish
olive oil tends to be more
robust in flavor. Grecian olive
oil tends to have a thicker
texture but a lighter taste.
French olive oil is often
peppery or spicy.

As with oil, the flavor and
strength of vinegar can
dramatically change the taste
of the dressing, as follows:

Red Wine Vinegar: Versatile.
    Sharp, clean taste.
White Wine Vinegar: Similar
    to red wine; softer flavor.
Balsamic Vinegar: True
    balsamic comes from
    Modena, Italy, and is aged
    in oak casks. The older the
    vinegar, the sweeter the taste.
Sherry Vinegar: Strong, high
    acid, rich flavor.
Rice Vinegar: Low acid.
    Clean, mild taste.

Continued on next page

For a basic vinaigrette, combine 2 tablespoons vinegar, $^1/_2$ teaspoon salt and $^1/_4$ teaspoon freshly ground pepper in a bowl and mix well. Add 6 tablespoons oil gradually, whisking constantly. For a variation, add fresh or dried herbs, and/or use balsamic vinegar; replace vinegar with lemon or lime juice; or add grainy mustard.

ITALIAN PASTA SALAD WITH SAUSAGE AND ARTICHOKES

YIELD: 6 SERVINGS

6 cups water
$^1/_2$ teaspoon salt
$1^1/_2$ cups rotini pasta
1 (6-ounce) jar marinated artichoke hearts
1 cucumber
3 ounces Thuringer (sausage)
4 ounces mozzarella cheese, cut into
   $^1/_2$-inch cubes
1 cup shredded carrot
1 (4-ounce) can sliced black olives
$^1/_4$ cup (1 ounce) freshly grated Parmesan cheese
2 tablespoons white wine vinegar
1 teaspoon dry mustard
$^1/_4$ cup freshly cut basil
$^1/_2$ teaspoon minced garlic
$^1/_2$ teaspoon salt

Bring the water and $^1/_2$ teaspoon salt to a boil in a large saucepan. Stir in the pasta. Reduce the heat. Simmer for 10 minutes or until al dente; drain. Rinse with cold water and drain.

Drain the artichokes, reserving $^1/_4$ cup marinade. Coarsely chop the artichokes. Cut the cucumber into quarters and remove the seeds. Cut into $^1/_2$-inch-thick slices. Cut the Thuringer into $^1/_4$-inch-thick slices. Cut into $^1/_2$-inch cubes.

Combine the pasta, artichokes, cucumber, Thuringer, mozzarella cheese, carrot, olives and Parmesan cheese in a bowl and mix well.

Combine the reserved artichoke marinade, vinegar, dry mustard, basil, garlic and $^1/_2$ teaspoon salt in a jar. Cover and shake to combine. Pour into the salad and toss to combine.

Chill the salad, covered, for 8 to 12 hours. Toss just before serving.

ANTIPASTO SALAD

YIELD: 8 SERVINGS

DRESSING

1 cup olive oil
1/4 cup white wine vinegar
1 garlic clove, minced
1 teaspoon salt
1/2 teaspoon freshly ground black pepper
1/2 teaspoon celery salt
1/4 teaspoon ground red pepper
1/4 teaspoon dry mustard

SALAD

1 head leaf lettuce
1 cup grape tomatoes or cherry tomatoes,
    cut into halves
1/2 cup (2 ounces) shredded
    mozzarella cheese
1/2 cup (2 ounces) shredded
    provolone cheese
1 cup canned garbanzo beans, drained
4 ounces hard salami, chopped
1/2 cup chopped pepperoncini
1 (5-ounce) jar marinated
    mushrooms, drained
1 (5-ounce) jar marinated artichoke
    hearts, drained
1 (5-ounce) jar roasted red bell
    peppers, drained
1/2 cup small pitted black olives
1/4 cup chopped green onions

FOR THE DRESSING, whisk the olive oil, vinegar, garlic, salt, black pepper, celery salt, red pepper and dry mustard together in a bowl.

FOR THE SALAD, line a salad bowl with the lettuce leaves. Combine the tomatoes, mozzarella cheese, provolone cheese, beans, salami, pepperoncini, mushrooms, artichokes, roasted bell peppers, olives and green onions in a large bowl. Add the dressing and toss to coat. Spoon into the lettuce-lined salad bowl.

SMOKED TROUT AND APPLE SALAD

YIELD: 4 SERVINGS

SALAD
2 crisp apples, sliced
1/2 bunch watercress
4 cups mixed salad greens
1 (6-ounce) smoked trout, skinned
   and boned

DRESSING
1/2 cup plain yogurt
1 teaspoon lemon juice
1 tablespoon coarse grain horseradish sauce
Milk (optional)
Salt to taste
Pepper to taste

GARNISH
1 tablespoon chopped chives

FOR THE SALAD, combine the apples, watercress, greens and trout in a salad bowl.

FOR THE DRESSING, whisk the yogurt, lemon juice and horseradish sauce together in a bowl. Whisk in enough milk to make of the desired consistency. Season with salt and pepper.

Drizzle the dressing over the salad and toss to combine. Garnish with chopped chives.

WILD RICE CRAB CAKES ON GREENS

YIELD: 24 TO 30 CRAB CAKES

$1/2$ cup uncooked wild rice

2 cups water

$1/2$ teaspoon salt

1 pound crab meat, drained, shells removed
    and flaked

$3/4$ cup fresh bread crumbs

$1/2$ cup finely chopped red bell pepper

$1/4$ cup minced shallots

$1/4$ cup mayonnaise

2 tablespoons Dijon mustard

$1^1/2$ tablespoons lemon juice

$1/2$ teaspoon salt

$1/2$ teaspoon cumin

$1/8$ teaspoon ground red pepper

$1/8$ teaspoon black pepper

2 egg whites, lightly beaten

4 teaspoons olive oil

Combine the wild rice, water and salt in a saucepan and bring to a boil. Reduce the heat. Simmer for 45 minutes or until the rice grains open and are tender.

Combine the cooked wild rice, crab meat, bread crumbs, bell pepper, shallots, mayonnaise, mustard, lemon juice, $1/2$ teaspoon salt, cumin, red pepper, black pepper and egg whites in a large bowl and mix well. Shape by tablespoonfuls into bite-size cakes.

Heat 2 teaspoons of the olive oil in a large nonstick skillet over medium heat. Add enough cakes in a single layer to fill the skillet. Cook until brown on both sides, turning once. Repeat with the remaining oil and cakes.

Place on a bed of salad greens such as arugula or watercress. (See sidebar page 114.)

HOMEMADE MAYONNAISE

Beat 1 egg yolk in a bowl until blended. Add $1/2$ teaspoon salt, $1/2$ teaspoon Dijon mustard, $1^1/2$ teaspoons lemon juice and 1 teaspoon white wine vinegar and beat until thick. Add $3/4$ cup canola oil in a fine stream, beating constantly. You may add grated lemon zest and additional lemon juice, or an additional 2 tablespoons Dijon mustard, or 1 tablespoon minced tarragon for variations.

FRISÉE SALAD WITH POACHED EGGS AND WARM BACON DRESSING

YIELD: 4 SERVINGS

WARM BACON DRESSING
6 ounces thick-cut slices bacon
2 shallots, chopped
3 tablespoons red wine vinegar

SALAD
2 tablespoons distilled vinegar
4 eggs
8 ounces frisée lettuce, torn into
    bite-size pieces

GARNISH
1 tablespoon chopped fresh tarragon leaves

FOR THE DRESSING, cut the bacon into $1/4$-inch pieces. Cook in a skillet over medium heat until golden brown. Add the shallots. Cook for 1 minute, stirring frequently. Whisk in the vinegar. Remove from the heat and keep warm.

FOR THE SALAD, fill a medium saucepan half full with water. Stir in the vinegar. Bring to a simmer. Gently break 1 egg into the simmering water. Spoon hot water over the egg. Repeat with the remaining 3 eggs. Cook for 2 minutes for a runny yolk or 4 minutes for a firm yolk. Place eggs in a skillet of warm water to hold.

Divide the lettuce evenly among 4 salad plates. Remove an egg from the water and pat dry. Place over the lettuce on one of the plates. Repeat with the remaining eggs. Drizzle the warm dressing over the lettuce. Garnish with the tarragon.

WILTED SPINACH SALAD

YIELD: 4 SERVINGS

6 cups torn fresh spinach
1 cup sliced fresh mushrooms
1/4 cup sliced green onions
3 slices bacon
2 tablespoons vinegar
1 teaspoon sugar
1/4 teaspoon salt
1 hard-cooked egg, chopped

Combine the spinach, mushrooms and green onions in a bowl.

Cook the bacon in a 12-inch skillet until crisp. Remove the bacon, reserving the drippings. Crumble the bacon and set aside.

Stir the vinegar, sugar and salt into the reserved drippings in the skillet. Bring to a boil. Remove from the heat. Add the spinach mixture and toss to coat. Spoon into a serving dish. Sprinkle the egg and cooked bacon over the top. Serve immediately.

GRAND ROUNDS SCENIC BYPASS

The Grand Rounds Scenic Bypass feature 50.1 miles of continuous walking and biking trails around the various water byways of the Twin Cities. The Bypass is divided into five glorious sections, including some of the most beautiful riverfront and lake trails in the country.

MOLDED GAZPACHO SALAD

YIELD: 10 TO 12 SERVINGS

2^1/4 cups tomato juice

2 envelopes unflavored gelatin

^{1}/3 cup red wine vinegar

1 teaspoon salt

Tabasco sauce to taste

2 small tomatoes, peeled and chopped
    (about 1 cup)

1 cucumber, peeled and chopped
    (about 1 cup)

^{1}/2 green bell pepper, chopped
    (about ^{1}/2 cup)

^{1}/4 cup finely chopped red onion

1 tablespoon chopped chives

Pour ^{3}/4 cup of the tomato juice into a medium saucepan. Sprinkle the gelatin over the tomato juice to soften. Cook over low heat until the gelatin is dissolved, stirring constantly. Remove from the heat. Stir in the remaining 1^1/2 cups tomato juice, vinegar, salt and Tabasco sauce. Place saucepan in a bowl of ice. Let stand for 15 minutes or until the mixture thickens, stirring occasionally.

Fold the tomatoes, cucumber, bell pepper, onion and chives into the gelatin mixture. Rinse a 1^1/2-quart mold with cold water. Pour the gelatin mixture into the mold. Chill, covered, until set.

Always Superb: Recipes for Every Occasion

ASPARAGUS AND NEW POTATOES WITH TOASTED HAZELNUTS

YIELD: 12 SERVINGS

2 pounds small new potatoes, scrubbed
2 pounds asparagus, trimmed
1/2 cup hazelnut or walnut oil
2 tablespoons raspberry vinegar
1 teaspoon brown sugar
1 cardamom pod, crushed
1 cup hazelnuts, toasted

GARNISH
Chopped chives

Combine the potatoes with enough water to cover in a saucepan. Bring to a boil. Boil for 15 to 20 minutes or until tender; drain. Place in a large bowl.

Cut each asparagus spear diagonally into 2 or 3 pieces. Bring enough water to cover the asparagus to a boil in a saucepan. Add the asparagus. Cook for 1 to 2 minutes or until tender-crisp; drain. Set aside.

Whisk the hazelnut oil, vinegar, brown sugar and cardamom pod together in a bowl. Pour over the warm potatoes. Add the hazelnuts and toss to coat. Add the asparagus just before serving and toss to combine. Garnish with chopped chives.

ROASTED ASPARAGUS WITH GOAT CHEESE AND BACON

YIELD: 6 SERVINGS

6 slices bacon
2 pounds asparagus, trimmed
2 tablespoons olive oil
Salt to taste
Pepper to taste
4 ounces soft goat cheese, crumbled
2 teaspoons freshly squeezed lemon juice
1 tablespoon olive oil
1 teaspoon grated lemon zest

Cook the bacon in a skillet until crisp. Place on paper towels to drain. Crumble and set aside.

Arrange the asparagus on a baking sheet. Drizzle with 2 tablespoons olive oil, turning to coat. Sprinkle generously with salt and pepper. Roast at 500 degrees for 7 minutes or until tender-crisp. Arrange in a single layer on a serving platter.

Sprinkle the goat cheese and bacon over the asparagus. Drizzle with lemon juice and 1 tablespoon olive oil. Sprinkle the lemon zest over the top.

SMOKY HOT BEANS

YIELD: 8 SERVINGS

3/4 cup packed brown sugar
1/2 cup ketchup
1/3 cup light corn syrup
2 or 3 drops hot pepper sauce such as
    Tabasco sauce
2 to 3 teaspoons liquid smoke
1 onion, chopped
4 (15-ounce) cans lima beans, drained
4 to 6 slices bacon, cut into bite-size pieces

Combine the brown sugar, ketchup, corn syrup, hot pepper sauce, liquid smoke and onion in a bowl and mix well. Add the beans and mix well. Pour into a 2-quart baking dish. Arrange the bacon pieces over the top. Bake at 325 degrees for 1 hour.

GLAZED BEETS

YIELD: 6 SERVINGS

6 red beets
2 tablespoons vegetable oil
1/4 cup water
1/2 cup balsamic vinegar
3 tablespoons brown sugar
Salt to taste
Pepper to taste

Rinse the unpeeled beets and place in a shallow baking dish. Stir the oil and water together in a small bowl. Pour over the beets, turning to coat. Bake at 400 degrees for 1 hour or until tender. Let stand until cool enough to handle. Remove the peel from the beets. Cut crosswise into thin slices.

Combine the vinegar and brown sugar in a saucepan and mix well. Bring to a boil over medium heat, stirring to dissolve the brown sugar. Boil until reduced by one-third. Remove from the heat.

Warm a serving bowl. Place the beets in the warm bowl. Drizzle with the glaze.

BROCCOLI WITH LEMON CREAM SAUCE

YIELD: 8 SERVINGS

2 pounds fresh broccoli
Salt to taste
6 ounces cream cheese, softened
6 tablespoons milk
1 teaspoon grated lemon zest
1 tablespoon lemon juice
1/2 teaspoon ground ginger
1/2 teaspoon cardamom
1 tablespoon butter
1/2 cup sliced almonds

Trim and peel the ends of the broccoli spears. Bring enough water to cover the spears to a boil in a large saucepan. Add a small amount of salt. Add the broccoli. Cook for 5 minutes or until tender-crisp; drain. Arrange with the spears pointing in one direction in a large shallow baking dish.

Combine the cream cheese, milk, lemon zest, lemon juice, ginger and cardamom in a mixing bowl and beat until smooth. Spoon over the broccoli stems. Bake, covered, at 350 degrees for 15 minutes.

Heat the butter in a skillet until melted. Add the almonds. Sauté until toasted. Sprinkle over the cooked broccoli just before serving.

BROCCOLI PURÉE

YIELD: 6 TO 8 SERVINGS

1 large bunch fresh broccoli
3 tablespoons butter
3 tablespoons flour
Salt to taste
Pepper to taste
1/4 cup (1/2 stick) butter, melted
1/4 cup sour cream
7 tablespoons grated Parmesan cheese

Trim the broccoli stems. Bring enough water to cover the broccoli to a boil in a large saucepan. Add the broccoli. Cook until tender; drain.

Heat 3 tablespoons butter in a heavy 1-quart saucepan until melted. Stir in the flour. Cook until the flour browns, stirring constantly. Remove from the heat.

Purée the broccoli in a food processor. Add the flour mixture and process to combine. Add the salt, pepper, 1/4 cup melted butter, sour cream and 4 tablespoons of the Parmesan cheese and mix well. Pour into an 8-inch square baking dish. Sprinkle the remaining 3 tablespoons Parmesan cheese over the top. Bake at 350 degrees for 30 minutes.

ROASTED BRUSSELS SPROUTS WITH PANCETTA

YIELD: 6 TO 8 SERVINGS

1 pound brussels sprouts, trimmed and cut
   into halves
2 ounces pancetta, minced
1 shallot, minced
$^{1}/_{2}$ tablespoon olive oil
Salt to taste
Pepper to taste
$^{1}/_{4}$ cup chicken broth

Toss the brussels sprouts, pancetta, shallot, olive oil, salt and pepper together in a bowl. Place in a single layer in an 11×17-inch baking pan. Bake at 450 degrees in the upper third of the oven for 25 minutes, stirring after 10 minutes.

Pour the chicken broth over the brussels sprouts, scraping up any browned bits. Serve immediately.

WALKING AND BIKING IN THE TWIN CITIES

The Twin Cities is home to nearly 700 miles of walking and biking paths, many abutting the nearly 950 lakes within the metro region. The trails are shared by athletic enthusiasts, children in strollers, and individuals commuting to work on foot or by bike. Most of the trails are open to the public year-round and often get cleared of snow before the neighborhood streets are plowed. In addition, during the winter months, it's common to see people cross-country skiing, snowshoeing, ice boating, or ice skating on the many frozen lakes and ponds.

HISTORY OF MINNEAPOLIS

Minneapolis was originally settled by Father Louis Hennepin in 1860 in St. Anthony Falls, the current site of Downtown Minneapolis. The city of Minneapolis was incorporated in 1867, named for the Dakota word "Minne" ("of the waters") and the Greek word "polis" ("city"). The city is affectionately referred to as the City of Lakes, as its city limits cover almost sixty square miles, including at least eighteen lakes and over one hundred fifty parks. The Twin Cities' unique location near the wheat fields of the Dakotas and on the banks of both the mighty Mississippi and Minnesota Rivers helped distinguish Minneapolis as the "Flour Milling Capital of the World" during the 1870s.

CORN PUDDING

YIELD: 6 TO 8 SERVINGS

4 eggs
2 cups milk
$1/2$ cup (scant) sugar
1 tablespoon flour
1 teaspoon salt
2 cups corn
$1/4$ cup ($1/2$ stick) butter, melted

Beat the eggs lightly in a mixing bowl. Beat in the milk. Combine the sugar, flour and salt in a separate bowl and mix well. Beat into the egg mixture. Stir in the corn and butter. Pour into a baking dish. Bake at 350 degrees for 1 hour or until the pudding is puffed and golden. This recipe freezes well.

BRANDIED CARROTS

YIELD: 8 TO 10 SERVINGS

3 pounds carrots, cut into large pieces
3 cups water
2 tablespoons sugar
1 teaspoon salt
6 tablespoons butter
3 tablespoons honey
1 1/2 tablespoons brown sugar
3 tablespoons brandy
Heavy cream (optional)
3 tablespoons parsley

Combine the carrots, water, sugar, salt and
3 tablespoons of the butter in a saucepan.
Bring to a boil. Reduce the heat. Simmer,
covered, for 10 minutes or until the carrots
are tender; drain.

Heat the remaining 3 tablespoons butter,
honey and brown sugar in a skillet over
medium heat until the butter melts and the
brown sugar dissolves, stirring constantly. Add
the cooked carrots and brandy. Cook for
3 minutes or until the carrots are coated with
the glaze. Add enough heavy cream to make
of the desired consistency. Sprinkle with
the parsley.

GINGERED CARROTS

YIELD: VARIABLE

1 to 2 pounds carrots, peeled and chopped
1/4 cup (1/2 stick) butter, melted
1 cup white wine
1 tablespoon ginger
1 teaspoon cardamom
1/2 teaspoon salt
1 teaspoon pepper

Bring enough water to cover the carrots to
a boil in a saucepan. Add the carrots. Cook
for 6 to 8 minutes or until tender-crisp. Drain
and return to the saucepan.

Combine the butter, wine, ginger, cardamom,
salt and pepper in a bowl and mix well. Pour
over the carrots.

Cook the carrots over low heat for 15 minutes.
Serve warm or cold.

CARROT SOUFFLÉ

YIELD: 8 SERVINGS

2 pounds carrots, peeled
2 teaspoons lemon juice
2 tablespoons minced scallions
$^{1}/_{2}$ cup (1 stick) butter, softened
$^{1}/_{4}$ cup sugar
1$^{1}/_{2}$ tablespoons flour
$^{1}/_{2}$ teaspoon salt
$^{1}/_{4}$ teaspoon cinnamon
1 cup milk
3 eggs
1 egg white, stiffly beaten

Bring enough water to cover the carrots to a boil in a saucepan. Add the carrots. Cook until tender; drain. Purée the carrots in a food processor or blender.

Combine the puréed carrots, lemon juice, scallions, butter, sugar, flour, salt, cinnamon, milk and eggs in a bowl and mix well. Fold in the egg white.

Pour the carrot mixture into a greased 2-quart baking dish. Bake at 350 degrees for 50 to 60 minutes or until the center is firm. Serve immediately.

BAUNJAUN BOURANEE

YIELD: 6 SERVINGS

2 cups plain yogurt
3 garlic cloves, finely chopped
2^1/2 teaspoons salt
1^1/2 eggplants
^{1}/2 cup vegetable oil
1 onion, chopped
^{1}/4 cup chopped red bell pepper
^{1}/4 cup chopped green bell pepper
^{1}/2 cup tomato sauce
^{1}/4 cup (or more) water
Pepper to taste

Place the yogurt in a strainer over a bowl and let stand for 1 hour or longer. Discard the liquid in the bowl. Combine the yogurt, garlic and 1 teaspoon of the salt in a bowl and mix well. Set aside.

Peel the eggplants and cut into ^{1}/2-inch-thick slices. Score the slices lightly and arrange in a single layer on baking sheets. Sprinkle with ^{1}/2 teaspoon of the salt. Let stand for 15 minutes; pat dry.

Heat 1 tablespoon of the oil in a large skillet. Arrange the eggplant slices in a single layer in the hot oil. Cook until light brown on both sides, turning once. Remove the eggplant and set aside, reserving the oil in the skillet. Repeat with the remaining oil and eggplant.

Add the onion and bell peppers to the reserved hot oil in the skillet. Cook until tender, stirring frequently. Stir in the remaining 1 teaspoon salt, tomato sauce and water. Add the browned eggplant. Cook until the eggplant is tender, adding water as needed. Season with pepper.

Spread ^{1}/2 of the yogurt mixture on a platter. Arrange the eggplant slices over the yogurt. Spread the remaining yogurt mixture over the eggplant slices. Spoon any remaining tomato sauce over the top.

NOTE: You may brush the eggplant slices with olive oil, arrange in a single layer on a baking sheet and bake at 350 degrees for 15 to 20 minutes instead of cooking in the skillet.

LEMON GREEN BEANS

YIELD: 4 TO 6 SERVINGS

1 large bunch fresh string green beans
1 tablespoon extra-virgin olive oil
Juice of $1/2$ lemon
1 teaspoon kosher salt, or to taste
Freshly ground pepper to taste

Trim and rinse the beans. Place a vegetable steamer in a large saucepan. Add 1 inch of water. Cover and bring to a boil. Uncover and add the beans. Steam, covered, until the beans are tender-crisp. Place in a serving bowl. Drizzle with the olive oil and lemon juice. Sprinkle with the kosher salt and pepper. Toss to coat the beans.

ORIENTAL GREEN BEANS

YIELD: 4 SERVINGS

1 pound green beans, trimmed
1 tablespoon vegetable oil
1 tablespoon chopped fresh chives
1 tablespoon minced garlic
1 tablespoon soy sauce
$1/2$ teaspoon sugar
2 teaspoons sesame seeds, toasted

Steam the beans in a steamer until tender-crisp. Drain and set aside. Heat the oil in a wok or large skillet. Add the chives and garlic. Sauté until the garlic is tender. Stir in the soy sauce and sugar. Add the beans. Cook for 1 minute, tossing gently to coat. Sprinkle with sesame seeds. Serve immediately.

TRADITIONAL GREEN BEAN CASSEROLE

YIELD: 4 SERVINGS

1 (16-ounce) package frozen French green
   beans, or 1 pound fresh green beans
1 tablespoon butter
1/2 cup minced onion
1 teaspoon salt
1/8 teaspoon pepper
2 teaspoons flour
1/4 teaspoon grated lemon zest
1/2 cup sour cream
1 tablespoon cooking sherry
1/2 cup bread crumbs
1/2 cup (2 ounces) shredded Cheddar cheese

Steam the beans in a steamer until tender-
crisp. Heat the butter in a skillet until melted.
Add the onion and cook until tender. Stir in
the salt, pepper, flour and lemon zest. Stir
in the sour cream. Cook over low heat for
2 minutes. Stir in the sherry. Add the beans
and toss to combine. Spoon into an 8-inch
square baking dish. Sprinkle the bread crumbs
and Cheddar cheese over the top. Bake at
350 degrees for 20 minutes.

Entertaining

WHAT THE HECK IS A HOT DISH?

The "hot dish" is
Minnesota's equivalent to the
Philly cheese steak or the
Chicago deep-dish pizza.
It's the staple of most church
potlucks, family reunions,
and many neighborhood
gatherings. The beauty of the
"hot dish" is that it can
generally be prepared ahead
of time, serves a large number
of people, and is easy to
make. The basic recipe
includes some type of ground
meat, diced vegetables, and/or
potatoes, maybe some noodles
or rice and ALWAYS some
type of canned cream soup.
It's good, you betcha!

MUSHROOM STRUDEL

YIELD: 8 SERVINGS

1 pound mushrooms, finely chopped
$^1/_4$ cup ($^1/_2$ stick) unsalted butter
$^1/_4$ cup white wine
$1^1/_2$ teaspoons chives
$1^1/_2$ teaspoons parsley
$^1/_2$ teaspoon salt
$^1/_8$ teaspoon pepper
$^1/_2$ cup sour cream
4 phyllo sheets
$^1/_4$ to $^1/_2$ cup ($^1/_2$ to 1 stick) unsalted
    butter, melted
12 tablespoons bread crumbs
Butter
$^1/_2$ cup chopped mushrooms

Combine 1 pound mushrooms, $^1/_4$ cup butter and wine in a skillet. Cook for 30 to 45 minutes or until the liquid has evaporated. Remove from the heat. Stir in the chives, parsley, salt, pepper and sour cream. Divide into 4 equal portions.

Cover 3 of the phyllo sheets with waxed paper topped with a damp towel. Place the remaining phyllo sheet on a damp towel. Brush generously with the melted butter. Sprinkle with 3 tablespoons of the bread crumbs. Spoon 1 portion of the mushroom filling along one end, leaving 2 inches from the edge. Fold the edge over and roll up, brushing the ends and opposite edge with butter to seal. Place in a buttered rimmed baking pan. Brush the outside with melted butter. Cover loosely with waxed paper. Repeat with the remaining phyllo sheets. Remove the waxed paper. Bake at 375 degrees for 20 minutes or until golden. Place on a serving platter.

Heat a small amount of butter in a skillet until melted. Add $^1/_2$ cup mushrooms. Cook until tender. Spoon over the strudels.

BALSAMIC APRICOT GLAZED ONIONS

YIELD: 4 SERVINGS

2 Vidalia or other sweet onions
   (about 1 pound)
2 tablespoons olive oil
2 tablespoons balsamic vinegar
3 tablespoons apricot preserves
1/4 cup packed brown sugar

Peel the onions and cut into halves lengthwise. Place cut sides down in a baking dish. Drizzle with the olive oil, turning to coat. Bake at 400 degrees for 30 minutes or until tender.

Combine the vinegar, preserves and brown sugar in a bowl and mix well. Pour over the hot onions. Serve immediately.

FENNEL POTATOES

YIELD: 6 TO 8 SERVINGS

2 fresh fennel bulbs
2 pounds new red potatoes
2 tablespoons fennel seeds
Salt to taste
Pepper to taste
2 1/2 tablespoons regular or garlic-flavored
   olive oil

Cut the tops off the fennel bulbs; discard. Remove the leaves and reserve. Cut the fennel into thin slices. Cut the potatoes into wedges or slices. Combine the fennel, potatoes, fennel seeds, salt, pepper and olive oil in a bowl and toss to mix. Arrange in an even layer in a large rimmed baking pan. Bake at 425 degrees for 30 to 40 minutes or until the potatoes are tender. Place in a serving bowl. Garnish with the reserved fennel leaves.

SMASHED RED POTATOES WITH GORGONZOLA CHEESE

YIELD: 6 SERVINGS

1 1/2 pounds small red potatoes, cut
   into halves
Salt to taste
3 tablespoons butter or margarine, softened
1/3 cup buttermilk
4 ounces Gorgonzola cheese, crumbled
1/2 teaspoon salt
Dash of pepper

Combine the potatoes with enough water
to cover in a 3-quart saucepan. Add a small
amount of salt. Cover and bring to a boil.
Reduce the heat. Simmer for 20 minutes or
until the potatoes are tender; drain. Shake the
potatoes in the saucepan over low heat until
dry. Add the butter, buttermilk, Gorgonzola
cheese, 1/2 teaspoon salt and pepper and
mash lightly leaving some large pieces.

NOTE: You may prepare this recipe in advance
and keep the potatoes warm in the top of
a double boiler over simmering water or in
a slow cooker on Low for 2 to 3 hours.
You may sprinkle toasted chopped walnuts
or chopped fresh chives over the top for
a special touch.

ASIAGO AU GRATIN POTATOES

YIELD: 6 SERVINGS

2 pounds Yukon Gold potatoes
1/4 cup (1/2 stick) butter
1 tablespoon flour
1 teaspoon salt
1 teaspoon white pepper
2 cups half-and-half
2 cups (8 ounces) shredded asiago cheese

Scrub the potatoes. Combine the potatoes with enough cold water to cover in a saucepan. Bring to a boil. Boil for 30 to 35 minutes or until tender; drain. Let stand until cool. Peel and cut into slices. Arrange in a buttered 2-quart baking dish.

Heat the butter in a medium saucepan over medium heat until melted. Stir in the flour, salt and white pepper. Bring to a boil, stirring constantly. Stir in the half-and-half. Bring to a boil, stirring constantly. Boil for 1 minute, stirring constantly. Remove from the heat. Add the asiago cheese, stirring until melted. Pour over the potatoes.

Bake at 350 degrees for 30 to 35 minutes or until bubbly.

LEMON OREGANO POTATOES

YIELD: 4 SERVINGS

3 pounds Yukon Gold potatoes, peeled and chopped (about 6 medium)
1/4 cup freshly squeezed lemon juice
1/4 cup olive oil
2 teaspoons salt
1/2 teaspoon pepper
1 1/2 teaspoons oregano
4 or 5 garlic cloves, minced
1 1/2 cups water

Combine the potatoes, lemon juice, olive oil, salt, pepper, oregano and garlic in a bowl and mix well. Spoon into an 8×12-inch baking dish sprayed with nonstick cooking spray. Pour the water over the potatoes. Bake at 475 degrees for 1 hour, stirring occasionally.

NOTE: You may substitute cilantro or basil for the oregano.

BAKED GOAT CHEESE POTATOES

YIELD: 8 TO 10 SERVINGS

2 tablespoons butter
2 shallots, chopped
8 ounces goat cheese, crumbled
1 cup cream
1 cup milk
1 cup sour cream
3 pounds yellow potatoes, thinly sliced
2 teaspoons salt
1 teaspoon pepper

Heat the butter in a skillet until melted. Add the shallots. Sauté until tender; do not brown. Whisk in the goat cheese, cream, milk and sour cream.

Layer the potatoes, salt, pepper and cheese sauce in a buttered baking dish. Bake, covered with foil, at 350 degrees for 45 minutes. Remove the foil and bake for 45 minutes longer or until the potatoes are tender.

BAKED BUTTERNUT SQUASH WITH APPLES

YIELD: 12 SERVINGS

2^1/2 to 2^3/4 pounds butternut squash
Salt to taste
2^1/4 pounds Granny Smith apples, peeled
    and sliced
^{3}/4 cup dried craisins
^{1}/4 teaspoon grated nutmeg
^{1}/2 teaspoon cinnamon
^{1}/4 cup packed brown sugar
^{1}/4 teaspoon salt
Pepper to taste
^{3}/4 cup maple syrup
^{1}/4 cup (^{1}/2 stick) butter
1^1/2 tablespoons freshly squeezed
    lemon juice

Peel the squash and cut into quarters lengthwise. Remove and discard the seeds. Cut crosswise into ^{1}/4-inch-thick slices.

Bring enough water to cover the squash to a boil in a large saucepan. Add a small amount of salt. Add the squash. Cook for 3 minutes or until almost tender; drain. Combine the squash, apples and craisins in a large bowl and toss to mix. Spoon into a 9×13-inch baking dish. Sprinkle the nutmeg, cinnamon, brown sugar, ^{1}/4 teaspoon salt and pepper over the squash mixture.

Heat the maple syrup, butter and lemon juice in a heavy saucepan over low heat until the butter melts, whisking constantly. Pour over the squash mixture and toss to coat evenly.

Bake at 350 degrees for 1 hour or until the squash and apples are very tender, stirring occasionally.

NOTE: You may prepare 1 day in advance and store, covered, in the refrigerator. Reheat in a 350-degree oven for 30 minutes.

SKY WHAT? Skyways. Similar to a sci-fi movie, the downtowns of Minneapolis and St. Paul, feature climate-controlled walkways connecting the businesses and shops. Since 1962, the skyways have allowed shoppers and businesspeople alike to move from one location to the other without ever having to go outside. They're the one place in Minnesota where you don't have to wear your coat in the winter.

SWEET POTATO SOUFFLÉ

YIELD: 6 TO 8 SERVINGS

SWEET POTATOES
3 cups mashed cooked sweet potatoes
$1/2$ cup sugar
2 eggs
$1/4$ cup ($1/2$ stick) butter, melted
$1/2$ cup milk
$1/2$ teaspoon salt
1 teaspoon vanilla extract
$1/2$ teaspoon ground ginger, or to taste

TOPPING
1 cup packed brown sugar
$1/3$ cup flour
$1/4$ cup ($1/2$ stick) butter, melted
$1/3$ cup pecan halves or chopped pecans

FOR THE SWEET POTATOES, beat the sweet potatoes, sugar, eggs, butter, milk, salt, vanilla and ginger together in a mixing bowl. Pour into a greased 8- or 9-inch square baking dish.

FOR THE TOPPING, combine the brown sugar, flour and butter in a bowl and mix well. Stir in the pecans. Sprinkle over the sweet potato mixture.

Bake at 350 degrees for 30 minutes.

ARTICHOKE VEGETABLE DISH

YIELD: 6 TO 8 SERVINGS

6 canned artichoke bottoms
1 tablespoon olive oil
$^1/_2$ to 1 cup sliced fresh mushrooms
4 to 6 mushroom caps
2 teaspoons salt
1 teaspoon pepper
2 tablespoons butter
2 tablespoons flour
1 cup milk
2 (10-ounce) packages frozen chopped
    spinach, thawed and drained
1 cup mayonnaise
1 cup sour cream
1 teaspoon lemon juice
Dash of cayenne pepper, or to taste

Drain the artichoke bottoms. Arrange in a single layer over the bottom of a 9×13-inch baking pan.

Heat the olive oil in a skillet. Add the sliced mushrooms and mushroom caps. Sprinkle with salt and pepper. Cook until the mushrooms are tender, stirring frequently. Remove from the heat. Set the mushroom caps aside.

Heat the butter in a saucepan until melted. Stir in the flour. Add the milk gradually, stirring constantly. Cook until the sauce thickens, stirring constantly. Stir in the spinach and cooked sliced mushrooms. Pour over the artichokes.

Combine the mayonnaise, sour cream, lemon juice and cayenne pepper in a saucepan and mix well. Cook over low heat until heated through. Pour over the layers. Top with the mushroom caps.

Bake at 350 degrees for 15 to 20 minutes.

WILD RICE

Wild rice is actually the seed from grass that grows wild along lakes in Minnesota, Wisconsin, and Canada, traditionally harvested by local Indians. There is also commercial wild rice production in California. Wild rice is long-grained and loved for its rich, nutty flavor and chewy texture. Wild rice must be rinsed before it is cooked. It does take longer than other rice to cook, but the wait is well worth it. However, overcooking the rice may result in stickiness. Garnish the cooked rice with blanched carrots, celery, and onion, or dress it up with dried cranberries, raisins, or almonds. While it may be more costly than traditional white or brown rice, the flavor is worth the cost.

ORZO AND WILD RICE

YIELD: 12 SERVINGS

4 ounces wild rice
Salt to taste
4 ounces orzo
1 cup pecan halves
$^1/_2$ cup dried cranberries
$^1/_4$ cup snipped fresh parsley
$^1/_4$ cup sliced green onions
$^1/_4$ cup sliced celery
$^1/_2$ cup raspberry vinegar
$^1/_2$ cup orange juice
2 tablespoons olive oil
2 tablespoons sugar
Pepper to taste

Bring enough water to cover the wild rice to a boil in a saucepan. Add a small amount of salt. Add the wild rice. Cook for 40 minutes or until tender; do not overcook. Drain and rinse with cold water. Drain and set aside.

Bring enough water to cover the orzo to a boil in a saucepan. Add a small amount of salt. Add the orzo. Cook for 8 to 10 minutes or until tender. Drain and rinse with cold water. Drain and set aside.

Place the pecans in a nonstick skillet. Cook until toasted, stirring frequently; do not burn. Set aside to cool.

Combine the cooked wild rice, cooked orzo, toasted pecans, dried cranberries, parsley, green onions and celery in a bowl.

Whisk the vinegar, orange juice, olive oil, sugar, salt and pepper together in a bowl. Pour over the wild rice mixture and toss to combine. Chill, covered, for 8 to 12 hours.

THREE-GRAIN CASSEROLE

YIELD: 6 TO 8 SERVINGS

2 tablespoons butter
1 garlic clove, minced
$^1/_3$ cup wild rice
$^1/_3$ cup brown rice
$^1/_3$ cup pearl barley
8 ounces mushrooms
1 onion, cut into $^1/_4$-inch rings
3 cups chicken broth
1 teaspoon thyme
Salt to taste
Pepper to taste

Heat the butter in a skillet until melted. Add the garlic and sauté for 2 minutes. Add the wild rice, brown rice and barley. Cook for 3 minutes, stirring constantly. Remove from the heat.

Stir the mushrooms, onion, broth, thyme, salt and pepper into the rice mixture and mix well. Spoon into a baking dish. Bake at 350 degrees for 1$^1/_2$ hours.

NOTE: You may prepare ahead and keep warm.

JUST RIGHT RICE

Short-grain rice, such as basmati, risotto and Japanese moochi, has almost round grains, is highest in starch content, and is usually moist but very sticky. Medium-grain rice produces a more fluffy rice, but it may begin to get sticky as it cools. Long-grain rice is the least starchy of all.

To prepare long-cooking whole grains, such as brown rice, ahead, cook in the morning while having breakfast. Cover, refrigerate, and then reheat for dinner by steaming in a sieve set over a pan of boiling water. To keep cooked rice hot and fluffy, lay a slice of dry bread on top and cover tightly.
To add flavor, cook the rice in stock or add a bouillon cube to the water as the rice cooks. To keep grains from sticking, add 1 tablespoon butter or vegetable oil to the water. Don't stir rice while simmering; the result is sticky rice. Use a heavy pan to avoid scorching. If the rice is watery, fluff with a fork while on low heat until the water evaporates.

Chapter Five

ENTRÉES

Paella (*recipe on page 206*)

HORSERADISH SAUCE

Horseradish sauce is the perfect accompaniment to any beef dish and also livens up an otherwise drab sandwich. Combine $^1/_2$ cup mayonnaise, $^1/_2$ cup sour cream, 2 tablespoons minced horseradish (or to taste) and a dash of pepper in a bowl and mix well.

TERRIFIC BEEF TENDERLOIN TUREEN

YIELD: 8 TO 10 SERVINGS

1 cup (2 sticks) butter
5 garlic cloves, pressed or chopped
1 (2$^1/_2$- to 3-pound) beef tenderloin
Seasoned salt to taste
Flour for sprinkling
1$^1/_2$ cups water
$^3/_4$ cup hearty red wine
$^1/_2$ cup milk
3 tablespoons flour
1 pound fresh mushrooms, sliced
6 green onions, sliced
2 tablespoons butter

Melt 1 cup butter in the bottom of a roasting pan in a 375-degree oven. Add the garlic.

Cut the tenderloin into halves. Sprinkle with seasoned salt and flour. Place the tenderloins in the prepared pan. Bake at 375 degrees for 30 minutes. Place the tenderloins on a cutting board.

Combine the pan juices, water and wine in a bowl and mix well. Combine the milk and 3 tablespoons flour in a separate bowl and mix well. Stir into the wine mixture.

Sauté the mushrooms and green onions in 2 tablespoons butter in a skillet until tender-crisp. Set aside.

Cut the tenderloins into thin slices and arrange in the roasting pan. Pour the wine mixture over the slices. Top with the mushroom mixture. Chill, covered, for 8 to 12 hours.

Bake, covered, at 375 degrees until heated through. Serve immediately.

NOTE: You may also serve this in a chafing dish with buns for elegant buffet sandwiches. Any leftovers freeze well.

BEEF TENDERLOIN WITH GREEN PEPPERCORN SAUCE

YIELD: 6 TO 8 SERVINGS

BEEF TENDERLOIN
1 (2¹/₂- to 3-pound) beef fillet,
    trimmed and tied
Salt to taste
Pepper to taste

GREEN PEPPERCORN SAUCE
3 tablespoons butter
3 tablespoons minced shallots
3 tablespoons brandy
1 tablespoon mashed green peppercorns
2 teaspoons Dijon mustard
1 bouillon cube, crushed
1 cup heavy cream
1 tablespoon butter, softened

FOR THE BEEF, place the beef on a rack in a broiler pan. Season with salt and pepper. Broil until brown. Reduce the oven temperature to 450 degrees. Roast for 10 to 12 minutes for rare.

FOR THE SAUCE, heat 3 tablespoons butter in a skillet until melted. Sauté the shallots in the butter. Stir in the brandy. Cook over high heat until reduced by half. Add the peppercorns, mustard, bouillon and cream. Cook over low heat until thickened, stirring constantly. Whisk in 1 tablespoon butter.

Cut the beef into slices and arrange on a serving platter. Serve with the sauce.

KNOW YOUR BUTCHER AND YOUR MEAT

There's no substitute for a good butcher. When purchasing meat, generally purchase a half-pound of meat per person or perhaps a bit less if the cut contains little fat and no bone (such as ground veal). Cuts that have more bones (ribs or lamb shanks) may require up to one pound per person. With the exception of cured meats, such as ham or bacon, meat should be wrapped loosely and stored for no more than a few days. Large cuts such as loins or roasts generally keep longer than smaller cuts such as chops or fillets. For the most tender selections, choose cuts such as tenderloin. Tougher cuts, such as chuck steak from the shoulder, need to be tenderized and cooked slowly to extract the most flavor. While it is best to avoid fatty pieces of meat, a moderate marbling of fat dissolves as it cooks, internally basting the meat and enhancing its flavor.

WINE PAIRINGS

Wine lovers agree any meal is better when served with a glass of wine. However, it is important to choose a wine that complements the flavors of the meal rather than one that competes with the food. As a general rule, white wines pair nicely with fish, chicken, and seafood. Red wines complement most red meat, certain rich fish, and chocolate. Meals with strong spices or flavors, such as in Indian cuisine, require strongly flavored wines to match the flavor intensity. Blush or white zinfandel actually matches the spicy flavors of Thai food very nicely. Foods rich in fat can be paired with an acidic white wine, such as German Gewürztraminer, or a full-bodied red wine, such as a burgundy or côtes du Rhone. Even picnic-bound wine lovers can be served a lighter red wine such as beaujolais or vapoliciella with a char-grilled burger. Above all, drink a wine you enjoy.

ORANGE BLACK PEPPER-GLAZED FILETS MIGNONS

YIELD: 4 SERVINGS

1 tablespoon olive oil
2 shallots, finely chopped
2 garlic cloves, finely chopped
1 tablespoon grated gingerroot
$^{1}/_{4}$ cup dark rum
1 cup freshly squeezed orange juice
$^{1}/_{3}$ cup dark molasses
1 tablespoon coarsely crushed peppercorns
4 (6- to 8-ounce) filets mignons
1 tablespoon olive oil
Salt to taste
Pepper to taste

Heat 1 tablespoon olive oil in a saucepan over medium heat. Add the shallots and cook for 4 minutes or until tender, stirring frequently. Add the garlic and gingerroot and cook for 2 minutes. Stir in the rum. Cook until almost all of the liquid has evaporated. Stir in the orange juice, molasses and peppercorns. Simmer for 15 to 20 minutes or until reduced and the desired consistency. Let stand until room temperature.

Brush the filets with 1 tablespoon olive oil. Sprinkle with salt and pepper. Place on a grill rack. Grill over hot coals for 5 minutes. Turn the filets over and grill for 4 minutes. Spoon the glaze over the filets until it runs down the sides. Grill for 1 minute. Steaks will be medium-rare. Serve immediately with any remaining glaze on the side.

GINGER BEEF STEW

YIELD: 8 SERVINGS

1 tablespoon olive oil
3 pounds lean boned chuck roast, trimmed
2 tablespoons flour
2 (14-ounce) cans chopped tomatoes
3 cups vertically-sliced onions
2 teaspoons pepper
2 teaspoons salt
2^{1}/2 cups water
^{1}/2 cup molasses
^{1}/3 cup white vinegar
2^{1}/2 cups thinly sliced carrots
  (about 1 pound)
^{3}/4 cup raisins
^{1}/2 teaspoon ground ginger

Heat the olive oil in a large Dutch oven.
Dredge the roast in the flour. Brown the roast
on all sides in the hot oil. Add the tomatoes,
onions, pepper and salt.

Combine the water, molasses and vinegar in
a bowl and mix well. Pour over the roast.
Bring to a boil. Reduce the heat to low.
Simmer, covered, for 1 to 3 hours or until the
beef is fork tender.

Add the carrots, raisins and ginger. Simmer
for 30 minutes or until carrots are tender.

Remove the roast from the Dutch oven.
Shred the roast, removing and discarding
any fat. Return the shredded roast to the
Dutch oven. Serve immediately. This recipe
freezes well.

SUPERB SHORT RIBS

YIELD: 6 TO 8 SERVINGS

1 tablespoon vegetable oil
4 pounds beef short ribs
2 onions, cut into quarters
1 (8-ounce) can pineapple chunks in syrup
1 (14-ounce) can low-salt beef broth
^{1}/4 cup honey
^{1}/2 cup ketchup
3 tablespoons Worcestershire sauce
3 garlic cloves
1 tablespoon chili powder

Heat the oil in a large ovenproof pot over
medium-high heat. Add as many ribs as will
fit in a single layer in the hot oil. Cook for
10 minutes or until brown on both sides,
turning once. Remove and set aside. Repeat
with the remaining ribs.

Return the ribs to the pot. Add the onions,
undrained pineapple, beef broth, honey,
ketchup, Worcestershire sauce, garlic and
chili powder.

Bake the ribs, covered, at 350 degrees for
1 hour. Remove the cover. Bake for 1 hour
longer or until the ribs are tender.

MARINATED BUFFALO RIBEYES WITH GRILLED POLENTA

YIELD: 4 SERVINGS

MARINADE
1 tablespoon olive oil
$^1/_2$ cup minced red onion
4 garlic cloves, minced
$^1/_2$ cup balsamic vinegar
$^1/_2$ cup coffee
$^1/_4$ cup molasses
$2^1/_2$ tablespoons lemon juice
$^1/_2$ tablespoon freshly ground pepper
$^1/_4$ teaspoon allspice
1 teaspoon salt

RIBEYE STEAKS
4 (10- to 12-ounce) buffalo or beef ribeye
  steaks, $1^1/_4$ inches thick

POLENTA
4 cups low-salt chicken broth
1 cup polenta
$^1/_3$ cup chopped chives
$^1/_2$ cup chopped moist sun-dried tomatoes
$2^1/_2$ tablespoons chopped Italian parsley
Salt to taste
Pepper to taste

ASSEMBLY
Olive oil for grilling

FOR THE MARINADE, heat the olive oil in a medium saucepan over medium-high heat. Add the onion and garlic. Sauté for 5 minutes or until tender. Add the vinegar, coffee, molasses, lemon juice, pepper, allspice and salt. Bring to a boil, stirring frequently. Reduce the heat. Simmer for 10 minutes or until slightly thickened. Let stand until cool. Reserve $^1/_3$ cup of the marinade.

FOR THE STEAKS, place the steaks in a single layer in a shallow dish. Pour the remaining marinade over the steaks. Marinate, covered, in the refrigerator for 6 hours or longer.

FOR THE POLENTA, bring the chicken broth to a boil in a saucepan. Whisk in the polenta. Cook for 25 minutes or until creamy, stirring frequently. Stir in the chives, sun-dried tomatoes and parsley. Season with salt and pepper. Pour into an 8-inch square pan. Chill, covered, for 5 hours or longer.

TO ASSEMBLE, cut the polenta into 8 triangles. Brush with olive oil. Drain the steaks, discarding the marinade. Place on a grill rack. Grill over medium-hot coals for 6 minutes on each side for medium-rare. Grill the polenta for 5 minutes on each side or until heated through.

Serve the steaks and the polenta with the reserved marinade.

MARINATED RACK OF LAMB

YIELD: 4 TO 6 SERVINGS

MARINADE
1/4 cup olive oil
1 tablespoon Dijon mustard
1 tablespoon freshly squeezed lemon juice
1 or 2 fresh peppermint leaves
1/2 teaspoon oregano
1/2 teaspoon thyme
1/2 teaspoon rosemary
Pinch of cayenne pepper
2 tablespoons Worcestershire sauce
2 garlic cloves

LAMB
2 pounds rack of lamb

FOR THE MARINADE, combine the olive oil, mustard, lemon juice, peppermint, oregano, thyme, rosemary, cayenne pepper, Worcestershire sauce and garlic in a bowl and mix well.

FOR THE LAMB, place the lamb in a sealable plastic bag. Pour the marinade over the lamb and seal the bag. Marinate in the refrigerator for 8 to 10 hours.

Drain the lamb, discarding the marinade. Wrap the bone tips in foil. Place on a grill rack. Grill over hot coals for 15 to 18 minutes or to the desired degree of doneness.

HISTORY OF ST. PAUL

With humble beginnings as a trading post along the Mississippi River for fur traders and Native Americans in the late 1700s, Pig's Eye Landing gained new status as an outpost to the Northwest Territory of the United States in 1819. As the 5th Regiment began construction on Fort Snelling, at the junction of the Mississippi and Minnesota Rivers, French priest Reverend Lucien Galtier changed the name of the river town to Saint Paul, in honor of his favorite saint. Shortly thereafter, in March of 1849, Minnesota was named a territory and Saint Paul its capital. Throughout its history, Saint Paul has maintained an old-world charm reflected in the lovely Victorian homes still gracing Summit Avenue, the European styling of the Saint Paul Cathedral, and the Gothic design of the state capitol.

Herbs and spices are any cook's secret weapon. Dried herbs and spices should be stored in a cool, dry place and should have a pungent fragrance. Dried herbs do lose their flavor over time, so try to purchase small amounts of less frequently used spices. Fresh herbs usually have a deeper flavor and can also serve as a festive garnish. However, when cooking with fresh herbs, use about two times the amount suggested for the dried version. Most herbs are easy to grow and can be maintained all year in a sunny window box in the kitchen.

LAMB KABOBS

YIELD: 4 TO 6 SERVINGS

2 pounds lamb, cut into large cubes
2 teaspoons cumin
2 teaspoons coriander
2 tablespoons lemon juice
2 tablespoons lime juice
1 cup olive oil
$^1/_2$ teaspoon salt
$^1/_2$ teaspoon garlic powder

Arrange the lamb in a single layer in a shallow dish. Whisk the cumin, coriander, lemon juice, lime juice, olive oil, salt and garlic powder together in a bowl. Pour over the lamb. Marinate, covered, in the refrigerator for 8 to 12 hours. Drain the lamb, discarding the marinade.

Thread the lamb onto skewers. Place on a grill rack. Grill over hot coals for $7^1/_2$ minutes; turn. Close the lid on the grill and reduce the flame to low. Grill for 11 minutes longer. Place on a serving platter. You may serve this with yogurt mixed with chopped fresh mint or hummus.

NOTE: You may use the marinade as a salad dressing by whisking in 1 teaspoon of balsamic vinegar.

MOROCCAN STEW

YIELD: 6 SERVINGS

1/4 cup vegetable oil
1 onion, chopped
1 to 2 pounds lamb or chicken, cut into bite-
   size pieces
2 cups water
1 teaspoon salt
1/2 teaspoon cinnamon
1/2 teaspoon ground cloves
1/2 teaspoon cumin
1/2 teaspoon ground cardamom
2 tablespoons vegetable oil
1 teaspoon sugar
2 carrots, julienned
1 cup dark raisins
2 tablespoons blanched almonds
1 cup basmati or long grain rice
1 1/2 teaspoons salt
1/8 teaspoon saffron
1 tablespoon blanched pistachios

Heat 1/4 cup oil in a large skillet. Add the onion and sauté until tender. Add the lamb and cook until brown on all sides, stirring frequently. Stir in the water, 1 teaspoon salt, cinnamon, cloves, cumin and cardamom. Bring to a simmer. Simmer, covered, until the lamb is tender. Remove from the heat. Drain, reserving the pan juices.

Heat 2 tablespoons oil in a small saucepan. Add the sugar and carrots. Cook until the carrots are light brown and tender, adding water if needed. Remove the carrots. Add the raisins to the saucepan and cook until plump. Remove the raisins. Add the almonds to the saucepan and cook until the almonds are light brown. Remove the almonds, reserving the pan juices.

Bring the reserved lamb pan juices and reserved carrot pan juices to a boil in a large pot. Add the rice and 1 1/2 teaspoons salt. Add enough water to bring 2 inches above the rice. Bring to a boil. Reduce the heat. Cook, covered, until the liquid is absorbed and the rice is tender. Stir in the saffron gently.

Layer the lamb mixture, rice, carrots and raisins in a large baking dish. Bake at 300 degrees for 20 to 30 minutes or until heated through. Spoon onto a serving platter. Crush the pistachios if desired. Sprinkle the pistachios and almonds over the top.

PLATING THE MEAL

Any plated meal looks more appealing when careful thought has been given to the color, texture, and taste of the meal. For example, a white plate drizzled with a balsamic reduction is not only eye appealing, it also enhances the flavor of the dish. Mixing and matching colorful pottery or antique china can dress up an otherwise drab meal. Colorful kale, sprigs of fresh herbs, or a wedge of citrus adds color and texture without distracting from the essence of the entrée.

GRILLED GINGER LAMB CHOPS

YIELD: 4 SERVINGS

8 small loin lamb chops
2 teaspoons minced gingerroot
2 teaspoons minced garlic
8 teaspoons vegetable oil
2 teaspoons soy sauce
2 teaspoons red wine vinegar
1 teaspoon brown sugar
Pepper to taste

Arrange the lamb chops in a single layer in a shallow dish.

Whisk the gingerroot, garlic, oil, soy sauce, vinegar, brown sugar and pepper together in a bowl. Pour over the lamb chops. Marinate, covered, in the refrigerator for 1 hour. Drain the lamb chops, reserving the marinade. Bring the reserved marinade to a boil in a saucepan. Boil for 2 to 3 minutes, stirring constantly.

Place the lamb chops on a grill rack. Grill over hot coals for 7 minutes. Turn and brush with the reserved cooked marinade. Grill for 7 minutes or to the desired degree of doneness.

LAMB SHANKS WITH WHITE BEANS

YIELD: 6 TO 8 SERVINGS

1 pound dried Great Northern beans
    or cannellini
1 tablespoon olive oil
6 to 8 lamb shanks
Salt to taste
Pepper to taste
5 garlic cloves, minced
4 carrots, chopped
3 ribs celery, chopped
1 large onion, chopped
1$^1/_2$ cups dry red wine
1 (28-ounce) can whole plum tomatoes in
    tomato purée
3 cups chicken broth
3 sprigs of fresh rosemary
2 bay leaves

Sort and rinse the beans; drain. Combine the beans with enough water to cover in a bowl. Let stand for 8 to 12 hours; drain.

Heat the olive oil in a skillet over medium-high heat. Sprinkle the shanks with salt and pepper. Arrange enough shanks in a single layer in the skillet to fill the skillet. Cook for 10 minutes or until brown on all sides, turning occasionally. Remove the browned shanks and repeat with the remaining shanks. Set the shanks aside.

Add the garlic, carrots, celery and onion to the drippings in the skillet. Sauté until tender. Add the wine and cook for 2 minutes. Add the tomatoes, breaking them up with a wooden spoon. Stir in the soaked beans, chicken broth, rosemary and bay leaves. Add the shanks. Bring to a boil. Reduce the heat. Simmer for 2 to 3 hours or until the beans and lamb are tender; the lamb should be falling off the bones.

Remove and discard the bay leaves and rosemary sprigs from the lamb mixture. Season with salt and pepper. Serve immediately. You may serve this over white rice.

MEDITERRANEAN CHILI

YIELD: 5 SERVINGS

1 tablespoon olive oil
1 large onion, chopped
1 pound ground lamb
1 teaspoon allspice
2 garlic cloves, chopped
1 teaspoon oregano
1/2 teaspoon thyme
1 teaspoon cumin
2 bay leaves
1/4 teaspoon pepper
1 (14-ounce) can Italian-style stewed
   tomatoes
1 (14-ounce) can diced tomatoes
1 (14-ounce) can artichoke hearts, chopped
1 (15-ounce) can garbanzos, rinsed and
   drained
1/4 cup pitted kalamata olives, chopped, or
   1 (2-ounce) can sliced black olives

GARNISH
Small bowl of crumbled feta cheese
Tortilla chips or crusty bread

Heat the olive oil in a large pot over medium heat. Add the onion and cook until tender, stirring frequently. Add the lamb and allspice. Increase the heat to high. Cook until the lamb is brown and crumbly, stirring constantly.

Stir the garlic, oregano, thyme, cumin, bay leaves, pepper, tomatoes, artichoke hearts, garbanzos and olives into the lamb mixture. Reduce the heat to medium. Cook for 15 minutes, stirring occasionally. Remove and discard the bay leaves.

Ladle the chili into bowls. Garnish with feta cheese and tortilla chips.

HAWAIIAN PORK ROAST

YIELD: 8 TO 10 SERVINGS

1 (3-pound) boneless pork roast
1 cup teriyaki sauce
3 tablespoons brown sugar
1 teaspoon ground ginger
3 tablespoons dry sherry
1 garlic clove, minced

Pierce the pork roast with a fork in several places. Place in a sealable plastic bag. Combine the teriyaki sauce, brown sugar, ginger, sherry and garlic in a bowl and mix well. Pour over the pork roast. Seal the bag, pressing out the air. Turn to coat the pork roast with the marinade. Marinate in the refrigerator for 8 hours or longer. Drain, reserving the marinade.

Bring the reserved marinade to a boil in a saucepan. Boil for 2 to 3 minutes, stirring constantly.

Place the pork roast in a shallow baking dish. Cover with foil. Bake at 350 degrees for 30 minutes. Remove the foil. Bake for 60 minutes longer or to 170 degrees on a meat thermometer.

Slice the pork roast and serve with the boiled marinade.

PORTION PERFECTION

When in doubt, never overload the plate. Smaller servings arranged on a larger plate create a lovely presentation for the diner. As a guideline, suggested portion sizes are as follows:

Meat = $^1/_2$ pound per person.
Carbohydrates and veggies = $^1/_2$ to 1 cup per person.
Salad = 1 cup per person.
Appetizers = 8 single appetizers per person per hour.

SWEET-AND-SOUR PORK TENDERLOIN

YIELD: 8 TO 12 SERVINGS

4 (1-pound) pork tenderloins
$^1/_2$ cup honey
$^3/_4$ cup freshly squeezed lemon juice
$^1/_2$ cup soy sauce
1 bunch green onions, chopped
2 bay leaves, crushed
1 teaspoon dry mustard
$^1/_2$ teaspoon ground ginger
$^1/_2$ teaspoon garlic powder

Place the tenderloins in a shallow dish. Combine the honey, lemon juice, soy sauce, green onions, bay leaves, mustard, ginger and garlic powder in a bowl and mix well. Pour over the tenderloins. Marinate, covered, in the refrigerator for 8 to 12 hours, turning occasionally. Drain, reserving the marinade.

Bring the reserved marinade to a boil in a saucepan. Boil for 5 minutes, stirring constantly.

Place the tenderloins on a grill rack. Grill over medium-hot coals, turning frequently; do not burn. Cut the tenderloins into $^1/_2$-inch-thick slices. Arrange in a fan on a serving platter. Pour the cooked marinade over the slices or serve on the side.

PORK TENDERLOIN WITH CHINESE FIVE-SPICE

YIELD: 4 SERVINGS

1 (1-pound) pork tenderloin
Salt to taste
1 tablespoon flour
1 tablespoon brown sugar
1/2 teaspoon salt
1 teaspoon Chinese five-spice powder
2 tablespoons brown sugar
1/4 cup orange juice
3 tablespoons balsamic vinegar
1 tablespoon olive oil

Cut the tenderloin diagonally into 8 thin slices. Sprinkle with salt to taste.

Combine the flour, 1 tablespoon brown sugar, 1/2 teaspoon salt and five-spice powder in a bowl and mix well. Rub over the pork slices.

Combine 2 tablespoons brown sugar, orange juice and vinegar in a separate bowl and stir until the brown sugar dissolves.

Heat the olive oil in a nonstick skillet over medium-high heat. Add the pork slices and cook for 2 minutes. Turn and cook for 2 minutes longer. Pour the orange juice mixture over the pork. Cook for 2 minutes or until the sauce thickens and the pork is cooked through.

CHINESE FIVE-SPICE POWDER

This fragrant mix of five ground spices is a common flavor enhancer in Chinese cooking. Generally, it consists of equal parts of cinnamon, cloves, fennel seeds, star anise, and Szechuan peppercorns. However, you may find other spices substituted. Prepared five-spice powder is available in Asian markets and most supermarkets.

PESTO PERFECTO

Don't throw away extra herbs. Instead, make this easy pesto and freeze it in single portion servings to enhance pasta, hearty soups, or even breakfast. Plus, don't forget that in addition to basil, parsley, and cilantro, even puréed roasted ancho chiles can be used to make delicious sauces for pasta, rice, or bruschetta. Try different nuts in your pesto also. Rather than pine nuts, add walnuts, cashews, or even pecans to change the flavor of the pesto sauce.

For basic pesto, process 2 cups rinsed and dried packed fresh basil, 2/3 cup olive oil, 1/2 cup pine nuts, toasted and cooled, 1/3 cup freshly grated Parmesan cheese, 1 tablespoon lemon juice and a dash of salt in a food processor until smooth. Spoon into greased ice cube sections of an ice cube tray and freeze.

PESTO-PACKED PORK CHOPS

YIELD: 4 SERVINGS

1/4 cup (1 ounce) crumbled feta cheese
1/4 cup pesto
2 tablespoons pine nuts, toasted
1/4 cup jalapeño jelly
2 tablespoons balsamic vinegar
2 to 3 tablespoons pesto
4 (1 1/2-inch-thick) bone-in or boneless pork loin chops (about 2- to 2 1/2-pounds total with bones)
1/4 cup Cajun seasoning

GARNISH
Fresh basil leaves

Combine the feta cheese, 1/4 cup pesto and pine nuts in a bowl and mix well. Set aside.

Heat the jelly in a saucepan over low heat until melted. Stir in the vinegar and the desired amount of the 2 to 3 tablespoons pesto. Cook until heated through. Set aside.

Trim the pork chops. Cut each chop horizontally to the bone, creating a pocket. Spoon the feta cheese mixture evenly into the pockets, securing the opening with a wooden pick if needed. Rub each filled chop with the Cajun seasoning. You may wrap in plastic and chill for up to 8 hours at this point.

Place the pork chops on a grill rack. Grill over indirect medium heat for 10 minutes. Turn and grill for 10 minutes longer or until the juices run clear, brushing with the jalapeño jelly mixture during the last 3 to 5 minutes. Garnish with basil leaves.

FIESTA STEW

YIELD: 6 SERVINGS

3 tablespoons flour
$1/2$ teaspoon cumin
$1/2$ teaspoon chili powder
$1/2$ teaspoon garlic powder
$1/4$ teaspoon cinnamon
$1^{1}/4$ pounds pork, cut into 1-inch cubes
2 tablespoons vegetable oil
1 cup fat-free beef broth
$1/2$ cup apple juice
8 small white potatoes, peeled and
     quartered
2 sweet potatoes, peeled and chopped
1 green bell pepper, seeded and cut into
     2-inch strips
1 red bell pepper, seeded and cut into
     2-inch strips
1 onion, thinly sliced
1 (10-ounce) can tomatoes with green chiles
1 (8-ounce) can tomato sauce
2 tablespoons honey
2 Granny Smith apples, cut into 1-inch pieces
1 (15-ounce) can dark red kidney beans,
     drained
2 tablespoons chopped flat-leaf parsley

GARNISH
Shredded Cheddar cheese
Coarsely chopped black olives

Combine the flour, cumin, chili powder, garlic powder and cinnamon in a large bowl and mix well. Add the pork and toss to coat.

Heat the oil in a large heavy pot over medium-high heat. Arrange as many pork cubes as will fit in a single layer in the pot. Cook until brown on all sides. Remove the browned pork and repeat with the remaining pork cubes. Return the browned pork to the pot. Add the beef broth and apple juice. Bring to a simmer over medium heat. Simmer, covered, for 1 hour or until the pork is tender.

Add the white potatoes, sweet potatoes, bell peppers, onion, tomatoes with green chiles, tomato sauce and honey to the pork mixture and stir to combine. Simmer, covered, for 30 to 35 minutes or until the potatoes are tender.

Add the apples and beans to the stew. Simmer, covered, for 15 minutes or until the apples are tender. Stir in the parsley.

Ladle the stew into shallow bowls. Garnish with Cheddar cheese and olives.

BARBECUE PORK SANDWICHES

YIELD: 4 SERVINGS

2 cups chopped cooked pork or beef
1 cup ketchup
1/4 cup packed brown sugar
1/4 cup vinegar
2 tablespoons Worcestershire sauce
4 onion rolls or Kaiser rolls

Combine the pork, ketchup, brown sugar, vinegar and Worcestershire sauce in a saucepan. Cook over low heat for 30 minutes, stirring occasionally. Cut the rolls into halves horizontally. Spoon the barbecue evenly over the bottom halves of each roll. Top with the remaining halves.

BLACK-EYED PEAS WITH HAM

YIELD: 10 SERVINGS

1 pound dried black-eyed peas
1 tablespoon olive oil
1 large ham hock
1 cup chopped onion
1/2 cup chopped celery
1/2 cup chopped green bell pepper
1 tablespoon chopped garlic
6 cups (or more) chicken stock
1 bay leaf
1 teaspoon thyme
1 teaspoon salt
1 teaspoon black pepper
1 teaspoon cayenne pepper
6 cups cooked rice

GARNISH
3 tablespoons finely chopped green onions

Combine the peas with enough water to cover in a bowl. Let stand for 8 to 12 hours; drain.

Heat the olive oil in a large pot. Add the ham hock and sear on all sides for 5 minutes. Add the onion, celery, bell pepper and garlic. Cook for 5 minutes. Add the soaked peas, 6 cups chicken stock, bay leaf, thyme, salt, black pepper and cayenne pepper. Bring to a boil. Reduce the heat. Simmer for 50 to 60 minutes or until the peas are creamy and tender, stirring occasionally and adding water or additional chicken stock as needed. Adjust the seasonings if desired. Remove and discard the bay leaf. Serve over the rice. Garnish with green onions.

STROMBOLI SANDWICH

YIELD: 6 TO 8 SERVINGS

1 pound mild Italian sausage,
   casings removed
8 ounces ground beef
1 cup chopped green bell pepper
1 cup chopped onion
1 cup sliced fresh mushrooms
1 (8-ounce) can tomato sauce
1 (6-ounce) can tomato paste
1/4 cup water
1/4 cup (1 ounce) grated Parmesan cheese
1/4 teaspoon oregano
1/4 teaspoon rosemary
1/4 teaspoon salt
1 (1 1/2-pound) loaf Vienna bread
3 cups (12 ounces) shredded
   mozzarella cheese

Brown the sausage and ground beef in a
skillet, stirring until crumbly; drain. Add the
bell pepper, onion and mushrooms. Sauté
for 5 minutes.

Stir the tomato sauce, tomato paste, water,
Parmesan cheese, oregano, rosemary and salt
into the sausage mixture. Bring to a simmer.
Simmer for 10 minutes, stirring occasionally.

Cut the bread into halves lengthwise. Scoop
out the centers to form bread shells, reserving
the bread centers for another use. Layer 1/2 of
the mozzarella cheese, sausage mixture and
remaining mozzarella cheese in the bottom
shell. Top with the remaining shell. Wrap in foil.
Bake at 400 degrees for 6 to 8 minutes or
until heated through.

THE STATE CAPITOL

The elaborate marble and
granite structure overlooking
the city of Saint Paul is
actually Minnesota's third
statehouse. Ground was
initially broken for the capitol
in 1896, but the cornerstone
was not actually laid until two
years later. The building was
designed in the Italian
Renaissance tradition by Cass
Gilbert of Saint Paul. Gilbert
was one of the outstanding
architects of the period and
was also responsible for
designing the United States
Supreme Court Building in
Washington, D.C. The capitol
took six years to build and
was completed in 1904
at a cost of approximately
$4.5 million. Governor
Samuel VanSant was the first
chief executive to occupy the
current building, and the
legislature has met there
since 1905.

TIPS FOR COOKING WILD GAME

Wild game is delicious if prepared properly. In addition to the very sizable portion of the state's population that enjoys fishing and hunting, Minnesota is also a destination for hunters and fishermen from around the world. The rolling hills in the southwest part of the state make the perfect habitat for pheasant, partridge, and other winged prey. Ducks, geese, and other waterfowl enjoy the more than ten thousand lakes, marshes, and ponds across the state. Deer, elk, and even moose are hunted in the more wooded parts of the state. Game meats, including wild birds, venison, elk, and even buffalo, are very low in fat and thus must be basted often while cooking to avoid drying out the meat.

Continued on next page

VENISON STROGANOFF

YIELD: 10 SERVINGS

4 pounds boneless venison
$^1/_2$ cup (1 stick) butter, or $^1/_2$ cup corn oil
2 yellow onions, julienned
4 garlic cloves, minced
Salt to taste
Pepper to taste
1 cup flour
1 cup red wine
1 bay leaf
8 cups brown sauce
1 tablespoon tarragon
2 pounds mushrooms, sliced
2 cups sour cream

Cut the venison into 1×1×2-inch strips. Heat the butter in a heavy pan until melted. Add the onions and garlic. Sauté until the onions are tender. Remove the onions and garlic and set aside, reserving the butter in the pan.

Sprinkle the venison with salt and pepper. Dredge the venison in the flour to coat. Shake to remove the excess flour. Place in the hot reserved butter in the pan. Cook for 1 to 2 minutes or until brown on both sides. Remove the venison and set aside, reserving the drippings in the pan.

Add the wine to the reserved hot drippings, stirring to delgaze the pan. Continue to simmer until all of the brown bits have been scraped from the bottom of the pan. Remove from the heat.

Combine the browned venison, bay leaf, onion mixture and brown sauce in a stockpot. Bring to a boil. Reduce the heat. Simmer for 30 to 45 minutes or until the venison is tender. Add the tarragon and mushrooms, stirring to combine. Simmer for 10 minutes.

Place the sour cream in a bowl. Pour 1 cup of the hot sauce into the sour cream gradually, stirring rapidly. Pour the sour cream mixture into the venison mixture gradually, stirring rapidly. Remove the bay leaf and discard. Serve over wild rice, your favorite pasta or roasted garlic mashed potatoes.

Always Superb: Recipes for Every Occasion

Entertaining

MUFFULETTA

YIELD: 8 TO 12 SERVINGS

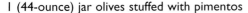

1 (44-ounce) jar olives stuffed with pimentos
1 (8-ounce) jar marinated cocktail
    onions, drained
4 ribs celery, chopped
3 tablespoons capers, drained
4 large garlic cloves, minced
1 tablespoon oregano
1 teaspoon pepper
3 tablespoons red wine vinegar
$1/3$ cup olive oil
8 ounces mortadella, sliced
8 ounces Capricola, sliced
8 ounces Genoa salami, sliced
8 ounces provolone cheese, sliced
4 loaves round Italian bread, cut into
    halves horizontally

Drain the olives, reserving $3^{1}/2$ tablespoons of the liquid. Pulse the olives 1 cup at a time in a food processor or blender until coarsely chopped. Place in a large bowl. Process the onions in a food processor or blender until minced. Add to the olives. Add the celery, capers and garlic to the olive mixture and mix well.

Whisk the reserved olive liquid, oregano, pepper and vinegar together in a bowl. Add the olive oil in a fine stream, whisking constantly. Pour over the olive mixture and toss to combine. Store in a tightly covered container in the refrigerator.

Layer 2 ounces of the mortadella, 2 ounces of the Capricola, 2 ounces of the salami and 2 ounces of the provolone cheese on the bottom half of each loaf of bread. Spoon $3/4$ cup of the olive mixture evenly over the top half of each loaf of bread. Place loaf tops on the loaf bottoms to form sandwiches.

Place the sandwiches on baking sheets. Bake at 350 degrees until the provolone cheese melts.

Similarly, the meat is often tough, so it must be tenderized and cooked slowly to produce the most tender meat. Soaking game in milk prior to cooking will not only reduce the strong flavor of the meat; it also improves its tenderness. In addition to being a refreshing drink, dark sodas like cola make a perfect base for slow-cooking game, whether in the oven or in a slow cooker. Tart jellies also complement the rich flavor of most game. Dredging fresh fish fillets in cornmeal seasoned with a dash of salt and pepper, frying it in a beer-based batter, or broiling the entire fish with a side of dill sauce will produce an entrée that will please almost any guest.

CHICKEN ENCHILADAS

YIELD: 5 TO 6 SERVINGS

5 boneless skinless chicken breasts
3 to 4 tablespoons vegetable oil
$3/4$ cup chopped green onions
1 (4-ounce) can chopped green chilies
2 garlic cloves, chopped
1 tablespoon coriander
$2^1/2$ teaspoons cumin
$1/8$ to $1/4$ teaspoon pepper
$1^1/4$ cups raisins
3 cups chicken broth
1 tablespoon cornstarch (optional)
1 tablespoon water (optional)
5 or 6 flour tortillas
Sour cream (optional)
Hot sauce (optional)
Guacamole (optional)
Shredded Monterey Jack cheese (optional)

Cut the chicken into 2-inch strips. Heat 2 tablespoons of the oil in a skillet until hot. Add the chicken strips and sauté until brown on both sides and the strips are cooked through.

Heat the remaining oil in a skillet until hot. Add the green onions, green chilies and garlic. Sauté until the green onions are tender. Add the coriander, cumin, pepper, raisins and chicken broth, stirring to combine. Bring to a boil. Add the chicken strips. Bring to a boil. Whisk the cornstarch and water together in a bowl. Stir into the chicken mixture. Cook until the mixture is the desired consistency.

Spoon the chicken mixture down the middle of 5 or 6 tortillas. Top with sour cream, hot sauce, guacamole and Monterey Jack cheese. Roll to enclose the filling. You may reheat by placing on a microwave-safe plate and microwaving until warm.

CHICKEN SATAY WITH THREE SAUCES

YIELD: VARIABLE

PEANUT SAUCE

8 ounces peanut butter

1 1/2 teaspoons garlic powder

1 1/2 teaspoons ground ginger

1/4 teaspoon cayenne pepper

2 tablespoons soy sauce

2 tablespoons rice vinegar

3/4 cup hot water

CARIBBEAN BARBECUE SAUCE

1 red onion, chopped

4 garlic cloves

1 tablespoon freshly squeezed lime juice

1 tomato, chopped into 1/2-inch pieces

4 cups tomato sauce

1 cup chili paste

Dash of pepper

CURRY SAUCE

2 roasted red peppers, peeled and seeded

4 1/2 ounces gingerroot, sliced

9 garlic cloves

1/2 cup chili paste

3 tablespoons curry powder

2 teaspoons cardamom

2 teaspoons salt

3 (10-ounce) cans coconut milk

CHICKEN SATAY

Boneless skinless chicken breasts

FOR THE PEANUT SAUCE, whisk the peanut butter, garlic powder, ginger, cayenne pepper, soy sauce and vinegar together in a bowl. Whisk in the water gradually.

FOR THE BARBECUE SAUCE, coarsely purée the onion, garlic and lime juice in a food processor. Pour into a bowl. Add the tomato, tomato sauce, chili paste and pepper and mix well.

FOR THE CURRY SAUCE, purée the red peppers, gingerroot, garlic, chili paste, curry powder, cardamom and salt in a food processor. Add the coconut milk and mix well.

FOR THE SATAY, cut the chicken into bite-size pieces. Thread 4 to 6 pieces of chicken on a water-soaked bamboo skewer. Repeat with the remaining chicken. Place on a grill rack. Grill over hot coals for 8 to 10 minutes or until the chicken is cooked through. Serve with the sauces.

CRISPY SESAME CHICKEN

YIELD: 8 SERVINGS

1 1/4 cups cornflake crumbs
1/4 cup sesame seeds
3/4 teaspoon paprika
1/4 teaspoon salt
1/4 teaspoon ground ginger
Dash of red pepper
1/2 cup plain nonfat yogurt
2 tablespoons honey
8 boneless skinless chicken breasts
2 tablespoons margarine, melted

Combine the cornflake crumbs, sesame seeds, paprika, salt, ginger and red pepper in a sealable plastic bag and mix well.

Combine the yogurt and honey in a shallow bowl and mix well.

Dip the chicken into the yogurt mixture, turning to coat. Discard the remaining yogurt mixture. Place the chicken in the cornflake mixture and seal the bag. Shake to coat the chicken.

Arrange the chicken in a single layer on a baking sheet sprayed with nonstick cooking spray. Drizzle the margarine over the chicken.

Bake at 400 degrees for 30 to 40 minutes or until the juices run clear.

GINGER-PEANUT CHICKEN WRAPS

YIELD: 8 SERVINGS

PEANUT SAUCE

3 tablespoons sugar

2 tablespoons minced gingerroot

6 tablespoons freshly squeezed lime juice

2 tablespoons soy sauce

$1/2$ teaspoon salt

$1/2$ teaspoon red pepper

1 garlic clove, crushed

$1/2$ cup creamy peanut butter

$1/4$ cup water

WRAPS

1 teaspoon olive oil

6 (4-ounce) boneless skinless chicken
   breast halves

1 cup chopped seeded peeled cucumber

$3/4$ cup chopped red bell pepper

3 tablespoons chopped fresh cilantro

8 (8-inch) flour tortillas

4 cups chopped romaine lettuce

FOR THE SAUCE, process the sugar, gingerroot, lime juice, soy sauce, salt, red pepper and garlic in a blender until smooth. Add the peanut butter and water. Process until smooth, scraping down the sides.

FOR THE WRAPS, heat the olive oil in a large nonstick skillet over medium-high heat. Add the chicken. Cook for 5 minutes on each side or until the juices run clear. Remove the chicken and let stand until cool. Shred into bite-size pieces.

Combine the chicken, cucumber, bell pepper and sauce in a bowl and mix well. Add the cilantro and toss to combine.

Place the tortillas on a microwave-safe plate. Cover with a paper towel. Microwave on High for 5 to 10 seconds per tortilla or until warm. Spoon $1/2$ cup of the chicken mixture onto each tortilla. Top with $1/2$ cup lettuce. Roll to enclose the filling.

WINE AND FOOD PAIRINGS

Light-bodied white wines, such as pinot grigio, Riesling, or chardonnay, pair nicely with subtly flavored and more delicate foods, including pasta with an olive-oil finish, shellfish, such as oysters and scallops, white fish, and grilled vegetables.

A more full-bodied white wine, such as Pouilly-Fume or Sauvignon Blanc, matches the flavors of pasta with cream sauces, seafood, such as crab or lobster, salmon and tuna, chicken dishes, and roasted meats, including pork and turkey.

A robust red wine, such as a Zinfandel, Cabernet Sauvignon, or a Burgundy, match the more robust flavors of red meats, including beef and veal, hearty stews, and many tomato-based pasta dishes.

HAWAIIAN CHICKEN BARBECUE

YIELD: 10 TO 12 SERVINGS

10 boneless skinless chicken breasts
36 ounces barbecue sauce
1 (20-ounce) can crushed pineapple
1 green bell pepper, chopped
1/2 red bell pepper, chopped
1 red onion, chopped
2 carrots, chopped
1 tablespoon crushed garlic
Parsley to taste
Marjoram to taste
Pepper to taste
Onion salt to taste

Place the chicken in a 5-quart slow cooker. Combine the barbecue sauce, pineapple, bell peppers, onion, carrots, garlic, parsley, marjoram, pepper and onion salt in a bowl and mix well. Pour over the chicken.

Cook on Low for 8 to 9 hours, stirring occasionally and shredding the chicken. You may serve with sourdough bread.

MADEIRA CHICKEN

YIELD: 6 SERVINGS

2 tablespoons butter
3 whole chicken breasts, split
   (2$^{1}/_{2}$ to 3 pounds)
1 teaspoon salt
$^{1}/_{4}$ teaspoon pepper
12 ounces mushrooms
2 teaspoons lemon juice
1 tablespoon butter
2 tablespoons chopped shallots
1 tablespoon flour
$^{3}/_{4}$ cup madeira
$^{3}/_{4}$ cup heavy cream
$^{3}/_{4}$ cup (3 ounces) shredded Swiss cheese

Heat 2 tablespoons butter in a large skillet. Add the chicken. Cook over medium-high heat for 10 minutes on each side or until brown. Sprinkle with salt and pepper. Arrange in a single layer in a 7×11-inch baking dish.

Trim the mushrooms. Toss with the lemon juice in a bowl. Add 1 tablespoon butter to the skillet. Add the shallots. Sauté for 3 minutes. Add the mushrooms. Cook for 5 minutes or until light brown, stirring constantly.

Stir the flour into the mushroom mixture. Add the wine and cream. Cook until thickened and bubbly, stirring constantly. Stir in $^{1}/_{2}$ cup of the Swiss cheese. Spoon over the chicken. Sprinkle the remaining $^{1}/_{4}$ cup Swiss cheese over the top.

Bake at 400 degrees for 20 to 30 minutes or until the chicken is tender. You may serve this with cooked brown rice or parslied new potatoes, spinach salad and steamed carrots.

MANGO CHICKEN SALAD

YIELD: 4 SERVINGS

10 cups red and green leaf lettuce, torn into
    bite-size pieces
2 ounces arugula, torn into bite-size pieces
3 mangoes
$1/4$ cup rice wine vinegar
3 tablespoons vegetable oil
2 tablespoons honey
1 teaspoon snipped fresh mint
1 teaspoon snipped fresh chives
4 boneless skinless chicken breasts, grilled
    and cut into strips

Toss the lettuce and arugula together in a
large salad bowl.

Peel and pit the mangoes. Cut into slices.
Chop enough of the mango slices to measure
$1/2$ cup.

Process the chopped mango, vinegar, oil,
honey, mint and chives in a blender until
smooth. Drizzle half the dressing over the
greens and toss to coat.

Divide the greens evenly among 4 plates.
Arrange the remaining sliced mango
and chicken over the greens. Drizzle with
the remaining dressing.

NOTE: You may substitute papaya or pineapple
for the mango.

Always Superb: Recipes for Every Occasion

SPANISH SOFT TACOS

YIELD: 6 TO 8 SERVINGS

4 whole chicken breasts (3 to 4 pounds)
Salt to taste
Black pepper to taste
12 ounces white corn
1 (8-ounce) can cream-style corn
2 ounces chopped mild green chiles
$^1/_2$ cup slivered almonds
$^2/_3$ cup grated onion
2 teaspoons chili powder
$^1/_2$ teaspoon cumin
1 teaspoon salt
$^1/_2$ teaspoon black pepper
$^1/_4$ teaspoon cayenne pepper
$^1/_4$ cup minced fresh cilantro
2 cups sour cream
$2^1/_2$ teaspoons Worcestershire sauce
2 cups (8 ounces) shredded Cheddar cheese
12 flour tortillas
Sour cream

GARNISH
Fresh cilantro

Sprinkle the chicken with salt and pepper to taste. Place in a baking dish. Cover with foil. Bake at 350 degrees for 30 minutes or until tender. Let stand until cool. Shred the chicken, discarding the skin and bones.

Combine the cooked chicken, white corn, cream-style corn, green chiles, almonds, onion, chili powder, cumin, 1 teaspoon salt, $^1/_2$ teaspoon black pepper, cayenne pepper, cilantro, 2 cups sour cream and Worcestershire sauce in a bowl and mix well. Spoon into a 9×13-inch baking pan. Sprinkle the Cheddar cheese over the top. Bake at 350 degrees for 45 minutes.

Spoon the chicken mixture into the tortillas. Top with a dollop of sour cream. Roll to enclose the filling. Garnish with fresh cilantro.

TANDOORI CHICKEN

YIELD: 4 SERVINGS

3 whole chicken breasts
   (about 1 pound each)
$^1/_4$ cup freshly squeezed lemon juice
1 cup plain low-fat yogurt
1 tablespoon grated gingerroot
$1^1/_2$ teaspoons paprika
3 garlic cloves, minced
$1^1/_4$ teaspoons coriander
$1^1/_4$ teaspoons cumin
$1^1/_4$ teaspoons curry powder
$^1/_4$ teaspoon cayenne pepper

Pat the chicken dry. Cut slits in the chicken.
Rub with the lemon juice.

Combine the yogurt, gingerroot, paprika,
garlic, coriander, cumin, curry powder and
cayenne pepper in a bowl and mix well.
Spoon into a shallow dish. Place the chicken
in the yogurt mixture, turning to coat.
Chill, covered, for 2 hours or longer,
turning occasionally.

Remove the chicken from the marinade.
Arrange skin side up in a buttered baking pan.
Bake at 400 degrees for 15 minutes. Turn the
chicken and bake for 15 minutes. longer
Reduce the oven temperature to 350
degrees. Turn the chicken and bake for 15
minutes longer or until cooked through.

Place the chicken on a serving platter. You may
serve with yellow rice and a salad.

WHITE CHILI WITH CHICKEN AND CORN

YIELD: 8 SERVINGS

2 cups dried Great Northern beans
1 tablespoon olive oil
1 large onion, chopped
3 garlic cloves, crushed
1 green bell pepper, seeded and chopped
8 cups chicken broth
$1/2$ teaspoon red pepper flakes
$1/2$ teaspoon oregano
2 teaspoons cumin
2 teaspoons chili powder
1 teaspoon salt
$1/4$ teaspoon black pepper
2 cups chopped cooked chicken breasts
1 (7-ounce) can chopped green chilies
2 cups canned or frozen corn
2 tablespoons cornstarch
$1/4$ cup water

GARNISH
Fresh cilantro leaves
Red pepper flakes

Sort and rinse the beans. Combine the beans with enough water to cover in a bowl. Let stand for 8 to 12 hours; drain.

Heat the olive oil in a large stockpot over medium heat. Add the onion, garlic and bell pepper. Sauté until tender; do not brown.

Add the broth, beans, red pepper flakes, oregano, cumin, chili powder, salt, black pepper and chicken to the onion mixture. Bring to a boil. Reduce the heat. Simmer, covered, for 45 minutes or until the beans are tender, stirring occasionally.

Add the green chilies and corn to the chili. Whisk the cornstarch and water together in a small bowl until the cornstarch is dissolved. Stir into the chili. Simmer for 5 minutes.

Ladle the chili into soup bowls. Garnish with cilantro and red pepper flakes.

MISSISSIPPI RIVER

The Great River Road follows the scenic Mississippi River through the towns and cities of Minnesota. The mighty Mississippi River travels over 2,500 miles from its head in Itasca State Park in northern Minnesota to its mouth at the Gulf of Mexico in Louisiana. The Mississippi is the longest river in North America, passing through ten states. In addition, the Mississippi-Missouri River system is the fourth longest in the world, surpassed only by the Nile, the Amazon, and the Yangtze Rivers. The Mississippi River continues to serve as a primary transportation route for grain and other food products that are shipped across the country and around the world.

PHEASANT IN MADEIRA WINE

YIELD: 2 SERVINGS

2 tablespoons butter
1/4 cup olive oil
2 garlic cloves
1/4 cup finely chopped onion
2 pheasant breasts, cut into bite-size pieces
1/4 cup madeira
1/2 cup heavy cream
1/2 cup pine nuts (optional)
Salt to taste
Pepper to taste

GARNISH
Parsley sprigs

Heat the butter and olive oil in a skillet over medium heat. Add the garlic and onion. Sauté for 7 minutes or until tender. Add the pheasant. Increase the heat to medium-high. Brown the pheasant on all sides. Add the madeira to the skillet, stirring to coat the pheasant. Cook until the madeira evaporates.

Add the cream and pine nuts to the pheasant mixture. Cook for 5 minutes or until the liquid is reduced; do not overcook the pheasant or it will become tough. Season with salt and pepper. Garnish with parsley sprigs. Serve immediately.

NOTE: You may substitute duck or capon for the pheasant. This is excellent served with Minnesota wild rice.

SPICY NO-BEAN CHILI WITH TURKEY

YIELD: 4 SERVINGS

1 (4-ounce) can chopped green chiles
Olive oil for spraying
1 large onion, chopped
1 green bell pepper, chopped
3 large garlic cloves, minced
20 ounces ground turkey or ground beef
1 1/2 tablespoons chili powder
1/2 teaspoon oregano
1/2 teaspoon thyme
1/4 teaspoon cayenne pepper
1/4 teaspoon (heaping) cumin
3 (14-ounce) cans diced tomatoes

GARNISH
Shredded cheese
Sour cream
Chopped cilantro
Sliced green onions

Drain the green chiles and rinse. Return the chiles to the can and fill with water. Spray a skillet with olive oil. Heat the olive oil. Add the onion, bell pepper, green chiles in water and garlic. Sauté over medium heat for 5 minutes or until the onion and bell pepper are tender.

Add the ground turkey to the onion mixture. Add the chili powder, oregano, thyme, cayenne pepper and cumin. Cook until the ground turkey is brown and crumbly, stirring frequently. Pour in the undrained tomatoes.

Bring the chili to a boil, stirring occasionally. Reduce the heat. Simmer for 45 minutes. Ladle into soup bowls. Garnish with cheese, sour cream, cilantro and green onions.

HONEY-GLAZED SALMON

YIELD: 2 TO 3 SERVINGS

$^1/4$ cup packed dark brown sugar
1 tablespoon honey
2 tablespoons butter
2 tablespoons Dijon mustard
1 tablespoon soy sauce
1 tablespoon olive oil
1 teaspoon ground ginger
$^1/4$ cup bourbon (optional)
1 (1-pound) salmon fillet

Combine the brown sugar, honey and butter in a saucepan. Cook over low heat until the butter melts and the sugar dissolves, stirring constantly. Stir in the mustard, soy sauce, olive oil, ginger and bourbon.

Place the salmon skin side down on heavy-duty foil. Cut the foil to outline the fish, leaving enough to fold up and create an edge. Fold the edges of the foil up. Spread $^1/2$ of the glaze over the salmon.

Place the salmon on a grill rack over medium-high heat on a gas grill or 4 to 6 inches from medium-hot coals. Grill, covered, for 8 minutes or until the salmon flakes easily. Serve with the remaining glaze. You may serve with grilled asparagus or zucchini.

INDIVIDUAL SALMON WELLINGTONS WITH WHITE DILL SAUCE

YIELD: 4 SERVINGS

FILLING
2 tablespoons butter
1 cup fresh mushrooms, stemmed
    and chopped
2 cups fresh or thawed frozen spinach
Salt to taste
Pepper to taste

WELLINGTON
2 sheets frozen puff pastry, thawed
4 (6-ounce) skinless salmon fillets
1 egg
1 tablespoon water
4 thin lemon slices

SAUCE
2/3 cup bottled clam juice
1/2 cup white wine
1 1/4 cups crème fraîche
3 tablespoons minced fresh dill
1 tablespoon freshly squeezed lemon juice

FOR THE FILLING, heat the butter in a saucepan until melted. Add the mushrooms. Sauté until tender. Add the spinach and cook until wilted. Increase the heat to high. Cook until the liquid evaporates, stirring frequently. Season with salt and pepper. Set aside.

FOR THE WELLINGTONS, unroll the puff pastry and cover 1 sheet with waxed paper topped with a damp towel. Roll the remaining puff pastry sheet into a 12-inch square on a lightly floured surface. Cut into 4 equal squares. Spoon the filling equally into the center of each square. Place a salmon fillet over the filling in each square. Bring the corners of each square up over the salmon; the salmon will not be completely covered.

Roll the remaining pastry sheet into a 13-inch square on a lightly floured surface. Cut into 4 equal squares. Place each square on top of a salmon fillet and tuck under. Pinch to enclose the fillets completely.

Whisk the egg and water together in a small bowl. Brush over the tops of the Wellingtons. Place each seam side down on a buttered baking sheet. Chill for 30 minutes.

Bake the Wellingtons at 400 degrees for 15 minutes. Place 1 lemon slice on each Wellington. Bake for 15 to 20 minutes or to 145 degrees on a meat thermometer. Place on individual dinner plates.

FOR THE SAUCE, bring the clam juice and wine to a boil in a saucepan. Boil until reduced to 1/3 cup. Stir in the crème fraîche. Boil until reduced to 1 cup. Stir in the dill and lemon juice. Spoon around the Wellingtons.

POACHED SALMON WITH CUCUMBER CREAM SAUCE

YIELD: 6 SERVINGS

SALMON
3 cups dry white wine
2 cups water
5 lemon slices
1 white onion, cut into halves
8 sprigs of fresh dill
8 sprigs of fresh flat-leaf parsley
2 fresh bay leaves
15 peppercorns
$1^1/2$ teaspoons coarse kosher salt
1 (2-pound) fresh salmon fillet,
   skinned and boned

CUCUMBER CREAM SAUCE
1 cucumber, chilled
$^1/2$ cup whipping cream, chilled
2 tablespoons apple cider vinegar, chilled
$^1/4$ teaspoon salt
$^1/8$ teaspoon white pepper

FOR THE SALMON, combine the wine, water, lemon slices, onion, dill, parsley, bay leaves, peppercorns and salt in a nonreactive skillet large enough to allow the salmon to lay flat. Bring to a boil. Reduce the heat and simmer. Add the salmon. Cook, covered, for 10 to 12 minutes or until the salmon flakes easily. Remove and discard the bay leaves. Remove the salmon and place on a large platter. Chill, covered, until ready to serve.

FOR THE SAUCE, peel the cucumber and cut into halves. Remove the seeds. Chop the cucumber and drain. Beat the cream in a mixing bowl until thick but not stiff. Add the vinegar gradually, beating constantly. Beat in the salt and white pepper. Fold in the cucumbers. Serve immediately with the salmon.

HALIBUT STEAKS WITH MANGO SALSA

YIELD: 4 SERVINGS

SALSA
1 garlic clove, minced
1 mango, chopped
1 tomato, chopped
$^1/_2$ cup finely chopped onion
2 tablespoons finely chopped cilantro
Juice of $^1/_2$ lime
$^1/_4$ teaspoon fine sea salt
Pinch of sugar

HALIBUT
1$^1/_2$ pounds halibut fillets
$^1/_4$ cup virgin olive oil
2 teaspoons dill
$^1/_4$ teaspoon salt
$^1/_4$ teaspoon pepper

FOR THE SALSA, combine the garlic, mango, tomato, onion, cilantro, lime juice, sea salt and sugar in a bowl and mix well. Chill, covered, for 2 hours or longer.

FOR THE HALIBUT, place the halibut skin side down on a piece of foil large enough to enclose the halibut. Drizzle the olive oil over the halibut. Sprinkle with the dill, salt and pepper. Fold the foil over the halibut to enclose. Poke small holes in the bottom of the foil.

Place the halibut on a grill rack. Grill over hot coals for 15 minutes or until the halibut flakes easily. Serve with the salsa.

NOTE: You may substitute salmon for the halibut.

The internationally known Mall of America, located in Bloomington, Minnesota, a southern suburb of the Twin Cities, is one of the largest entertainment and retail centers in the United States. In addition to featuring over 500 retail and specialty stores and numerous dining spots, the Mall of America, the "Megamall" to locals, is also the home of Camp Snoopy, the largest indoor theme park in the country. In addition, the LEGO Imagination Center attracts many visitors each year. If you can't find it at the Mall of America, it probably doesn't exist!

GINGERED SEA BASS

YIELD: 4 TO 6 SERVINGS

1 1/2 pounds sea bass
1/4 cup soy sauce
Tops of 4 green onions
1 small piece of gingerroot
    (about the size of a thumb)
1/4 cup soy sauce

Rinse the sea bass and pat dry. Cut into 4 pieces. Place in a shallow dish. Pour 1/4 cup soy sauce over the sea bass.

Cut each green onion top into quarters lengthwise. Cut the gingerroot diagonally into slices and chop.

Pour enough water in a pan with a steaming rack to almost reach the rack. Pour 1/4 cup soy sauce into the water. Cover and bring to a boil. Place the sea bass on the rack. Sprinkle with the green onions and gingerroot. Steam, covered, for 15 minutes or until the sea bass flakes easily.

ALMOND-CRUSTED TROUT WITH ROMESCO SAUCE

YIELD: 6 SERVINGS

ROMESCO SAUCE

1 tablespoon extra-virgin olive oil

1 slice French bread

$^1/4$ cup almonds, toasted

1 cup chopped seeded peeled tomatoes

1 garlic clove, minced

2 teaspoons sweet paprika

$^1/4$ teaspoon red pepper flakes

3 tablespoons red wine vinegar

$^1/4$ cup extra-virgin olive oil

Salt to taste

Black pepper to taste

TROUT

3 eggs

Salt to taste

Pepper to taste

6 whole trout

$^1/2$ cup flour

2 cups almonds, finely chopped

1 tablespoon unsalted butter

1 tablespoon olive oil

FOR THE SAUCE, heat 1 tablespoon olive oil in a skillet. Add the bread. Cook for 2 to 3 minutes or until golden brown on both sides. Place in a food processor container. Add the almonds, tomatoes, garlic, paprika and red pepper flakes to the bread. Process for 1 minute. Add the vinegar and $^1/4$ cup olive oil in a fine stream, processing constantly. Process for 1 minute longer. Season with salt and black pepper. Pour into a serving bowl. Let stand for 1 hour or longer.

FOR THE TROUT, whisk the eggs in a shallow dish. Season with salt and pepper. Dredge 1 trout in the flour, shaking to remove the excess. Dip into the eggs to coat. Dredge in the almonds. Repeat with the remaining trout.

Heat the butter and olive oil in a large heavy skillet over medium heat until the butter is melted. Add the trout. Cook until the trout flake easily and are golden on both sides, turning once. Serve with the sauce.

SWORDFISH WITH SAFFRON AND CAPER SAUCE

YIELD: 4 SERVINGS

SAFFRON AND CAPER SAUCE
1 tablespoon water
1 or 2 saffron threads
3/4 cup mayonnaise
1/4 cup capers
1 teaspoon minced garlic
2 teaspoons lemon juice
1/4 teaspoon white pepper

SWORDFISH
1/2 cup olive oil
4 (8-ounce) swordfish steaks
2 teaspoons lemon pepper

FOR THE SAUCE, bring the water and saffron to a simmer in a small saucepan. Let stand until cool. Combine the saffron mixture and mayonnaise in a bowl and mix well. Drain the capers, reserving 1 teaspoon of the liquid. Add the drained capers, reserved liquid, garlic, lemon juice and white pepper to the mayonnaise mixture and mix well. Chill, covered, for up to 2 days.

FOR THE SWORDFISH, drizzle the olive oil over the steaks. Sprinkle with lemon pepper. Place on a grill rack. Grill over hot coals for 3 to 4 minutes on each side or to the desired degree of doneness. Serve with the sauce.

PAN-FRIED WALLEYE WITH TARTAR SAUCE

YIELD: 4 SERVINGS

TARTAR SAUCE
2 cups mayonnaise

1/4 white onion, chopped

6 gherkins, finely chopped, or an equivalent
   amount of pickle relish

1 rib celery, finely chopped

1 teaspoon capers

1 teaspoon finely chopped parsley

1 teaspoon finely chopped chives

1 teaspoon tarragon vinegar

Dash of Tabasco sauce

WALLEYE
4 medium walleye fillets

1 extra-large egg, or 2 small eggs, beaten

15 saltine crackers, crushed

Vegetable oil for frying

GARNISH
1 lemon, cut into wedges

FOR THE TARTAR SAUCE, combine the mayonnaise, onion, gherkins, celery, capers, parsley, chives, vinegar and Tabasco sauce in a bowl and mix well.

FOR THE WALLEYE, dip the fillets in the eggs and then in the saltines. Heat enough oil in a skillet to cover half the fillet. Cook the fillets in the hot oil for 5 minutes or until golden brown on both sides, turning once; drain. Garnish with lemon wedges. Serve with the tartar sauce.

NOTE: You may substitute pickles of choice for the gherkins.

MINNESOTA WALLEYE

Walleye, a member of the perch family, is one of Minnesota's most-loved seafood. The walleye is a light, flaky white fish that is native to the many lakes and rivers of the upper Midwest. It is served as an elegant entrée in many Twin Cities restaurants, or it may be pan-fried around the campfire. The scientific name, *Stizostedion vitreum,* means a pungent, throated fish with large glassy, silvery eyes. Generally, walleye caught on local lakes weigh six to nine pounds and range in size from fifteen to twenty-six inches long.

LUTEFISK

In many parts of Minnesota, you can smell Christmas coming. Lutefisk, a Scandinavian specialty, has a very distinct odor and taste. A centuries-old Yuletide delicacy in Norway, Denmark, and Sweden, lutefisk is traditionally prepared during the holidays using dried unsalted cod. The cod is soaked in cold fresh water for up to eight days. It is then soaked in a mixture of water and potash lye for two more days and finally soaked for an additional two days in fresh water. (Note: You can also purchase pre-soaked lutefisk that is ready to cook.) Finally, the fish is simmered for ten to fifteen minutes until it becomes translucent. To serve, the lutefisk is sprinkled with allspice, salt, and white pepper. Like many Scandinavian meals, it is often accompanied by a basic white sauce and boiled potatoes.

GRILLED TUNA WITH SOY MARINADE

YIELD: VARIABLE

6-ounce tuna fillets
1 cup sake (Japanese rice vinegar)
1/2 cup natural soy sauce or tamari
1 tablespoon grated gingerroot
2 garlic cloves, mashed
1 tablespoon dark brown sugar
1/2 teaspoon sesame oil
Lemon wedges (optional)

Rinse the tuna in cold water. Arrange in a single layer in a glass dish. Combine the sake, soy sauce, gingerroot, garlic, brown sugar and sesame oil in a bowl and mix well. Pour over the tuna. Marinate, covered, in the refrigerator for 1 to 3 hours, spooning the marinade over the tuna occasionally.

Drain the tuna. Place on foil on a grill rack. Grill over hot coals until the tuna flakes easily or to the desired degree of doneness, squeezing the lemon wedges over the tuna.

NOTE: You may broil the tuna if desired.

SHRIMP ÉTOUFFÉ

YIELD: 4 SERVINGS

1/2 cup (1 stick) butter
1/4 cup flour
1 cup chopped onion
1/2 cup chopped green bell pepper
1/2 cup chopped celery
1 tablespoon finely chopped garlic
1 pound (25- to 30-count) shrimp, shelled
    and deveined
1 teaspoon salt
1/2 teaspoon black pepper
1/4 teaspoon cayenne pepper
1 tablespoon lemon juice
1/2 cup thinly sliced scallions
2 tablespoons minced parsley
1 cup cold water
Salt to taste
Hot cooked rice

Heat the butter in a 5-quart saucepan until melted. Stir in the flour. Cook over medium heat for 30 to 35 minutes or until the roux turns a rich dark brown, stirring constantly and decreasing the heat near the end; do not burn.

Stir the onion, bell pepper, celery and garlic into the roux. Sauté for 20 minutes. Add the shrimp, 1 teaspoon salt, black pepper, cayenne pepper, lemon juice, scallions, parsley and cold water and mix well. Bring to a boil. Reduce the heat. Simmer for 10 to 12 minutes or until the shrimp turn pink, stirring occasionally. Season with salt to taste. Serve over hot cooked rice.

SHRIMP LINGUINI WITH SUN-DRIED TOMATOES

YIELD: 4 SERVINGS

1/2 cup oil-packed sun-dried tomatoes
3 tablespoons unsalted butter
2 tablespoons olive oil
1 small onion, chopped
3 garlic cloves, minced
1/4 cup minced fresh parsley
1 tablespoon capers
1/2 cup dry white wine
1 pound jumbo shrimp, shelled and deveined
2 tablespoons Dijon mustard
1/2 cup heavy cream
1/2 teaspoon salt
1/2 teaspoon freshly ground pepper
16 ounces linguini

Drain the sun-dried tomatoes and cut into thin strips. Heat the butter and oil in a large heavy skillet until the butter melts. Add the onion, garlic, sun-dried tomatoes, parsley and capers. Sauté until the onion is tender. Add the wine. Bring to a simmer and simmer for 2 minutes. Add the shrimp. Cook until the shrimp turn pink.

Add the mustard and cream to the shrimp mixture. Cook for 2 minutes or until the sauce thickens, stirring frequently. Stir in the salt and pepper. Cook the linguini using the package directions until al dente. Drain and stir into the shrimp mixture. Cook over medium heat until heated through, tossing to coat the linguini with the sauce.

NOTE: You may substitute scallops for the shrimp.

PAELLA

YIELD: 4 TO 6 SERVINGS

Although the list of ingredients is long, most of the work can be done ahead as it is in three or four basic steps which are outlined in the recipe. In Spain, paella is the meal itself and needs no accompaniment, but in America, you notice restaurants offer other tapas (appetizers) with it. In addition, other meats of the cook's choice may be substituted for the fish ingredients with no problem in flavor or texture—same goes for the sausage—any strong-flavored one will do.

SOFRITO
1/4 cup olive oil
1 1/4 ounces lean, boneless pork,
     cut into 1/4-inch cubes
1/3 cup finely chopped onion
2/3 teaspoon minced garlic
1 red bell pepper, cut into
     1/4-inch-wide strips
1 green bell pepper, cut into
     1/4-inch-wide strips
1 tomato, peeled, seeded and chopped

FOR THE SOFRITO, heat the olive oil in a skillet until hot. Add the pork and cook until brown on all sides. Add the onion, garlic, bell peppers and tomato. Cook until the mixture is thick, stirring constantly. You may prepare this in advance and refrigerate for up to 6 hours.

PAELLA

1 1/2 pounds lobster tails and claws
1 1/4 teaspoons salt
1/4 teaspoon thyme
1 1/4 teaspoons paprika
Freshly ground black pepper to taste
1 1/2 pounds chicken, cut into bite-size pieces
1/4 cup olive oil
1/4 to 1/2 teaspoon saffron threads
5 cups chicken broth
3 tablespoons olive oil
2 cups short grain rice
4 medium shrimp, shelled and deveined,
   tails intact
4 small clams, scrubbed
4 mussels, scrubbed and debearded
2 chorizo sausages, cut into 1/4-inch rounds
1/3 cup peas

GARNISH
Lemon wedges

FOR THE PAELLA, cut the lobster tail from underneath crosswise into 1-inch-thick slices; do not remove the shell. Combine the salt, thyme, paprika and black pepper in a shallow dish and mix well. Add the chicken pieces and toss to coat. Heat 1/4 cup olive oil in a skillet until hot. Add the chicken and cook until brown on all sides. Remove and set aside. Add the lobster and cook over high heat for 2 to 3 minutes or until the shell begins to turn

pink. Remove and set aside. Discard the pan drippings. You may prepare this in advance and refrigerate for up to 6 hours.

Pulverize the saffron with a mortar and pestle. Heat the chicken broth in a saucepan. Stir in the saffron and bring to a boil. Heat 3 tablespoons olive oil in a separate skillet. Add the rice and cook until translucent, stirring frequently. Add the boiling chicken broth, stirring constantly. Add the sofrito and stir to combine. Spoon into a paella dish.

Arrange the lobster, chicken, shrimp, clams, mussels and sausage over the rice mixture. Scatter the peas over the top. Bake at 400 degrees for 30 minutes; do not stir. Remove and place a towel loosely over the top of the paella. Let stand for 5 minutes.

Garnish the sides with lemon wedges. You may want to prepare extra lemon wedges to serve in a separate dish as the Spanish do. The freshly squeezed lemon juice gives the paella a delicious flavoring.

SEAFOOD STEW

YIELD: 10 SERVINGS

2 cups ($^1/_2$-inch) pieces butternut squash
   (about 1$^1/_4$ pounds whole squash)
2 tablespoons extra-virgin olive oil
$^3/_4$ cup chopped onion
$^3/_4$ cup chopped fennel bulb
2 garlic cloves, minced
2 tablespoons tomato paste
2 teaspoons chopped fresh thyme
1 bay leaf
3 cups bottled clam juice
1 (14-ounce) can diced tomatoes
1 cup dry white wine
$^1/_2$ cup dry sherry
$^1/_2$ cup water
24 small clams, mussels or a
   combination, scrubbed
$^1/_4$ teaspoon saffron threads, crushed
1$^1/_2$ pounds sea bass fillets, cut into
   1-inch pieces
Salt to taste
Pepper to taste

GARNISH
Fennel fronds

Steam the squash in a steamer for 10 minutes or until tender-crisp. Let stand until cool. You may prepare this 1 day in advance and chill, covered, in the refrigerator.

Heat the olive oil in a large heavy pot over medium heat. Add the onion, fennel and garlic. Sauté for 3 minutes or until tender. Add the tomato paste, thyme and bay leaf. Cook for 1 minute, stirring constantly. Stir in the clam juice, tomatoes, wine, sherry and water. Bring to a boil. Reduce the heat. Simmer, covered, for 20 minutes. Remove and discard the bay leaf.

Add the clams and saffron to the tomato mixture. Cook, covered, for 4 minutes or until the clams open, discarding any clams that do not open. Add the sea bass and steamed squash. Simmer, covered for 5 minutes or until the squash is tender and the sea bass is opaque in the center. Season with salt and pepper. Garnish with fennel fronds.

ARTICHOKE CHEESE FETTUCCINI

YIELD: 4 SERVINGS

1 (14-ounce) can artichokes in water,
   drained
1 tablespoon butter
1^1/$_2$ cups sliced fresh mushrooms
1 teaspoon salt
^{1}/$_2$ teaspoon freshly ground pepper
^{1}/$_3$ cup dry leak soup mix
^{1}/$_2$ teaspoon basil
^{1}/$_4$ teaspoon dill
1^1/$_2$ cups skim milk
^{1}/$_2$ cup (2 ounces) shredded Cheddar cheese
^{1}/$_2$ cup (2 ounces) grated Parmesan cheese
1 tablespoon flour
2 teaspoons salt
8 ounces fettuccini

Chop the artichoke hearts. Heat the butter in a 3-quart saucepan over medium heat until melted. Add the chopped artichokes, mushrooms, 1 teaspoon salt and pepper. Cook for 2 to 3 minutes or until the mushrooms are tender, stirring occasionally. Add the soup mix, basil and dill and mix well. Add the milk, Cheddar cheese and Parmesan cheese. Cook until the cheeses melt, stirring constantly.

Sprinkle the flour over the artichoke mixture. Cook until the sauce thickens, stirring constantly. Reduce the heat to low. Simmer until ready to serve, stirring occasionally.

Fill a 2^1/$_2$-quart saucepan half full with water. Bring to a boil. Add 2 teaspoons salt. Add the fettuccini. Cook for 10 to 12 minutes or until tender; drain.

Divide the fettuccine evenly among 4 dinner plates. Spoon the artichoke sauce over the fettuccini.

PORTOBELLO RISOTTO

YIELD: 4 TO 5 SERVINGS

2 tablespoons unsalted butter
2 tablespoons olive oil
^{1}/2 cup finely chopped onion
1 garlic clove, minced
6 ounces portobello mushrooms, cut into
   ^{1}/2-inch pieces
1^1/2 cups arborio rice
^{1}/2 cup dry white wine
3^1/2 to 4 cups hot low-salt chicken broth
3 tablespoons chopped fresh lemon thyme
^{1}/4 cup (1 ounce) freshly grated
   Parmigiano-Reggiano cheese
Salt to taste
Pepper to taste
^{1}/4 cup (1 ounce) freshly grated
   Parmigiano-Reggiano cheese

Heat the butter and olive oil in a large heavy saucepan over medium heat until the butter is melted. Add the onion and garlic. Sauté for 10 minutes or until the onion is golden brown. Add the mushroom pieces and rice. Sauté for 5 minutes or until the rice becomes translucent. Stir in the wine. Cook until almost all of the liquid has evaporated, stirring constantly.

Stir in ^{1}/2 to ^{3}/4 cup hot broth. Cook until the broth is absorbed, stirring constantly. Repeat with the remaining broth. Cook until the rice is tender and the mixture is creamy. This process will take 15 to 20 minutes.

Stir the lemon thyme and ^{1}/4 cup Parmigiano-Reggiano cheese into the risotto. Season with salt and pepper. Serve with ^{1}/4 cup Parmigiano-Reggiano cheese.

VEGETARIAN CHILI

YIELD: 15 TO 20 SERVINGS

1 large white onion, chopped

1 or 2 garlic cloves, minced, or $1/2$ teaspoon
   oil-packed minced garlic

2 tablespoons olive oil

6 to 8 ribs celery, chopped

1 small package fresh mushrooms, peeled
   and quartered

1 green bell pepper, chopped

1 red bell pepper, chopped

Dash of salt

4 or 5 zucchini, quartered and sliced

3 or 4 yellow squash, quartered and sliced

1 (4-ounce) can chopped jalapeño
   chiles, drained

1 (4-ounce) can chopped green
   chilies, drained

2 (14-ounce) cans chopped tomatoes

1 (6-ounce) can tomato paste

2 to 3 tablespoons chili powder

Freshly ground pepper to taste

1 (15-ounce) can kidney beans, rinsed
   and drained

1 (15-ounce) can chili beans, rinsed
   and drained

GARNISH
Shredded Cheddar cheese
Sour cream

Sauté the onion and garlic in the olive oil in a large pot over medium-high heat until the onion is tender. Add the celery and cook for 6 minutes, stirring frequently. Reduce the heat to medium. Stir in the mushrooms, bell peppers and salt. Bring to a simmer and cook for 6 minutes or until the bell peppers are tender. Add the zucchini, squash, jalapeño chiles and green chiles. Simmer, covered, for 5 to 7 minutes or until the squash is tender, stirring occasionally. Stir in the tomatoes, tomato paste, chili powder and pepper. Stir in the beans. Simmer for 3 minutes or until ready to serve. Ladle into soup bowls. Garnish with cheese and a dollop of sour cream.

NOTE: This requires a very large pot. If you don't have one, use smaller quantities.

VEGETABLE LASAGNA

YIELD: 12 SERVINGS

1 tablespoon olive oil
1/2 bell pepper, chopped
1 onion, chopped
2 garlic cloves, minced
8 ounces mushrooms
15 ounces ricotta cheese
8 ounces cottage cheese
1 cup (4 ounces) grated Parmesan cheese
2 eggs
1 (10-ounce) package frozen chopped
    spinach, thawed and drained
1 teaspoon basil
1 (15-ounce) can whole tomatoes, drained
Vegetable oil for spraying
2 (26-ounce) jars spaghetti sauce
16 ounces lasagna noodles
4 cups (1 pound) shredded
    mozzarella cheese
1/4 cup minced fresh parsley

Heat the olive oil in a large saucepan. Add the bell pepper, onion and garlic. Sauté until the onion and bell pepper are tender. Add the mushrooms and sauté until tender.

Combine the ricotta cheese, cottage cheese, 1/2 cup of the Parmesan cheese, eggs, spinach, basil, and the mushroom mixture in a bowl and mix well.

Cut the tomatoes into halves. Spray the bottom of a 9×13-inch baking pan with vegetable oil. Spread 1 cup of the spaghetti sauce over the bottom of the pan. Layer 1/3 of the lasagna noodles, 1/2 of the ricotta cheese mixture, 1/2 of the tomatoes, 2 1/4 cups of the remaining sauce and 1 cup of the mozzarella cheese in the prepared pan. Continue layering with 1/2 of the remaining noodles, the remaining ricotta cheese mixture, the remaining tomatoes, 2 1/2 cups of the remaining sauce, and 1 cup of the remaining mozzarella cheese in the prepared pan. Continue layering with the remaining noodles and the remaining sauce. Sprinkle the remaining 2 cups mozzarella cheese, remaining 1/2 cup Parmesan cheese and parsley over the layers.

Cover the pan tightly with foil sprayed with nonstick cooking spray. Bake at 350 degrees for 1 hour. Remove the foil. Bake for 30 minutes longer or until hot and bubbly. Let stand for 15 minutes before cutting.

Always Superb: Recipes for Every Occasion

GINGER PANCAKES

YIELD: 4 SERVINGS

PANCAKES
2 cups baking mix
I egg
1^1/$_3$ cups milk
^{1}/$_4$ cup molasses
1^1/$_2$ teaspoons ground ginger
I teaspoon cinnamon
^{1}/$_2$ teaspoon ground cloves

LEMON SAUCE
I cup sugar
3 tablespoons lemon juice
^{1}/$_2$ cup (I stick) margarine or butter
^{1}/$_4$ cup water
I egg, beaten

FOR THE PANCAKES, combine the baking mix, egg, milk, molasses, ginger, cinnamon and cloves in a large mixing bowl and mix well. Pour ^{1}/$_4$ to ^{1}/$_2$ cup of the butter at a time onto a hot lightly greased griddle. Cook until brown on both sides, turning once.

FOR THE LEMON SAUCE, combine the sugar, lemon juice, margarine and water in a medium saucepan. Bring to a boil, stirring frequently. Remove from the heat. Stir a small amount of the hot mixture into the beaten egg. Stir the egg into the hot mixture. Cook until thickened and heated through, stirring constantly. Serve warm with pancakes.

The Twin Cities, home to many artisans, features numerous outdoor art fairs during the warmer months of the year. Almost every weekend between June and September, art enthusiasts can visit local parks and neighborhoods to view one-of-a-kind art, including photography, paintings, jewelry, pottery, sculpture, and much more. The Metris Uptown Art Fair, held during the first weekend of August, is one of the most popular. In addition, the St. Paul Art Crawl offers a self-guided tour of nearly 200 artists' studios in the St. Paul downtown neighborhood known as Lowertown. Tours are also common at the many art studios and galleries in the Warehouse and northeast neighborhoods of Minneapolis.

MINNESOTA BED AND BREAKFAST OVEN FRENCH TOAST

YIELD: 8 SERVINGS

1 (1-pound) loaf cinnamon bread
8 eggs
3 cups milk
1/4 cup sugar
1 teaspoon cinnamon
1 teaspoon vanilla extract

Cut the bread into 1-inch-thick slices. Arrange in a single layer in a greased 9×13-inch baking pan.

Beat the eggs, milk, sugar, cinnamon and vanilla together in a bowl. Pour over the bread. Chill, covered, for 4 to 12 hours.

Bake, uncovered, at 325 degrees for 45 minutes.

EASIEST EGGS BENEDICT

YIELD: 8 SERVINGS

4 English muffins, split and lightly toasted
16 thin slices Canadian bacon
8 eggs
$1/4$ cup ($1/2$ stick) butter
$1/4$ cup flour
1 tablespoon paprika
$1/2$ teaspoon nutmeg
$1/8$ teaspoon white pepper
2 cups milk
2 cups (8 ounces) shredded Swiss cheese
$1/2$ cup white wine
$1/2$ cup crushed cornflakes
1 tablespoon butter, softened

Arrange the muffins cut side up in a single layer in a greased 9×13-inch baking dish. Place 2 slices bacon on each muffin half.

Fill a 10-inch skillet half full with water. Bring the water to a boil. Break an egg into a custard cup. Slide the egg into the water carefully. Repeat with 3 of the remaining eggs. Simmer for 3 minutes or until the eggs are set. Place each egg on a muffin stack. Repeat the process with the remaining 4 eggs.

Heat $1/4$ cup butter in a medium saucepan until melted. Stir in the flour, paprika, nutmeg and white pepper. Pour in the milk gradually, whisking constantly. Cook until the mixture is thickened and bubbly, stirring constantly. Add the Swiss cheese. Cook until the Swiss cheese is melted, stirring constantly. Stir in the wine. Spoon over the muffin stacks.

Combine the cornflakes and 1 tablespoon butter in a small bowl and mix well. Sprinkle over the top. You may chill, covered, for 8 to 12 hours at this point and bring to room temperature before baking.

Bake, uncovered, at 375 degrees for 20 to 25 minutes or until heated through.

BASILICA/CATHEDRAL

The Twin Cities is home to
many remarkable houses of
worship. Two of the largest
and most striking are the
Basilica of St. Mary and the
Cathedral of Saint Paul.
The Basilica of St. Mary in
Minneapolis is a nationally
recognized historic landmark.
Built in 1914, it was the first
basilica in America and is still
undergoing renovations
today. The Cathedral of Saint
Paul sits on a hill overlooking
the city of Saint Paul at the
foot of Summit Avenue. The
Cathedral was begun in 1907,
and the first Mass was
conducted on Palm Sunday in
1915. Both churches were
envisioned by Archbishop
John Ireland and were
designed with input from
Emmanuel L. Masqueray, a
French-born architect whom
Archbishop Ireland met at the
1904 World's Fair and who
brought the unmistakable
grandeur and beauty of
French cathedrals to the
Twin Cities.

FRITTATA

YIELD: 6 SERVINGS

1 tomato, sliced
Salt to taste
Pepper to taste
4 eggs
2 egg whites
2 cups heavy cream
2 teaspoons hot sauce
1/4 cup (1 ounce) grated mozzarella cheese
3 tablespoons julienned fresh basil
1/2 cup (2 ounces) goat cheese
1/4 cup (1 ounce) grated Parmesan cheese

Spray an ovenproof 9-inch slope-sided sauté
pan generously with nonstick cooking spray;
do not touch the inside of the pan after
spraying or the seal will break.

Sprinkle the tomato slices with salt and
pepper. Combine the eggs, egg whites, cream
and hot sauce in a bowl and mix well. Pour
half the egg mixture into the prepared pan.
Layer the mozzarella cheese and tomato slices
over the egg mixture. Sprinkle with the basil.
Place dollops of goat cheese on the layers.

Pour the remaining egg mixture over the
layers; the egg mixture should reach the rim
of the pan. Sprinkle the Parmesan cheese over
the top.

Bake at 350 degrees for 45 minutes or until
the top is firm.

CRUSTLESS QUICHE

YIELD: 8 SERVINGS

2 tablespoons butter
$^1/_2$ cup chopped onion
$^1/_2$ cup sliced fresh mushrooms
4 eggs
1 cup sour cream
1 cup small curd cottage cheese
$^1/_2$ cup (2 ounces) grated Parmesan cheese
$^1/_4$ cup flour
$^1/_4$ teaspoon salt
4 drops of Tabasco sauce
2 cups (8 ounces) shredded
   Monterey Jack cheese
1 cup chopped cooked ham, bacon
   or sausage

Heat the butter in a skillet until melted. Add
the onion and sauté until tender. Add the
mushrooms. Sauté for 2 minutes.

Process the eggs, sour cream, cottage cheese,
Parmesan cheese, flour, salt and Tabasco sauce
in a food processor. Pour into a bowl. Add the
cooked onion mixture, Monterey Jack cheese
and ham and mix well.

Pour the ham mixture into a buttered 9-inch
square pan. Bake at 350 degrees for
45 minutes.

Chapter Six

DESSERTS

BAKLAVA

YIELD: 12 SERVINGS

FILLING
1 cup sugar
1 teaspoon cinnamon
$1/8$ teaspoon ground cloves
2 cups chopped walnuts, almonds
 or pistachios

BAKLAVA
1 (1-pound) package frozen phyllo
 dough, thawed
2 cups (4 sticks) butter, melted

SYRUP
$1/2$ cup water
$1/3$ cup packed brown sugar
$1/4$ cup sugar
$1/2$ cup honey
Grated zest of 1 lemon
Grated zest of 1 orange

FOR THE FILLING, combine the sugar, cinnamon, cloves and walnuts in a bowl and mix well.

FOR THE BAKLAVA, unroll the phyllo and cover with waxed paper topped with a damp towel. Keep the unused portion covered until needed.

Layer 6 of the phyllo sheets in a 9×12-inch baking pan, brushing each sheet with melted butter. Spread $1/3$ of the filling over the layers. Repeat the layers with the remaining phyllo sheets and filling, finishing with 2 or 3 phyllo sheets on top.

Cut the top layers into 2-inch diamond shapes; do not cut all the way through. Bake at 350 degrees for 30 to 45 minutes or until golden brown.

FOR THE SYRUP, combine the water, brown sugar, sugar, honey, lemon zest and orange zest in a saucepan. Bring to a boil. Boil for 5 minutes. Pour over the baked baklava.

Cut the bottom layers of the baklava following the diamond-shaped cut lines. Serve hot or cold.

NOTE: Thaw the phyllo dough, unopened, in the refrigerator overnight. It dries out very quickly, so do not open the package until the filling has been prepared.

CHOCOLATE BREAD PUDDING

YIELD: 4 SERVINGS

1/2 cup (3 ounces) semisweet
    chocolate chips
1/2 cup heavy cream
3/4 cup half-and-half
4 cups French bread cubes
1/2 cup sugar
1/4 teaspoon cinnamon
1 teaspoon vanilla extract
1 tablespoon bourbon
1 egg

Place the chocolate chips in a large bowl.
Heat the heavy cream and half-and-half in
a saucepan until almost boiling. Pour over the
chocolate chips. Stir until the chocolate chips
are melted. Add the bread cubes and stir
until coated.

Whisk the sugar, cinnamon, vanilla, bourbon
and egg together in a bowl. Add to the
chocolate mixture and mix well.

Pour the chocolate mixture into a 2-quart
baking dish. Chill for 15 to 30 minutes.

Bake at 350 degrees for 30 to 40 minutes or
until a wooden pick inserted in the center
comes out clean. Serve warm.

NOTE: Ice cream or a large dollop of whipped
cream is great served with this.

QUICK CRUST

Keep a package of prepared sugar cookie dough in the refrigerator to make an easy crust for fruit tarts and cheesecakes. Slice the roll of dough into individual disks according to the directions. Arrange the slices in the bottom of a springform or tart pan. Gently press the dough to cover the bottom of the pan evenly. Bake at 350 degrees for 12 to 14 minutes or until light brown. To create a chocolate crust, crush 12 chocolate sandwich cookies. Melt 3 tablespoons butter and add to the crushed cookies, tossing to mix well. Press into a lightly greased pan.

CRUSTLESS ITALIAN CHEESECAKE

YIELD: 8 TO 10 SERVINGS

16 ounces cream cheese, softened
2 cups sour cream
2 cups ricotta cheese, drained
3 tablespoons cornstarch
5 eggs
1 teaspoon vanilla extract
1 to 1 1/2 cups sugar

Beat the cream cheese in a mixing bowl until light and fluffy. Beat in the sour cream and ricotta cheese until smooth. Add the cornstarch, eggs, vanilla and the desired amount of sugar and mix well.

Pour the batter into a buttered and floured 12-inch springform pan. Bake at 350 degrees for 1 hour; do not overcook. Cool and remove the side of the pan before serving. You may bake in a 10-inch springform pan and increase the baking time.

Add to the crushed cookies, tossing to mix well.

LEMON SUPREME CHEESECAKE

CRUST
2 cups crushed graham cracker crumbs
6 tablespoons unsalted butter, melted

FILLING
24 ounces cream cheese, softened
1 1/2 cups sugar
3 eggs
1/4 cup fresh lemon juice
1 tablespoon grated lemon zest
2 teaspoons vanilla extract

TOPPING
2 cups sour cream
3 tablespoons sugar
1 teaspoon vanilla extract

GLAZE
3/4 cup water
1/3 cup freshly squeezed lemon juice
1 egg yolk
1/2 cup sugar
1 1/2 tablespoons cornstarch
1/4 teaspoon salt
1 tablespoon butter
2 teaspoons grated lemon zest

GARNISH
1 lemon

FOR THE CRUST, combine the graham cracker crumbs and melted butter in a bowl and mix well. Press over the bottom and up the side of a 9-inch springform pan. Bake at 350 degrees for 5 minutes.

FOR THE FILLING, beat the cream cheese in a large bowl until light and fluffy. Add the sugar gradually, beating constantly. Add the eggs 1 at a time, mixing well after each addition. Stir in the lemon juice, lemon zest and vanilla. Pour into the prepared pan. Bake for 60 to 75 minutes or until slightly puffed.

FOR THE TOPPING, combine the sour cream, sugar and vanilla in a bowl and mix well. Spread over the baked filling. Bake for 15 minutes. Cool for 30 minutes.

FOR THE GLAZE, combine the water, lemon juice and egg yolk in a small heavy saucepan and mix well. Stir in the sugar, cornstarch and salt. Bring to a boil over low heat, stirring constantly; this will take about 10 minutes. Stir in the butter and lemon zest. Cook until the butter melts, stirring constantly. Cool for 20 minutes. Spread over the cooled cheesecake. Chill the cheesecake, covered, for 8 to 12 hours. Remove the side of the pan.

TO GARNISH, cut the lemon into thin slices. Cut a slit in the bottom of each slice. Twist a slice and place on the top edge of the cheesecake. Repeat with the remaining slices until the circle around the edge is complete. Place 1 lemon twist in the middle of the cheesecake if desired.

CHOCOLATE CHEESECAKE

YIELD: 10 TO 12 SERVINGS

1/3 cup butter, melted
1 1/4 cups chocolate sandwich cookie crumbs
1/4 cup sugar
24 ounces cream cheese, softened
1 (14-ounce) can sweetened condensed milk
2 cups (12 ounces) semisweet chocolate
    chips, melted
4 eggs
2 teaspoons vanilla extract

GARNISH
Raspberry sauce

Combine the butter, cookie crumbs and sugar
in a bowl and mix well. Press firmly over the
bottom of a 9-inch springform pan.

Beat the cream cheese in a mixing bowl until
light and fluffy. Add the condensed milk and
beat until smooth. Add the melted chocolate
chips, eggs and vanilla and mix well. Pour into
the prepared pan.

Bake at 300 degrees for 65 minutes or until
the cheesecake springs back when lightly
touched. Let stand until room temperature.
Chill, covered, in the refrigerator. Remove the
side of the pan. Garnish with raspberry sauce.

CHERRIES IN THE SNOW

YIELD: 12 SERVINGS

MERINGUE
6 egg whites
$^1/2$ teaspoon cream of tartar
$1^1/2$ cups sugar
$^1/4$ teaspoon salt
1 teaspoon vanilla extract

FILLING
2 cups whipping cream
6 ounces cream cheese, softened
1 cup sugar
1 teaspoon vanilla extract
1 cup miniature marshmallows

TOPPING
1 (21-ounce) cherry pie filling
1 teaspoon almond extract

FOR THE MERINGUE, butter the bottom of a 9×13-inch baking pan. Beat the egg whites and cream of tartar in a mixing bowl until stiff. Add the sugar gradually, beating constantly. Add the salt and vanilla and mix well. Spread over the bottom of the prepared pan. Place in a 400-degree oven and turn the oven off. Let stand in the oven for 8 to 12 hours.

FOR THE FILLING, beat the whipping cream in a mixing bowl until stiff peaks form. Beat the cream cheese, sugar and vanilla in a separate mixing bowl until smooth. Fold in the whipped cream. Stir in the marshmallows. Spread over the meringue. Chill, covered, for 8 hours.

FOR THE TOPPING, combine the pie filling and almond extract in a bowl and mix well. Spread over the filling. Serve immediately.

Dessert wine generally refers to any sweet or fortified wine (i.e., brandy is added). However, in the United States dessert wine must legally be fortified even if it is not sweet. In addition to sparkling wines and Champagnes, which often accompany dessert, fortified wines, including port, sherry, madeira and marsala, make lovely accompaniments or substitutions for a sweet. In addition, botrytised wines (created when ripe grapes are consumed by mold, resulting in a deep honey-type flavor), including sauternes and late harvest wines, riesling or ice wine, complement any dessert or cheese course. Due to the high sugar content and subsequent intense flavor of many dessert wines, they are best enjoyed in small quantities.

RHUBARB STRAWBERRY CRUNCH

YIELD: 10 TO 12 SERVINGS

FILLING
1 cup sugar
3 tablespoons flour
3 cups chopped rhubarb
1 cup sliced strawberries

TOPPING
1 cup packed brown sugar
1 1/2 cups flour
1/2 cup (1 stick) butter
1 cup rolled oats

FOR THE FILLING, combine the sugar and flour in a bowl and mix well. Add the rhubarb and strawberries and toss to coat. Spoon evenly into a 9×13-inch baking pan.

FOR THE TOPPING, combine the brown sugar and flour in a bowl and mix well. Cut in the butter until crumbly. Stir in the oats. Sprinkle evenly over the filling.

Bake at 375 degrees for 45 minutes or until the topping is golden brown and the filling is bubbly.

NOTE: For oat crumble topping, combine 1 cup rolled oats, 3/4 cup flour, 3/4 cup packed brown sugar and 1/2 cup softened butter in a bowl and mix until crumbly.

AUTUMN PEAR CRISP

YIELD: 8 TO 10 SERVINGS

6 Anjou pears, chopped
Juice of 1 lemon
1/2 cup sugar
1 tablespoon cornstarch
1 teaspoon cinnamon
2/3 cup flour
1 cup packed brown sugar
2 teaspoons cinnamon
1 teaspoon salt
6 tablespoons chilled butter, cut into pieces
2/3 cup rolled oats
1/2 cup chopped pecans

Combine the pears and lemon juice in a large bowl and mix well.

Whisk the sugar, cornstarch and 1 teaspoon cinnamon together in a bowl. Add to the pears and toss gently to coat. Spoon into a 7×12-inch baking dish.

Place the flour, brown sugar, 2 teaspoons cinnamon and salt in a food processor container and pulse until mixed. Add the chilled butter pieces and pulse until mixed and chunky; do not pulse until smooth. Add the oats and pecans and pulse 2 times. Sprinkle over the pear mixture.

Bake at 375 degrees for 40 minutes or until the pears are tender and the topping is golden brown and bubbly. Cool for 20 minutes. Serve warm. You may serve this with cinnamon ice cream.

No one can say if it's the crisp cold air, the strong work ethic, or just good fortune, but Minnesota is blessed with one of the most generous populations in the country. The Twin Cities is home to nearly one hundred public and private philanthropic organizations, including four of the nation's largest: The McKnight Foundation, a private organization founded in Minnesota in 1953 by William L. McKnight, a founder of 3M, and his wife, Maude L. McKnight; The Bush Foundation, created in 1953 through the generosity of Archibald Granville Bush, also an early leader within 3M, and his wife, Edyth Bassler Bush; and two large community foundations, the Saint Paul Foundation and The Minneapolis Foundation, one of the oldest foundations and largest community foundations in the nation.

CHOCOLATE DESSERT WRAPS

YIELD: 4 SERVINGS

$^1/_2$ cup creamy peanut butter
4 (8-inch) flour tortillas
1 cup miniature marshmallows
$^1/_2$ cup miniature chocolate chips
Vanilla ice cream

GARNISH
Chocolate shavings

Spread 2 tablespoons peanut butter on each tortilla. Sprinkle $^1/_4$ cup of the marshmallows and 2 tablespoons of the chocolate chips over the peanut butter on each tortilla. Roll to enclose the filling. Wrap each tortilla in foil and seal tightly. You may chill the wrapped tortillas at this point.

Grill the foil-wrapped tortillas over hot coals for 5 to 10 minutes or until heated through. Unwrap and place on dessert plates. Place a scoop of vanilla ice cream next to each tortilla. Garnish with chocolate shavings.

NOTE: Tortillas may be baked at 350 degrees until heated through.

ALMOND STRAWBERRY PAIN PERDUE

YIELD: 4 SERVINGS

STRAWBERRY COMPOTE
1/4 teaspoon grated lime zest
2 tablespoons sugar
1 tablespoon lime juice
1 pint strawberries, cut into halves

PAIN PERDUE
2 eggs
2 tablespoons sugar
2 teaspoons vanilla extract
1/4 cup half-and-half
4 (3/4-inch-thick) slices egg bread
2 tablespoons butter
1/2 cup blanched almonds, coarsely chopped

ASSEMBLY
Whipped cream

GARNISH
Confectioners' sugar
Mint leaves

FOR THE COMPOTE, mash the lime zest into the sugar in a medium bowl. Add the lime juice and strawberries and mix well. Let stand for 10 minutes, tossing occasionally.

FOR THE PAIN PERDUE, whisk the eggs, sugar, vanilla and half-and-half together in a bowl. Pour into a large shallow dish. Arrange the bread slices in the egg mixture in a single layer. Soak for 10 minutes, turning occasionally.

Heat the butter in a nonstick skillet until melted. Place the almonds in a shallow dish. Dip one side of a bread slice into the almonds. Place almond side down in the hot butter. Cook over medium heat for 3 minutes or until golden brown. Turn and cook for 3 minutes longer. Place on a serving plate. Repeat with the remaining bread slices.

TO ASSEMBLE, spoon the compote evenly over the pain perdue. Place a dollop of whipped cream on the side. Garnish with confectioners' sugar and mint leaves.

BAKED LEMON CUSTARD

YIELD: 4 SERVINGS

2 egg yolks
1 cup milk
2 teaspoons grated lemon zest
3 tablespoons freshly squeezed lemon juice
1 1/2 tablespoons butter, melted
1/3 cup sugar
5 tablespoons flour
1/4 teaspoon baking powder
1/8 teaspoon salt
2 egg whites, at room temperature
1/3 cup sugar

Beat the egg yolks at high speed in a mixing bowl for 2 minutes or until thick and pale yellow. Add the milk, lemon zest, lemon juice and melted butter gradually, beating constantly.

Combine 1/3 cup sugar, flour, baking powder and salt in a separate bowl and mix well. Beat into the egg yolk mixture.

Beat the egg whites at high speed in a mixing bowl until foamy. Add 1/3 cup sugar, 1 tablespoon at a time, beating until stiff peaks form.

Fold 1/4 of the egg white mixture into the egg yolk mixture. Fold in the remaining egg white mixture.

Pour the batter into a greased 1-quart baking dish. Place the baking dish in a larger baking pan. Add enough hot water to the larger pan to fill to a depth of 1 inch. Bake at 375 degrees for 45 minutes or until the top is set. Remove the custard dish from the water bath. Serve warm.

CRÈME BRÛLÉE

YIELD: 6 SERVINGS

2 cups heavy cream
1 vanilla bean
6 egg yolks
12 tablespoons sugar

GARNISH
Fresh berries

Pour the cream into a saucepan. Split the vanilla bean and place in the cream. Cook over medium heat just until the cream begins to boil. Remove from the heat. Let steep for 20 minutes.

Beat the egg yolks and 6 tablespoons of the sugar in a mixing bowl until thick and pale yellow. Reheat the cream. Stir a small amount of the hot cream into the egg yolk mixture. Stir the egg yolk mixture into the hot cream. Strain the cream mixture into a bowl.

Pour the strained cream mixture evenly into 6 ramekins. Place the ramekins in a large shallow baking pan. Add enough water to the larger pan to come halfway up the side of the ramekins. Bake at 325 degrees for 20 to 25 minutes or until the custard is set. Let stand until completely cool. Chill, covered, for 4 hours or up to 3 days.

Sprinkle 1 tablespoon of the sugar evenly over one of the custards. Repeat with the remaining sugar and custards. Place the ramekins on a broiler pan. Broil for 30 seconds or until the sugar melts and begins to brown. Let stand until the sugar cools and hardens. Garnish with fresh berries. Serve immediately.

CRÈME CARAMEL

YIELD: 6 SERVINGS

$^1/2$ cup sugar
3 eggs, lightly beaten
$^1/3$ cup sugar
Dash of salt
1 teaspoon vanilla extract
$2^1/2$ cups milk
Nutmeg to taste

GARNISH
Fresh berries

Heat $^1/2$ cup sugar in a saucepan over low heat until melted and golden brown, stirring constantly; do not overcook. Divide evenly among 6 custard cups. Tilt each cup to coat the bottom with the syrup. Let stand for 10 minutes or until the syrup hardens.

Combine the eggs, $^1/3$ cup sugar, salt and vanilla in a bowl and mix well. Scald the milk in a saucepan over low heat; bubbles will form at the side and the milk will start to stick to the side when scalded.

Stir a small amount of the scalded milk into the egg mixture. Stir the egg mixture into the scalded milk. Pour into the prepared custard cups. Sprinkle the tops with nutmeg.

Place the filled custard cups in a 9×13-inch baking pan. Pour enough hot water into the pan to come $^1/2$ inch from the top of the custard cups.

Bake at 350 degrees for 45 minutes or until a knife inserted in the center comes out clean. Remove the cups from the water. Chill, covered, in the refrigerator.

Unmold the custard onto dessert plates; the caramel syrup will run down the sides of the custard to form a sauce. Garnish with fresh berries.

CRÈME À LA ORANGE

YIELD: 12 SERVINGS

8 egg yolks
1 cup sugar
1 tablespoon orange extract
4 cups heavy cream
Grated zest of 1 orange

GARNISH
Whipped cream
Mint leaves
Orange sections

Beat the egg yolks and sugar in a mixing bowl for 4 minutes or until thick and pale yellow. Add the orange extract and beat for 1 minute.

Heat the cream and orange zest in a saucepan until bubbles form around the edge. Remove from the heat. Stir a small amount of the hot cream into the egg yolk mixture. Stir the egg yolk mixture into the hot cream. Pour evenly into twelve 6-ounce custard cups.

Place the custard cups in a large baking pan. Pour enough hot water into the pan to fill to a depth of 1 inch. Bake at 350 degrees for 45 minutes or until set. Remove the custard cups from the water. Chill in the refrigerator.

To serve, garnish each custard cup with a dollop of whipped cream, mint leaves and orange sections.

NOTE: You may substitute 2% milk for the heavy cream. Milk and orange zest may be heated in a microwave-safe container to a temperature of 115 degrees instead of heated in a saucepan.

SAUTÉED BANANAS

YIELD: 8 SERVINGS

1 cup flaked coconut
1 egg, beaten
$^1/_4$ cup honey
4 firm ripe bananas
$^1/_2$ cup (1 stick) butter
8 scoops vanilla ice cream
Chocolate sauce

GARNISH
Mint leaves

Sprinkle the coconut evenly over a baking sheet. Bake at 350 degrees until the coconut is toasted.

Combine the egg and honey in a shallow bowl and mix well. Cut the bananas into halves and slice lengthwise. Dip the bananas into the honey mixture.

Heat the butter in a skillet until melted. Add the bananas. Sauté until golden brown on both sides.

Place a scoop of ice cream on a dessert dish. Arrange 2 cooked banana slices around the ice cream. Sprinkle with the toasted coconut. Drizzle with chocolate sauce. Garnish with a mint leaf. Repeat with the remaining ingredients.

INDOOR S'MORES

YIELD: 30 BARS

1 1/2 cups sugar
2 eggs
1 cup (2 sticks) butter, softened
2 teaspoons vanilla extract
2 cups flour
1 teaspoon baking powder
1 teaspoon salt
1 cup graham cracker crumbs
1 (13-ounce) package milk chocolate
   kisses, unwrapped
1 (7-ounce) jar marshmallow creme

Combine the sugar, eggs, butter and vanilla
in a bowl and mix well. Mix the flour, baking
powder, salt and graham cracker crumbs in
a separate bowl. Add to the egg mixture
gradually, beating constantly.

Spread half the dough over the bottom
of a 9×13-inch baking pan. Press the kisses
pointed side down into the dough.

Microwave the opened jar of marshmallow
creme on Defrost for 30 seconds to soften.
Spread over the kisses. Crumble the remaining
dough and sprinkle evenly over the
marshmallow creme.

Bake at 350 degrees for 30 to 40 minutes or
until brown on top.

RICE PUDDING

YIELD: 8 SERVINGS

2 tablespoons butter
1/3 to 1 cup cooked rice
4 eggs
2 cups milk
1/2 teaspoon salt
1/2 cup sugar
1/4 cup amaretto
Cinnamon to taste
Nutmeg to taste
Raisins to taste

Place the butter in an 8-inch square baking
dish. Place the dish in a 350-degree oven until
the butter melts. Tilt the dish to cover the
bottom with the butter.

Sprinkle the rice evenly over the melted
butter. Combine the eggs, milk, salt, sugar,
amaretto, cinnamon, nutmeg and raisins in
a bowl and mix well. Pour over the rice.

Bake at 350 degrees for 1 hour or until a
knife inserted in the center comes out clean.

LEMON SORBET WITH CRÈME DE CASSIS AND RASPBERRIES

YIELD: 4 SERVINGS

1/2 cup lemon juice
1/2 cup orange juice
1/4 cup sugar
1 teaspoon grated lemon zest
1/4 cup water
1 egg white, or an equivalent amount of
    meringue powder
2 tablespoons crème de cassis
Fresh raspberries

Combine the lemon juice, orange juice, sugar, lemon zest and water in a bowl and stir until the sugar is dissolved. Chill, covered, for 2 to 3 hours.

Beat the egg white in a mixing bowl until stiff. Fold into the chilled lemon mixture. Pour into an ice cube tray and freeze.

Remove the frozen cubes from the tray and place in a food processor. Process until smooth. Refreeze if necessary. Spoon into individual dessert dishes. Pour the crème de cassis over the sorbet. Arrange the raspberries around the sorbet. Serve immediately.

PAVLOVA

YIELD: 6 SERVINGS

$^1/_2$ cup sugar
$^3/_4$ teaspoon cornstarch
2 egg whites, at room temperature
$^1/_8$ teaspoon cream of tartar
$^1/_8$ teaspoon salt
$1^1/_2$ teaspoons vinegar
$^1/_2$ teaspoon vanilla extract
$^1/_2$ cup whipping cream
$^1/_2$ cup fresh berries
Sliced kiwifruit
$^1/_4$ cup confectioners' sugar

GARNISH
Mint leaves

Line a baking sheet with parchment paper and secure with tape. Trace six 3-inch circles on the parchment paper.

Mix the sugar and cornstarch in a bowl. Beat the egg whites, cream of tartar and salt in a mixing bowl until soft peaks form. Beat in the vinegar and vanilla. Add the sugar mixture 1 tablespoon at a time, beating constantly. Beat for 8 minutes longer or until the meringue is smooth and glossy.

Spread the meringue evenly over the 6 prepared parchment circles. Remove and discard the tape. Bake at 350 degrees for 5 minutes. Reduce the oven temperature to 300 degrees. Bake for 20 minutes longer; the meringues will be lightly browned, puffed and cracked on top and moist inside. Turn the oven off and set the door ajar. Let the meringues stand in the oven until completely cool.

Whip the cream in a mixing bowl until soft peaks form. Remove the pavlovas from the parchment paper and place each 1 on a dessert plate. Spoon a small amount of the whipped cream on each pavlova. Place the berries and kiwifruit on the whipped cream. Sprinkle with the confectioners' sugar. Garnish with mint leaves.

NOTE: Pavlovas can be made ahead and stored in an airtight container. They may also be frozen. To thaw, remove from the container and place on a plate. To make one 9- or 10-inch pavlova, double the ingredients. Bake at 350 degrees for 10 minutes and at 300 degrees for 30 to 40 minutes or until puffed and cracked on top.

Until the 9th century, sugar was an exotic and rare luxury in the Western world. Today, sugarcane and sugar beets are the most common sources of sugar. However, it is also derived from maple sap, corn, grapes, sorghum, fruit, and even milk (i.e., lactose). In addition to its role as a sweetening agent, sugar also stabilizes certain mixtures such as egg whites, contributes to the tenderness of dough, creates the warm golden surface on baked items, and helps preserve certain foods. Superfine sugar is preferred when sweetening cold liquid or meringue since it dissolves quickly. Confectioners' sugar (i.e., powdered sugar) is granulated sugar that is finely crushed into a powder and infused with a small amount of cornstarch. To substitute confectioners' sugar for granulated sugar, use 1³/4 cups of packed confectioners' sugar to equal 1 cup of granulated sugar.

Continued on next page

BERRIMISU

YIELD: 12 TO 16 SERVINGS

16 ounces mascarpone cheese
¹/4 cup sugar
1 cup heavy cream
¹/2 teaspoon vanilla extract
4 cups raspberries
¹/4 cup sugar
2 tablespoons light rum
2 (6-ounce) packages toasted almond
    cookies, such as almond biscotti
2 (2-ounce) packages sliced almonds, toasted

GARNISH
Raspberries
Mint leaves

Whisk the mascarpone cheese, ¹/4 cup sugar, cream and vanilla together in a large bowl.

Combine the raspberries, ¹/4 cup sugar and rum in a bowl and toss to coat the raspberries.

Layer the cookies, the raspberries, the almonds and the mascarpone cheese mixture ¹/2 at a time in an 8×11-inch serving dish. Chill, covered, for 2 to 24 hours. Garnish with raspberries and mint leaves.

NOTE: You may also prepare in individual serving dishes.

TIRAMISU

YIELD: 12 TO 16 SERVINGS

16 ounces mascarpone cheese
1/2 cup sugar
1 cup heavy cream
2 tablespoons light rum
1/2 teaspoon vanilla extract
2 (6-ounce) packages toasted almond
   cookies, such as almond biscotti
1 cup brewed espresso coffee
2 (2-ounce) packages sliced almonds, toasted
2 teaspoons baking cocoa

GARNISH
Sifted baking cocoa
Mint leaves

Whisk the mascarpone cheese, sugar, cream,
rum and vanilla together in a bowl.

Arrange 1/2 of the cookies in a single layer
in an 8×11-inch serving dish. Drizzle with
1/2 of the coffee. Sprinkle with 1/2 of the
almonds. Sift 1/2 of the baking cocoa through
a strainer over the almonds. Spread 1/2 of
the mascarpone cheese mixture over the
baking cocoa. Repeat the layers with the
remaining ingredients.

Chill, covered, for 2 to 24 hours. Garnish
with sifted baking cocoa and mint leaves.

Granulated sugar can also
be flavored with vanilla,
cinnamon, or even citrus
flavors to spice up any
dessert. Brown sugar is white
granulated sugar that has
been combined with a small
amount of molasses. One
firmly packed cup of brown
sugar can be substituted for
a single cup of granulated
sugar. Brown sugar has about
50 more calories per cup than
white granulated sugar. While
similar in color to brown
sugar, raw sugar is actually an
after-product, resulting
from the residue remaining
after the sugar has been
processed and the molasses
has been removed.

SUMMER BERRY TRIFLE

YIELD: 8 SERVINGS

1³/4 cups fresh blueberries
1 (14-ounce) can sweetened condensed milk
1 tablespoon brandy
1 (10-ounce) frozen loaf pound cake, thawed
1 (4-ounce) package white chocolate instant
    pudding mix
1¹/2 cups milk
¹/2 cup sour cream
1¹/2 cups fresh raspberries
1 cup fresh blackberries

Mash ¹/4 cup of the blueberries in a small bowl. Stir in 2 tablespoons of the condensed milk and the brandy.

Cut the pound cake into halves horizontally. Spread the blueberry mixture on the cut side of the bottom half. Place the top half over the blueberry mixture. Cut the cake lengthwise into 4 strips. Cut the cake crosswise into 1-inch-thick pieces.

Beat the remaining condensed milk, pudding mix and milk in a mixing bowl until smooth. Fold in the sour cream. Reserve ¹/2 cup of the pudding mixture.

Layer the pound cake pieces, remaining pudding mixture, remaining blueberries, raspberries and blackberries ¹/2 at a time in a 2- to 2¹/2-quart clear glass bowl. Spoon the reserved pudding mixture over the top.

Chill, covered, for 2 hours or longer.

AMISH COCONUT CAKE

YIELD: 10 TO 12 SERVINGS

CAKE
1 1/2 cups sugar
2 cups flour
1/2 cup shortening
2/3 cup milk
1 teaspoon salt
1 tablespoon baking powder
1/2 cup milk
2 eggs
1/2 teaspoon almond extract
1 teaspoon vanilla extract

FROSTING
4 cups sifted confectioners' sugar
1/2 cup (1 stick) butter, softened
1/4 cup cream
2 teaspoons vanilla extract
1 (7-ounce) package flaked coconut

FOR THE CAKE, beat the sugar, flour, shortening, 2/3 cup milk and salt at medium speed in a mixing bowl for 2 minutes. Add the baking powder, 1/2 cup milk, eggs, almond extract and vanilla and beat for 2 minutes.

Pour the batter into 2 greased and floured 8-inch round cake pans. Bake at 350 degrees for 30 minutes or until the layers spring back when lightly touched. Cool in the pans for 1 hour.

FOR THE FROSTING, beat the confectioners' sugar, butter, cream and vanilla in a mixing bowl until smooth.

TO ASSEMBLE, place 1 cake layer on a cake plate. Spread 1/2 of the frosting over the top and side of the layer. Sprinkle with 1/3 of the coconut.

Place the remaining cake layer over the frosted cake layer. Spread the remaining frosting over the top and side of the layer. Sprinkle the remaining coconut over the top and side of the cake.

STATE FAIR

The Minnesota State Fair not only marks the official end of summer, but it also represents a time for family and friends to remember Minnesota's agricultural roots. Not much can keep Minnesotans away from the State Fair, which has taken place almost every year since 1860—the year after Minnesota was granted statehood—with just a few notable exceptions: the Civil War and Dakota Indian Conflict in 1861 and 1862, scheduling conflicts with the World's Columbian Exposition in Chicago in 1893, wartime fuel shortages during 1945, and the polio epidemic of 1946. In the late 1800s, the fair was held in a different venue each year, including Rochester, Red Wing, Winona, and Owatonna, until it found its permanent home in the Midway region, centrally located between the Twin Cities.

APPLE CAKE

YIELD: 12 SERVINGS

3 cups flour
1 teaspoon salt
1 teaspoon cinnamon
1 teaspoon baking soda
1 1/2 cups vegetable oil
2 cups packed brown sugar
3 eggs
1 teaspoon vanilla extract
3 cups thickly sliced peeled apples

Sift the flour, salt, cinnamon and baking soda together.

Beat the oil and brown sugar in a mixing bowl. Add the eggs and beat until creamy. Stir in the flour mixture. Add the vanilla and mix well. Stir in the apple slices.

Pour the batter into a greased and floured tube pan. Bake at 350 degrees for 1 1/4 hours. Cool in the pan for 20 minutes. Invert onto a serving plate.

CARAMEL PECAN TURTLE CAKE

YIELD: 10 TO 12 SERVINGS

CAKE
2 cups flour
$1^3/4$ cups sugar
$^1/2$ cup baking cocoa
1 teaspoon salt
1 tablespoon baking soda
1 egg
$^2/3$ cup vegetable oil
1 cup buttermilk
1 cup hot coffee

FROSTING
$^1/2$ cup milk
1 cup sugar
6 tablespoons butter
2 cups (12 ounces) semisweet
    chocolate chips
1 or 2 teaspoons hot coffee (optional)

ASSEMBLY
3/4 cup unwrapped caramels
Milk (optional)
$1^1/2$ cups pecans, toasted

FOR THE CAKE, grease three 9-inch round cake pans and line with parchment paper. Combine the flour, sugar, baking cocoa, salt and baking soda in a bowl and mix well. Combine the egg, oil and buttermilk in a separate bowl and mix well.

Add the egg mixture to the dry ingredients and mix well. Pour the hot coffee into the batter slowly, stirring constantly. Pour the batter evenly into the prepared pans.

Bake at 350 degrees for 25 to 30 minutes or until a wooden pick inserted in the center comes out clean. Cool in the pans for 10 minutes. Remove to wire racks to cool completely.

FOR THE FROSTING, combine the milk and sugar in a saucepan and mix well. Add the butter. Bring to a boil. Remove from the heat. Add the chocolate chips and whisk until smooth. Whisk in the coffee if the frosting is too thick or grainy.

TO ASSEMBLE, microwave the caramels in a microwave-safe bowl on High until melted. Stir in a small amount of milk to make a drizzling consistency.

Place one cake layer on a cake plate. Pour $^1/3$ of the frosting over the layer allowing it to partially drip down the side. Sprinkle with $^1/2$ cup of the pecans. Drizzle with $^1/4$ cup of the caramel. Place one of the remaining cake layers over the frosted layer. Pour $^1/2$ of the remaining frosting over the layer allowing it to partially drip down the side. Sprinkle with $^1/2$ cup of the pecans. Drizzle with $^1/4$ cup of the caramel. Repeat with the remaining ingredients. This is delicious served with vanilla ice cream.

BLACK RUSSIAN BUNDT CAKE

YIELD: 12 SERVINGS

CAKE
1 (2-layer) package French vanilla
   cake mix
$^1/_2$ cup sugar
2 (3-ounce) packages chocolate cook-and-
   serve pudding mix
1 cup vegetable oil
$^1/_4$ cup vodka
$^1/_4$ cup Kahlúa
$^3/_4$ cup water
4 eggs

GLAZE
$^1/_2$ cup Kahlúa
$1^1/_2$ to 2 cups confectioners' sugar

GARNISH
Fresh raspberries or strawberries

FOR THE CAKE, combine the cake mix, sugar, pudding mixes, oil, vodka, Kahlúa, water and eggs in a mixing bowl. Beat until smooth and creamy.

Pour the batter into a greased bundt pan. Bake at 375 degrees for 35 to 45 minutes or until the cake tests done.

FOR THE GLAZE, combine the Kahlúa and $1^1/_2$ cups of the confectioner's sugar in a bowl and mix well. Add enough of the remaining confectioners' sugar to make of a thick and pourable consistency.

TO ASSEMBLE, poke holes in the bottom of the warm cake. Pour $^1/_3$ of the glaze over the bottom of the cake. Let stand for 20 minutes. Invert onto a cake plate. Pour the remaining glaze over the top of the cake. Decorate and surround the cake with raspberries or strawberries.

CHOCOLATE LAVA CAKE

YIELD: 6 CAKES

$1/4$ cup sugar
6 tablespoons butter or margarine
4 ounces semisweet chocolate
$1/4$ cup heavy cream
$1/4$ cup flour
$1/2$ teaspoon vanilla extract
2 eggs
2 egg yolks
$1/4$ cup sugar
Confectioners' sugar (optional)

Grease six 6-ounce ramekins and sprinkle with $1/4$ cup sugar.

Heat the butter, chocolate and cream in a medium saucepan over low heat until the butter and chocolate are melted and the mixture is smooth, stirring constantly. Remove from the heat. Whisk in the flour and vanilla.

Beat the eggs, egg yolks and $1/4$ cup sugar at high speed in a mixing bowl for 10 minutes or until thick and pale yellow. Fold into the chocolate mixture $1/3$ at a time.

Pour the batter into the prepared ramekins; filling about $3/4$ full. Place the ramekins on a baking sheet.

Bake at 400 degrees for 9 to 10 minutes or until the edges of the cakes are set but the center is not. Cool for 5 minutes.

Run a knife around the edge of each ramekin and invert onto a dessert plate. Sprinkle with confectioners' sugar. Serve immediately.

NOTE: Sprinkling the ramekins with sugar adds a crisp sugar coating to the dessert. As an option, try sprinkling the ramekins with baking cocoa.

DECORATING THE DESSERT

Any dessert plate can be beautified by "painting" fruit coulis or melted chocolate on the plate. Using a plastic squeeze bottle, create a circular pattern with the sauce and then draw a knife across the sauce for an eye-pleasing pattern. Fresh fruit is a lovely garnish. Prepare a simple granita to pair with fresh fruit for a healthy and light finish to the meal. Frozen pound cake can be dressed up with fresh berries and a dollop of crème fraîche with a fresh mint leaf. Place a paper doily or decorative design of paper on the top of any torte and sift confectioners' sugar or baking cocoa over the torte. Gently remove the doily or other design to reveal a lovely decorative presentation. Edible flowers also dress up any dessert.

CRANBERRY HOLIDAY CAKE

YIELD: 8 TO 12 SERVINGS

CAKE
3 tablespoons butter
1 cup sugar
2 cups flour
1 cup milk
1 tablespoon baking powder
1/4 teaspoon salt
3 cups cranberries

BUTTER SAUCE
1 cup sugar
1 tablespoon flour
1/2 cup (1 stick) butter
1/2 cup cream
1 tablespoon vinegar
1 teaspoon vanilla extract

FOR THE CAKE, combine the butter, sugar, flour, milk, baking powder and salt in a mixing bowl. Beat until smooth and creamy. Fold in the cranberries. Spread the batter evenly in a greased 8- or 9-inch square cake pan. Bake at 350 degrees for 35 to 40 minutes or until the cake tests done.

FOR THE SAUCE, combine the sugar and flour in a saucepan and mix well. Add the butter, cream and vinegar. Cook over high heat until hot and bubbly, stirring constantly. Stir in the vanilla.

TO ASSEMBLE, cut the cake into squares and place on individual serving plates. Spoon the warm sauce over the cake.

CRANBERRY ALMOND POUND CAKE

YIELD: 16 SERVINGS

CAKE
1/4 cup amaretto
1/2 cup dried cranberries
3 cups flour
1/4 teaspoon salt
1 1/4 teaspoons baking powder
1/2 teaspoon baking soda
4 ounces almond paste, at
   room temperature
3/4 teaspoon almond extract
2 1/2 cups sugar
1 cup plus 2 tablespoons unsalted butter
6 eggs
1 cup sour cream
2 cups cranberries

GLAZE
1 1/2 cups confectioners' sugar
3 to 3 1/2 tablespoons amaretto

GARNISH
Sprigs of fresh mint

FOR THE CAKE, heat the amaretto in a small saucepan. Add the dried cranberries. Let stand for 1 1/2 hours or until cool and all of the amaretto has been absorbed, stirring occasionally.

Butter and flour a 10-inch bundt pan, tapping out the excess flour.

Sift the flour, salt, baking powder and baking soda together. Beat the almond paste, almond extract and sugar at low speed in a mixing bowl until well mixed and granular. Add the butter and beat at medium speed for 3 minutes or until light and fluffy. Scrape the bowl down. Add the eggs one at a time, mixing well after each addition. Add the sifted dry ingredients and sour cream alternately 1/3 at a time, mixing well and scraping the bowl down after each addition. Beat for 20 seconds. Fold in the amaretto cranberries and cranberries.

Pour the batter into the prepared pan. Smooth the top and tap lightly on the counter. Bake at 325 degrees for 50 to 60 minutes or until a wooden pick inserted in the center comes out clean. Cool in the pan for 20 minutes. Invert onto a cake plate.

FOR THE GLAZE, sift the confectioners' sugar into a small bowl. Add the amaretto gradually, stirring constantly until smooth.

TO ASSEMBLE, drizzle the glaze over the warm cake. Garnish with mint. Serve with vanilla ice cream.

NOTE: You may bake the cake in individual fluted muffin cups for 20 to 30 minutes or until the cakes test done.

CRANBERRY CARAMEL CAKE

YIELD 8 SERVINGS

CAKE
2 cups flour
1 cup sugar
2 teaspoons baking powder
1/2 teaspoon salt
2/3 cup evaporated milk
1/3 cup water
1 tablespoon butter, melted
2 cups fresh cranberries

SWEET SAUCE
1/2 cup (1 stick) butter
1 cup sugar
2/3 cup evaporated milk
1 teaspoon vanilla extract

FOR THE CAKE, combine the flour, sugar, baking powder and salt in a bowl and mix well. Add the evaporated milk, water and butter and mix well. Stir in the cranberries. Spoon into a buttered 5x9-inch loaf pan. Bake at 350 degrees for 1 hour. Cool in the pan for 10 minutes. Remove to a wire rack to cool completely.

FOR THE SAUCE, heat the butter in a saucepan until melted. Stir in the sugar and evaporated milk. Bring to a boil. Boil for 1 minute, stirring constantly. Remove from the heat. Stir in the vanilla.

TO ASSEMBLE, cut the cake into slices and place on individual dessert plates. Spoon the warm sauce over the cake.

NOTE: Store any leftover cake and sauce in the refrigerator. The cake may be frozen or kept in the refrigerator for several weeks.

CRAZY BUTTERMILK CAKE

YIELD: 12 TO 15 SERVINGS

CAKE

2 cups sugar
2 cups flour
1 cup water
1/4 cup baking cocoa
1/2 cup (1 stick) butter
2 eggs
1 teaspoon vanilla extract
1/2 cup buttermilk
1 teaspoon baking soda

FROSTING

3 cups confectioners' sugar
1/2 cup (1 stick) butter
2 teaspoons vanilla extract
1/4 cup baking cocoa
6 tablespoons milk

FOR THE CAKE, combine the sugar and flour in a bowl and mix well. Bring the water, baking cocoa and butter to a boil in a saucepan, stirring frequently. Pour into the sugar mixture and mix well. Add the eggs, vanilla, buttermilk and baking soda. Beat until smooth and creamy. Pour into a 9×13-inch cake pan.

Bake at 350 degrees for 30 to 35 minutes or until a wooden pick inserted in the center comes out clean.

FOR THE FROSTING, combine the confectioners' sugar, butter, vanilla, cocoa and milk in a saucepan. Bring to a boil.

TO ASSEMBLE, pour the hot glaze over the hot cake.

NOTE: Prepare the frosting during the last 5 minutes of baking the cake and pour over the cake as soon as it is removed from the oven.

RUM CAKE

YIELD: 16 SERVINGS

CAKE
$^1/_2$ cup finely chopped pecans
1 (2-layer) package yellow cake mix
1 (4-ounce) package vanilla instant
   pudding mix
$^1/_2$ cup light rum
$^1/_2$ cup water
$^1/_2$ cup vegetable oil
4 eggs

GLAZE
$^1/_4$ cup light rum
$^1/_4$ cup water
1 cup sugar
$^1/_2$ cup (1 stick) butter

GARNISH
Pecans

FOR THE CAKE, spray a bundt pan with nonstick cooking spray. Sprinkle the pecans over the bottom of the pan. Combine the cake mix, pudding mix, rum, water, oil and eggs in a mixing bowl. Beat for 2 minutes. Pour into the prepared pan. Bake at 325 degrees for 50 minutes.

FOR THE GLAZE, combine the rum, water, sugar and butter in a saucepan. Bring to a boil. Boil for 2 minutes.

TO ASSEMBLE, pour $^1/_2$ of the glaze over the warm cake in the pan. Let stand for 30 minutes. Invert onto a cake plate. Pour the remaining glaze over the cake. Garnish with pecans.

PECAN PEACH CAKE WITH CARAMEL GLAZE

YIELD: 12 TO 16 SERVINGS

CAKE
1/4 cup (1/2 stick) butter, softened
1/2 cup sugar
1 egg
1 cup flour
3/4 teaspoon baking powder
1/2 teaspoon baking soda
1/2 teaspoon allspice
1/2 cup sour cream
3/4 cup chopped frozen peaches, thawed
3 tablespoons chopped pecans
3/4 teaspoon vanilla extract
1/4 teaspoon almond extract

CARAMEL GLAZE
2 tablespoons butter
2 tablespoons brown sugar
1 tablespoon milk
1/2 cup confectioners' sugar
1/4 teaspoon vanilla extract

FOR THE CAKE, beat the butter at medium speed in a mixing bowl until light and fluffy. Add the sugar gradually, beating constantly. Add the egg and mix well.

Combine the flour, baking powder, baking soda and allspice in a bowl and mix well. Add to the butter mixture alternately with the sour cream, mixing well after each addition and beginning and ending with the flour mixture. Stir in the peaches, pecans, vanilla and almond extract.

Pour the cake batter into a 6-cup bundt pan sprayed with nonstick cooking spray. Bake at 350 degrees for 45 minutes or until a wooden pick inserted in the center comes out clean. Cool in the pan on a wire rack for 10 minutes. Invert onto a cake plate. Cool completely.

FOR THE GLAZE, heat the butter in a saucepan until melted. Add the brown sugar. Cook over medium heat until the sugar dissolves, stirring constantly. Remove from the heat. Add the milk and mix well. Add the confectioners' sugar and vanilla. Beat at medium speed until the glaze is smooth.

TO ASSEMBLE, drizzle the hot glaze immediately over the cooled cake; the glaze will thicken as it cools.

NOTE: For a tropical flavor substitute mangoes for the peaches.

UPSIDE-DOWN PLUM CAKE

YIELD: 8 SERVINGS

5 large red plums
6 tablespoons unsalted butter, softened
1 cup packed light brown sugar
1 tablespoon honey
1 1/2 cups flour
2 teaspoons baking powder
1/2 teaspoon cinnamon
1/4 teaspoon salt
6 tablespoons unsalted butter, softened
1 cup sugar
2 eggs
1/2 teaspoon vanilla extract
1/4 teaspoon almond extract
1/2 cup milk
1 cup whipping cream
1/2 to 1 teaspoon confectioners' sugar

Cut the plums into halves. Cut each half into 6 wedges. Heat 6 tablespoons butter, brown sugar and honey in a heavy medium skillet over low heat until the butter melts and a thick smooth sauce is formed, stirring constantly. Pour evenly over the bottom of a 2-inch-deep 9-inch round cake pan. Arrange the plums skin side down in an overlapping concentric circle over the sauce.

Combine the flour, baking powder, cinnamon and salt in a bowl and mix well. Beat 6 tablespoons butter in a mixing bowl until light and fluffy. Add the sugar and beat until light and fluffy. Add the eggs and mix well. Beat in the vanilla and almond extract. Add the dry ingredients alternately with the milk, mixing just until blended after each addition; do not overmix.

Spoon the batter evenly over the plums. Bake at 350 degrees for 1 hour or until a wooden pick inserted in the center comes out clean. Cool in the pan on a wire rack for 30 minutes.

Loosen the cake from the side of the pan. Place a cake plate over the cake pan. Invert the cake pan and place the plate on a work surface. Let stand for 5 minutes. Remove the cake pan.

Pour the whipping cream into a chilled mixing bowl. Beat at high speed until soft peaks form. Add enough confectioners' sugar to make of the desired sweetness. Beat until stiff peaks form. Serve over the cake.

BLUEBERRIES AND CREAM PIE

YIELD: 6 SERVINGS

3 tablespoons flour
3 tablespoons unsalted butter, softened
1/2 cup chopped pecans
1 cup sour cream
2 tablespoons flour
3/4 cup sugar
1 egg, beaten
1 teaspoon vanilla extract
1/2 teaspoon grated lemon zest
1/4 teaspoon salt
2 1/4 cups blueberries
1 unbaked (9-inch) pie shell

Combine 3 tablespoons flour, butter and
pecans in a bowl and mix until crumbly.
Set aside.

Combine the sour cream, 2 tablespoons flour,
sugar, egg, vanilla, lemon zest and salt in a bowl
and mix until smooth. Fold in the blueberries.

Spoon the filling into the pie shell. Bake at 400
degrees for 25 minutes. Sprinkle with the
pecan mixture. Bake for 10 minutes. Let stand
until room temperature. Chill, covered, in
the refrigerator.

Agriculture is one of the economic mainstays of Minnesota's economy. Among the fifty states, Minnesota ranks in the top five in its production of soybeans, corn, wheat, sugar, beets, wild rice, milk cows and dairy products, pork, and turkeys. In addition, Minnesota exports more mink pelts than any state other than Wisconsin and Utah. The total receipts from agricultural products rank Minnesota sixth in the nation. Due to its northern location, the growing season in Minnesota is quite short, most fields are not planted until May, and harvesting generally takes place in September and early October.

CRANBERRY WALNUT PIE

YIELD: 8 TO 10 SERVINGS

2 cups cranberries
$1/2$ cup sugar
$1/2$ cup chopped walnuts
2 eggs
1 cup sugar
1 cup flour
$1/2$ cup (1 stick) butter, melted
$1/4$ cup vegetable oil

Sprinkle the cranberries, $1/2$ cup sugar and walnuts evenly over the bottom of a 9-inch pie plate.

Beat the eggs in a mixing bowl. Beat in the sugar. Add the flour and mix well. Add the melted butter and oil and mix well. Beat at low speed for 1 minute.

Pour the filling over the cranberries in the pie plate. Bake at 325 degrees for 45 minutes. You may serve this with whipped cream, cinnamon whipped cream, vanilla ice cream or cinnamon ice cream.

BUTTERSCOTCH CRUMB APPLE PIE

YIELD: 8 SERVINGS

PIE

6 cups sliced peeled tart cooking apples,
    such as Granny Smith
1 1/2 teaspoons lemon juice
1/2 cup sugar
1/4 cup flour
1 teaspoon cinnamon
1/8 teaspoon salt
1 unbaked (9-inch) deep-dish pie shell

TOPPING

1 cup (6 ounces) butterscotch chips
1/4 cup (1/2 stick) butter
3/4 cup flour
1/8 teaspoon salt

FOR THE PIE, combine the apples and lemon juice in a bowl and toss until the apples are coated. Add the sugar, flour, cinnamon and salt and mix well. Spoon into the pie shell. Cover the edge with foil. Bake at 375 degrees for 20 to 30 minutes or until the apples are tender and the filling is bubbly.

FOR THE TOPPING, place the butterscotch chips and butter over hot water. Cook until the chips are melted and the mixture is smooth, stirring frequently. Remove from the heat. Add the flour and salt and mix until crumbly.

TO ASSEMBLE, remove the foil from the edge of the pie. Crumble the topping over the pie. Bake at 375 degrees for 25 minutes. You may serve with whipped cream or ice cream.

PEAR TART

YIELD: 8 TO 10 SERVINGS

3 ounces almond paste
$1/3$ cup sugar
$1/2$ cup (1 stick) unsalted butter, softened
2 eggs
$3/4$ cup almonds, roasted and ground
1 teaspoon vanilla extract
$1/4$ cup melted bittersweet chocolate
1 unbaked (9-inch) tart shell
4 firm ripe winter pears, sliced
Juice of 1 lemon
4 ounces apricot preserves, melted and
    strained

Cream the almond paste and sugar in a mixing bowl. Add the butter and beat until smooth. Add the eggs and beat until smooth. Add the almonds and vanilla and mix well.

Brush the melted chocolate over the bottom of the tart shell. Pour the filling evenly over the chocolate. Bake at 350 degrees for 35 to 40 minutes or until the filling is set in the center and light brown. Cool on a wire rack.

Toss the pears with the lemon juice in a bowl to coat. Arrange the pear slices in concentric circles over the baked filling. Brush with the preserves.

FRESH STRAWBERRY PIE

YIELD: 8 SERVINGS

GRAHAM CRACKER CRUST
1¹/2 cups crushed graham crackers
2 to 4 tablespoons sugar
¹/4 cup (¹/2 stick) butter, melted

STRAWBERRY FILLING
5 to 6 cups Minnesota strawberries, hulled
1¹/2 cups water
³/4 cup sugar
3 tablespoons cornstarch
1 (3-ounce) package strawberry gelatin

FOR THE CRUST, combine the graham crackers, enough sugar to make of the desired sweetness and butter in a bowl and mix well. Press over the bottom and up the side of a large pie plate. Bake at 325 degrees for 10 minutes.

FOR THE FILLING, fill the prepared crust with the strawberries. Combine the water, sugar and cornstarch in a small saucepan and mix well. Bring to a boil over medium heat, stirring frequently. Boil for 2 minutes or until sauce is clear and thick. Remove from the heat. Add the gelatin and stir until dissolved. Pour over the strawberries.

Chill for 3 to 4 hours or until set. You may top this with whipped cream.

NOTE: You may substitute a purchased graham cracker pie shell for the home-made pie shell and decrease the strawberries to 4 cups and the water to 1 cup. You may substitute California strawberries for the Minnesota strawberries and increase the sugar to 1 cup.

RHUBARB MERINGUE TART

YIELD: 20 SERVINGS

SHORTBREAD CRUST
1 cup flour
2 tablespoons sugar
Pinch of salt
1/2 cup (1 stick) butter

FILLING
3 egg yolks
1/3 cup half-and-half
1 cup sugar
2 tablespoons flour
2 1/2 cups chopped fresh or frozen rhubarb

MERINGUE
3 egg whites
1/4 teaspoon cream of tartar
5 tablespoons sugar

GARNISH
Mint leaves

FOR THE CRUST, combine the flour, sugar and salt in a bowl and mix well. Cut in the butter until crumbly. Press over the bottom of an 8×10-inch baking pan. Bake at 325 degrees for 20 to 25 minutes or until light brown.

FOR THE FILLING, whisk the egg yolks, half-and-half, sugar and flour together in a saucepan. Stir in the rhubarb. Cook for 25 minutes or until the filling is thickened, stirring constantly; do not burn. Pour over the prepared crust.

FOR THE MERINGUE, beat the egg whites and cream of tartar in a mixing bowl until soft peaks form. Add the sugar gradually, beating constantly until stiff peaks form. Spoon over the filling and spread to the edge to seal. Bake at 325 degrees for 10 minutes. Garnish with mint leaves.

LEMON TART WITH STRAWBERRIES

YIELD: 8 TO 10 SERVINGS

CRUST

1 cup flour
1/3 cup sliced almonds
1/4 cup sugar
1/4 teaspoon salt
6 tablespoons unsalted butter
1/2 teaspoon almond extract
3 to 5 tablespoons cold water

TART

3 eggs
3 egg yolks
1 cup sugar
3/4 cup lemon juice
2 tablespoons grated lemon zest
Pinch of salt
6 tablespoons unsalted butter
2 cups sliced strawberries
3 tablespoons apricot jam
1 tablespoon water

GARNISH

Fanned strawberries, blackberries, star fruit,
    sliced kiwifruit, candied cranberries or
    lemon twists

FOR THE CRUST, process the flour, almonds, sugar and salt in a food processor until mixed. Add the butter and process until crumbly. Add the almond extract. Add the cold water 1 tablespoon at a time, pulsing until the mixture forms a ball. Chill, wrapped in plastic wrap, for 1 hour.

Roll into a 12-inch circle on a lightly floured surface. Fit into a 9-inch tart pan with a removable bottom sprayed with nonstick cooking spray, trimming the edge. Freeze for 30 minutes. Bake at 425 degrees for 20 to 25 minutes or until the crust begins to brown.

FOR THE TART, whisk the eggs, egg yolks, sugar, lemon juice, lemon zest and salt together in a large saucepan. Add the butter. Cook over medium-low heat for 8 to 10 minutes or until the filling thickens slightly, stirring constantly. Strain through a fine mesh sieve into the prepared crust. Bake at 325 degrees for 10 minutes or until the filling is set. Cool on a wire rack.

Arrange the strawberry slices in concentric circles over the baked filling. Whisk the apricot jam and water in a small microwave-safe bowl. Microwave on High until warm. Brush over the strawberries. Garnish with fanned strawberries, blackberries, star fruit, sliced kiwifruit, candied cranberries or lemon twists.

NOTE: To fan strawberries, make 5 to 7 slices from the tip to 1/4 inch from the stem and separate the sliced sections into a fan. For candied cranberries, heat 1/3 cup cranberries and 2 tablespoons sugar in a small saucepan over medium heat until the sugar begins to dissolve, stirring constantly. Roll the cranberries in additional sugar when cool enough to handle.

Situated approximately fifteen miles south of the Twin Cities in Chanhassen, the Minnesota Landscape Arboretum sits on more than one thousand acres of rolling prairie. The Arboretum is open to the general public but also serves as a teaching and research site for the University of Minnesota's Department of Horticultural Science. Not surprisingly, much of the research focuses on how plants survive or can be modified to sustain the cold weather. During warm weather, visitors can enjoy a hike through a native prairie, near a natural marsh, or through northern woodlands; during the winter, the Arboretum hosts many cross-country skiers, snowshoers, and winter hikers.

PECAN CRUNCH COOKIES

YIELD: 3 1/2 DOZEN

1 cup (2 sticks) butter or
　　margarine, softened
1/2 cup sugar
1 teaspoon vanilla extract
1/2 cup crushed potato chips
1/2 cup chopped pecans
2 cups sifted flour
Sugar
Red or green sugar crystals, pecans, or
　　candied cherry halves (optional)

Cream the butter, 1/2 cup sugar and vanilla in a mixing bowl until light and fluffy. Add the potato chips and 1/2 cup pecans and mix well. Stir in the flour.

Shape 1 tablespoon of the dough into a ball. Place on ungreased cookie sheets. Press flat with the bottom of a glass dipped in sugar. Repeat with the remaining dough.

Sprinkle with sugar crystals or top with a pecan or candied cherry half. Bake at 350 degrees for 16 to 18 minutes or until light brown.

ALMOND SUGAR COOKIES

YIELD: 2 TO 3 DOZEN

COOKIES
2^1/2 cups flour

1 teaspoon baking soda

1 teaspoon cream of tartar

1^1/2 cups confectioners' sugar

1 cup (2 sticks) unsalted butter, softened

1 egg

1 teaspoon vanilla extract

^{1}/2 teaspoon almond extract

ICING
2 cups confectioners' sugar

^{1}/2 teaspoon vanilla extract

^{1}/2 teaspoon almond extract

2 tablespoons butter, melted

2 to 3 tablespoons milk

FOR THE COOKIES, sift the flour, baking soda and cream of tartar together. Cream the confectioners' sugar and butter in a mixing bowl until light and fluffy. Add the egg, vanilla and almond extract and mix well. Beat in the sifted dry ingredients. Flatten the dough into a disk. Chill, wrapped in plastic wrap, for 3 hours.

Roll ^{1}/8-inch-thick on a floured surface. Cut with a cookie cutter into desired shapes. Place on nonstick cookie sheets. Bake at 375 degrees for 8 to 9 minutes or until light brown. Cool on wire racks.

FOR THE ICING, combine the confectioners' sugar, vanilla, almond extract and butter in a bowl and mix well. Add the milk 1 tablespoon at a time until the desired consistency, mixing well after each addition.

Dip the cooled cookies in the icing.

LEMON AND SPICE SUGAR COOKIES

YIELD: 3 DOZEN

COOKIES
$^1/_2$ cup (1 stick) butter, softened
$^3/_4$ cup sugar
1 egg
1 teaspoon milk
2 cups flour
$^1/_4$ teaspoon salt
$^1/_4$ teaspoon nutmeg
$^1/_4$ teaspoon baking powder

ICING
$^1/_4$ cup ($^1/_2$ stick) butter, softened
2 cups confectioners' sugar, sifted
$^1/_4$ cup heavy cream
2 teaspoons lemon juice
2 teaspoons vanilla extract
Food coloring (optional)

FOR THE COOKIES, cream the butter and sugar in a mixing bowl until light and fluffy. Add the egg and milk and mix well. Add the flour gradually, beating constantly. Add the salt, nutmeg and baking powder and mix well.

Roll the dough $^1/_8$-inch-thick on a floured surface. Cut with cookie cutters into desired shapes. Place on nonstick cookie sheets. Bake at 375 degrees for 11 to 13 minutes or until the cookies begin to brown on the edges. Cool on wire racks.

FOR THE ICING, cream the butter in a mixing bowl until light and fluffy. Add the confectioners' sugar alternately with the cream, mixing well after each addition. Beat until light and fluffy. Add the lemon juice, vanilla and food coloring and mix well. Spread over the cooled cookies.

Always Superb: Recipes for Every Occasion

SCANDINAVIAN TEA CAKES

YIELD: 2 DOZEN

1 cup (2 sticks) butter or
   margarine, softened
$^1/_3$ cup sugar
2 teaspoons water
2 teaspoons vanilla extract
2 cups flour
1 cup chopped nuts
Confectioners' sugar for rolling

Cream the butter and sugar in a mixing bowl until light and fluffy. Add the water and vanilla and mix well. Add the flour and mix well. Stir in the nuts. Chill the dough.

Shape the dough into 2 dozen balls and place on ungreased cookie sheets. Bake at 325 degrees for 20 minutes. Cool on wire racks. Roll in confectioners' sugar.

WHITE CHOCOLATE MACADAMIA NUT COOKIES

YIELD: 4 DOZEN

$^3/_4$ cup packed brown sugar
$^1/_2$ cup sugar
1 cup (2 sticks) butter, softened
$^1/_2$ teaspoon vanilla extract
$^1/_2$ teaspoon almond extract
2 extra-large eggs
$2^1/_2$ cups flour
1 teaspoon baking soda
$^1/_2$ teaspoon salt
$^3/_4$ cup coarsely chopped macadamia nuts
1 cup finely chopped white chocolate

Cream the brown sugar, sugar and butter in a mixing bowl until light and fluffy. Add the vanilla and almond extract and mix well. Add the eggs and beat until creamy.

Combine the flour, baking soda and salt in a bowl and mix well. Gradually add to the butter mixture, beating constantly at low speed. Stir in the macadamia nuts and white chocolate pieces.

Drop cookie dough by teaspoonfuls onto ungreased cookie sheets. Bake at 350 degrees for 10 minutes or until golden brown. Cool on wire racks.

A LOT OF CHOCOLATE

Chocolate is derived from the cocoa bean and literally means "bitter." The term "unsweetened chocolate" refers to chocolate that does not have sugar, milk, or other additives. When sugar, lecithin, or vanilla is added, chocolate is then classified as bittersweet, semisweet, or sweet chocolate, depending on the percentage of cocoa butter. Chocolate should have a pleasant lingering aftertaste and should be uniformly textured throughout. To ensure the flavor and texture, chocolate should be stored at 60 to 70 degrees, and should not be stored with foods with strong odors, as it will absorb the odor. Likewise, it may develop a pale gray film on its surface when stored at a higher temperature or may form tiny sugar crystals on its surface if stored in a damp location. Chocolate should be stored no more than nine months, due to milk solids.

CHOCOLATE TRUFFLE BARS

YIELD: 3 TO 4 DOZEN

BARS
10 eggs
$^1/_2$ cup sugar
1 tablespoon vanilla extract
$^1/_4$ cup flour
2 cups (4 sticks) butter
6 cups (36 ounces) semisweet
  chocolate chips

FROSTING
2 cups (12 ounces) semisweet
  chocolate chips
1 cup (2 sticks) butter

FOR THE BARS, beat the eggs, sugar and vanilla in a mixing bowl. Add the flour and mix well. Heat the butter and chocolate chips in a saucepan until melted, stirring constantly. Stir into the egg mixture. Pour into an ungreased 10×15-inch baking pan. Bake at 350 degrees for 20 minutes.

FOR THE FROSTING, melt the chocolate chips and butter in a saucepan over low heat, stirring constantly. Spread over the baked layer.

Cool the frosted layer in the pan. Cut into small bars.

NOTE: You may substitute fresh raspberries for the frosting.

GINGER SPiCE COOKIES

YIELD: 6 DOZEN

1 3/4 cups firmly packed dark brown sugar
1 1/2 cups (3 sticks) butter, softened
1 egg
1 tablespoon grated gingerroot
3 3/4 cups flour
1/2 cup finely ground walnuts
2 tablespoons ground ginger
1 tablespoon cinnamon
2 teaspoons freshly ground nutmeg
1/2 teaspoon ground white pepper
1/4 teaspoon freshly ground cloves
1/2 teaspoon salt
1 1/4 teaspoons baking powder
1/4 cup turbinado sugar (raw golden sugar),
   granulated sugar or red hot
   cinnamon candies

Cream the brown sugar and butter in a mixing bowl until light and fluffy. Add the egg and gingerroot and mix well.

Whisk the flour, walnuts, ginger, cinnamon, nutmeg, white pepper, cloves, salt and baking powder together in a bowl. Add to the butter mixture gradually, beating constantly until well mixed. Shape the dough into 2 disks. Chill, wrapped in plastic wrap, for 4 to 12 hours.

Remove one of the dough disks from the refrigerator. Let stand for 15 minutes. Remove the plastic wrap. Place the disk between two 10×15-inch sheets of waxed paper. Roll 1/8-inch-thick. If the dough cracks, let stand for 10 minutes longer before rolling. Slide the waxed paper with the rolled dough onto a cookie sheet. Freeze for 5 to 10 minutes or until the dough is stiff enough to be unsupported by the cookie sheet.

Peel the top sheet of waxed paper off the dough. Cut with a 2 inch gingerbread boy cookie cutter. Slide the boy off the waxed paper with a large spatula and place onto parchment-lined cookie sheets. Repeat with the remaining dough; the dough may be rerolled.

Sprinkle the gingerbread boys with turbinado sugar, granulated sugar or place a candy in the center of the tummy. Bake at 350 degrees for 8 to 10 minutes or until crisped and brown. Cool on wire racks.

NOTE: You may shape 1 teaspoon dough into a ball, place on parchment-lined cookie sheets and press flat with a glass dipped in sugar instead of cutting into gingerbread boys. You may shape the dough into logs instead of disks before chilling. Cut the chilled logs into 1/4-inch-thick slices, place the slices on parchment-lined baking sheets, sprinkle with sugar and bake for 10 minutes or until crisp. You may also sprinkle with granulated or confectioners' sugar after baking.

CRÈME DE MENTHE BARS

4 eggs
1 cup sugar
$^1/_2$ cup (1 stick) margarine, softened
1 cup flour
1 (16-ounce) bottle chocolate syrup
1 teaspoon vanilla extract
2 cups confectioners' sugar
$^1/_2$ cup (1 stick) margarine, softened
2 tablespoons milk
$^1/_2$ teaspoon peppermint extract
Green food coloring
1 cup (6 ounces) semisweet chocolate chips
6 tablespoons margarine

Beat the eggs in a mixing bowl. Add the sugar, $^1/_2$ cup margarine, flour, chocolate syrup and vanilla and mix well. Pour into a 9×13-inch baking pan. Bake at 350 degrees for 25 to 30 minutes. Cool completely.

Combine the confectioners' sugar, $^1/_2$ cup margarine, milk and peppermint extract in a bowl and mix until smooth. Add enough green food coloring to make of the desired tint and mix well. Spread over the cooled layer.

Heat the chocolate chips and 6 tablespoons margarine in a saucepan over low heat until the mixture is smooth, stirring constantly. Spread over the mint layer. Let stand until completely cool. Cut into bars.

DATE BARS

YIELD: 4 DOZEN

CRUST
$^3/_4$ cup (1$^1/_2$ sticks) butter or
    margarine, melted
3 tablespoons brown sugar
1$^1/_2$ cups flour

FILLING
2 eggs, lightly beaten
2 tablespoons flour
1 teaspoon vanilla extract
1$^1/_2$ cups packed brown sugar
2 cups chopped pitted dates
1 cup chopped nuts

FROSTING
$^1/_4$ cup ($^1/_2$ stick) butter or
    margarine, softened
2 tablespoons milk
2 cups confectioners' sugar
$^1/_2$ teaspoon vanilla extract
$^1/_4$ teaspoon almond extract

FOR THE CRUST, combine the melted butter, brown sugar and flour in a bowl and mix well. Spread over the bottom of a 9×13-inch ungreased baking pan. Bake at 350 degrees for 10 minutes.

FOR THE FILLING, combine the eggs, flour, vanilla and brown sugar in a bowl and mix well. Stir in the dates and nuts. Spread over the baked crust. Bake for 25 to 30 minutes. Cool for 30 minutes.

FOR THE FROSTING, beat the butter, milk, confectioners' sugar, vanilla and almond extract in a bowl until smooth. Spread over the baked layer. Let stand until completely cool. Cut into bars.

NUTTY GOOD BARS

YIELD: 40 TO 50 BARS

2 cups (12 ounces) semisweet
   chocolate chips
2 cups (12 ounces) butterscotch chips
2 cups creamy peanut butter
1 (12-ounce) can Spanish peanuts
1/2 cup (1 stick) butter
1/2 cup evaporated milk
1/4 cup vanilla instant pudding mix
2 (16-ounce) packages confectioners'
   sugar, sifted
1 teaspoon vanilla extract

Heat the chocolate chips and butterscotch
chips in a saucepan until melted, stirring
constantly. Add the peanut butter and mix
until smooth. Spread 1/2 of the chocolate
mixture over the bottom of a greased
10x15-inch baking pan. Chill in the
refrigerator. Stir the peanuts into the
remaining chocolate mixture and set aside.

Bring the butter, evaporated milk and pudding
mix to a boil in a saucepan, stirring frequently.
Boil for 1 minute. Remove from the heat. Beat
in the confectioners' sugar 1 cup at a time,
mixing well after each addition. Stir in the
vanilla. Spread over the chilled chocolate layer.

Spread the reserved chocolate mixture over
the layers. Chill, covered, until firm. Cut into
small bars. Store, covered, in the refrigerator.

KAHLÚA PRALINE BROWNIES

YIELD: 3 DOZEN

PRALINE CRUST
$^1/_3$ cup packed light brown sugar
$5^1/_3$ tablespoons butter, softened
$^2/_3$ cup flour
$^1/_2$ cup finely chopped pecans

BROWNIE FILLING
2 ounces unsweetened chocolate
$^1/_4$ cup shortening
$^1/_4$ cup ($^1/_2$ stick) butter
$^1/_2$ cup sugar
$^1/_2$ cup firmly packed brown sugar
1 teaspoon vanilla extract
2 eggs
$^1/_4$ cup Kahlúa
$^1/_2$ cup flour
$^1/_4$ teaspoon salt
$^1/_2$ cup chopped pecans

KAHLÚA BUTTERCREAM FROSTING
6 tablespoons butter, softened
2 cups sifted confectioners' sugar
1 tablespoon (or more) Kahlúa
1 tablespoon cream

FOR THE CRUST, combine the brown sugar, butter, flour and pecans in a bowl and mix well. Press over the bottom of a 9-inch square baking pan.

FOR THE FILLING, heat the chocolate, shortening and butter in a saucepan over low heat, stirring frequently. Remove from the heat. Let stand for 5 minutes to cool. Beat in the sugar, brown sugar and vanilla. Add the eggs one at a time, mixing well after each addition. Stir in the Kahlúa. Add the flour and salt and mix until smooth. Fold in the pecans. Pour over the crust. Bake at 350 degrees for 25 minutes; do not overbake. Cool completely.

FOR THE FROSTING, beat the butter, confectioners' sugar, 1 tablespoon of the Kahlúa and cream in a mixing bowl until smooth, adding additional Kahlúa if needed to make of desired spreading consistency. Spread over the brownies. Chill for 30 minutes. Cut into bars.

NOTE: You may drizzle the frosted bars with melted semisweet chocolate if desired.

ZESTY CITRUS BARS

YIELD: 12 TO 16 BARS

1/2 cup (1 stick) unsalted butter, softened
1 1/4 cups flour
1/2 cup quick-cooking rolled oats
1/2 cup packed brown sugar
1/4 teaspoon salt
8 ounces cream cheese, softened
1/3 cup sugar
1 egg white
4 teaspoons grated lemon zest
2 teaspoons grated orange zest
1 tablespoon lime juice
1/4 cup milk

Combine the butter, flour, oats, brown sugar
and salt in a bowl and mix until crumbly. Press
1/2 of the crumb mixture over the bottom of
an 8- or 9-inch square baking pan.

Combine the cream cheese, sugar, egg white,
lemon zest, orange zest, lime juice and milk in
a mixing bowl and beat until smooth and
creamy. Pour into the prepared pan. Sprinkle
with the remaining crumb mixture.

Bake at 350 degrees for 30 minutes. Cool
completely. Cut into bars. Store, covered, in
the refrigerator.

ENGLISH TOFFEE

YIELD: 3 TO 4 DOZEN

1 cup sugar
1 cup (2 sticks) butter
3 tablespoons water
1 teaspoon vanilla extract
1 1/2 cups (9 ounces) semisweet
    chocolate chips
1 cup finely chopped walnuts or
    pecans, toasted

Butter a 10x15-inch baking pan.

Combine the sugar, butter, water and vanilla in a heavy 2- or 3-quart saucepan. Bring to a boil over medium-high heat. Boil for 10 minutes or until the mixture registers 305 degrees on a candy thermometer hard-crack stage, stirring constantly. The mixture will darken and begin turning glossy. If you don't have a candy thermometer, drop some of the mixture and if it immediately hardens to a crack stage then it is ready.

Pour the hot candy in the prepared baking pan, spreading to a depth of 1/2 inch; the candy may not completely cover the pan. Sprinkle the chocolate chips immediately over the hot candy and spread over the top as they melt. Continue to spread until the candy is completely covered with chocolate. Sprinkle the walnuts over the warm chocolate.

Let the toffee stand in a cool area until hardened. Break into pieces and store in airtight containers. This candy has a long shelf life.

TASTY TOFFEE

Create a crunch toffee bar as an alternative to making candy: Spread graham crackers on a lightly greased foil-lined baking sheet. Combine 1 cup (2 sticks) butter and 1 cup packed brown sugar in a saucepan and bring to a boil. Boil for 3 minutes and pour over the graham crackers. Bake at 400 degrees for 6 minutes. Remove from the oven and immediately sprinkle with 1 cup (6 ounces) chocolate chips. As the chocolate chips soften, spread over the top. Sprinkle with a couple of handfuls of chopped nuts. Allow to cool and break into bite-size pieces.

The weather in Minnesota is extreme. The difference in temperature between summer and winter might be 120 degrees. In spite of these stark contrasts, Minnesota has four distinct seasons, each with its own rewards. While the average annual temperature of 45° F (7° C) makes Minneapolis the second coldest city in the United States, it's actually a great place to live, at least for six months out of the year!

Average Monthly Temperatures in the Twin Cities

Month	Fahrenheit	Celsius
January	12°	-11°
February	18°	-8°
March	31°	-1°
April	46°	8°
May	59°	15°
June	68°	20°
July	74°	23°
August	71°	22°
September	61°	16°
October	49°	9°
November	33°	1°
December	18°	-8°

HOMEMADE CHOCOLATE PEANUT BUTTER CUPS

YIELD: 1 DOZEN

^{1}/2 cup (1 stick) margarine
^{3}/4 cup peanut butter or other nut butter
^{3}/4 cup graham cracker crumbs
^{1}/4 cup sugar
2 cups (12 ounces) chocolate or carob chips
^{1}/2 cup soy milk
^{1}/4 cup chopped nuts (optional)

Heat the margarine in a small saucepan over medium heat until melted. Add the peanut butter, wafer crumbs and sugar and mix well. Spoon approximately 2 tablespoons of the peanut butter mixture into each of 12 paper-lined muffin cups.

Heat the chocolate chips and soy milk in a separate saucepan over medium heat until the chocolate chips are melted, stirring frequently. Spoon over the top of the peanut butter mixture in each cup. Sprinkle with the nuts.

Chill for 6 to 8 hours or until firm.

HEAVENLY CHOCOLATE SAUCE

YIELD: 2 CUPS

1 cup sugar
^{1}/3 cup baking cocoa
^{1}/4 cup (^{1}/2 stick) butter
^{1}/4 cup milk
1 tablespoon light corn syrup
1 teaspoon vanilla extract

Combine the sugar, baking cocoa, butter, milk and corn syrup in a saucepan. Bring to a simmer. Simmer for 1 minute, stirring constantly. Remove from the heat. Stir in the vanilla.

Store, covered, in the refrigerator for up to 2 weeks. You may serve this over ice cream or pound cake garnished with berries.

PISTACHIO BRITTLE

YIELD: 2 DOZEN

2¹/₂ cups shelled pistachios
1¹/₂ cups sugar
¹/₂ cup light corn syrup
¹/₂ cup cold water
3 tablespoons salted butter
1 teaspoon salt
¹/₄ teaspoon baking soda
1¹/₂ teaspoons vanilla extract

Place the pistachios in a single layer in a 10×15-inch baking pan. Bake at 250 degrees for 5 minutes. Turn the oven off, leaving the pistachios in the oven.

Butter a separate 10×15-inch baking pan.

Combine the sugar, corn syrup and water in a heavy 3-quart saucepan. Bring to a boil over medium heat, wiping down the sugar crystals from the side of the pan with a pastry brush dipped in cold water. Add the butter. Boil until the mixture registers 310 degrees on a candy thermometer, hard-crack stage, stirring frequently. Remove from the heat.

Stir the salt, baking soda and vanilla into the sugar syrup; the mixture will foam. Stir in the pistachios quickly.

Pour the hot mixture in the prepared pan, spreading with a nylon or wooden spatula to form a thin even layer. You may have gaps and irregular edges. Let stand until the brittle cools and hardens.

Break the cooled brittle into chunks. Store at room temperature in an airtight container.

NOTE: This has a wonderful greenish hue and is more unique than the common peanut brittle. It is also very quick to make.

Special Thank Yous

Special Thank Yous

Special thanks to the professionals who have donated their time, expertise, and support to the creation of this cookbook.

Ampersand—A charming gift and home decor store located in Edina, MN, 952-920-2118

Meg Brownson—A graduate of the Culinary Institute of America, Hyde Park, New York, owner of Alfresco Casual Living for Home and Garden, Stillwater, MN 55082, 651-439-0812

Thecla Forsman, Culinary student at Ai Minnesota

Identity Printing, Inc.

Monette Kollodge Design

LA Specialities Produce

Risdall Advertising Agency, New Brighton, MN, www.risdall.com, 1-888-RISDALL

Stuart Sandler— FontDiner.com

Steve Schenten — Photographer's Assistant

Matthew Slimmer—Studio Manager of Forsman Studios

Barbara Stark, Stark Raving Goodies, New Brighton, MN, 651-636-6059

Katie Sutton, Owner/Chef, LePoulet Coup Catering

Andrew Sutton, Executive Chef, Napa Rose Restaurant, Anaheim, California

T. R. Christian, Inc.—An elegant shop that carries dinnerware, glassware, and unusual gifts. Edina, MN, 1-800-788-9805, www.trchristian.com

Always Superb: Recipes for Every Occasion

Special Thank Yous

Red Mariposa all-purpose wine glasses from Ampersand (952-920-2118)

Napkin by LeJacquard Francaise from Ampersand

Simon Pearce dessert bowl from Ampersand

Props from T.R. Christian

Contributors

Thank you to all of the members, friends, and families of the Junior Leagues of Minneapolis and Saint Paul. We apologize for any errors or omissions.

Terry Aas
Julia Adams
Kaye Adams
Nancee Adelman
Kathleen Amundson
Patty Andersen
Anna Anderson
Ruth Anderson
Anna Andrew
Allen Andrews
Colleen Arey
Maureen Arnold
Trey Attenose
Dawn Bagaas
Crystal Baker
Janice Barker
Mary Bartlett
Florence Baskfield
Ellie Bathe
Cinda Baxter
Sherry Beck
Gretchen Beiswanger
Lely Beitner
Mary Ann Betts
Rebecca Bishop
Carolyn Blodgett
Sally Blood
Lisa Bock
Patricia Boehmer

Julie Boeshart
Leslie Boie
Patty Boo-Pryor
Dana Booth
Michelle Botkin
Elizabeth R. Boyd
Debbie Bradley
Penny Bradshaw
Erin Brass
Virginia Broberg
Marie Brodmerkel
Beth Bulach
Tory Bunce
Liz Burger
Ann Marie Butler
Pamela Byrnes
Katherine Calengor
Laura Cantrell
Dolores Cardon
Mary Carroll
Amy Carson
Danielle Carter
Kayleen Caulfield
Mary Cederberg
Patti Christianson
Mary Clanton
Annie Cleveland
Cynthia Coler
Nicole Cordero

Cynthia Courtney
Mary Cramer
Andrea Crockett-Sticha
Peggy Cummings
Molly Curren
Amy Cutter
Pauline Dahl
Diana Manuel Danielson
Laurie Danley
Amie Davis
Cathy Davis
Sandy Day
Polly Dean
Joaquin Delgado
Mei Delgado
Christine deVillers
Rebecca Diekmann
Adel Dimian
Nikki Dobbs
Michele Dobin
Kathleen Dodson-Smith
Lisa Dolan
Shannon Dollerschell
Cheryl Douglas
Deborah Dove
Jayne Dow
Carlon Doyle
Julie Drake
Christine Droubie

Always Superb: Recipes for Every Occasion

Jill Droubie
Jenna Dulas
Liz Duman
Shannon Dunleavy
Heather Durenberger
Roxanne Eggen
Carol Enck
Mary Enck
Joan Erdman
Cindy Ericson
Camie Eugster
Jamine Ewine
Sue Eull
Anne Farrar
Jane Farrell
Lisa Finsness
Pat Fleet
Laurie Fleming
Georgia Forchuk
Cynthia Forrest
Penny Freeman
Genevieve Freier
Susan Frommelt
Tamara Fuller
Susan Gabler
Lisa Gallmeyer
Kathryn Knoll Gantriis
Sue Ellen Gebert
Kathleen Gertz

Phyllis Giordano
Erica Giorgi
Candace Gislason
Fran Glover
Mary Sue Godfrey
Isabel Goepferd
Kristen Goetze
Kay Golden
Deb Grayson
Mary Hageman
Brandi Hagen
Margaret Haglund
Rosalie Haglund
Marcia Hall
Amy Hammerschmidt
Peggy Hansen
Kathie Harder
Sarah Hardy
Dana Harrison
Cheryl Harrison
Claire Harvey
Dorothy Hautman
Rachelle Heinen
Marla Heisterkamp
Anne-Marie Hendrickson
Patty Hergott
Shea Hermes
Laura Hewitt
Sue Hodder

Mary Lee Hoffman
Heidi Holley
Michelle Holm
Jane Hopkins
Elizabeth Horton
Carolyn Horttor
Andrea Hougaard
Jill Houliston
Heather Hoyt
Samantha Hubbard
Kim Hunnewell
Chris Ignatik
Jerri Jackson
Jennifer Jaffe
Anne Jennen
Amy Johnson
Dana Johnson
Joan Johnson
Jon Johnson
Julie Johnson
Karen Johnson
Karin Johnson
Lori Johnson
Mary Johnson
Jamie Jones
Karen Judge
Maura Juelich
Claire Justinaniano
Amy Kalgren

Contributors

Lindsay Whipple Kallas
Katy Kenagy
Kathleen Kenney
Betsy Kiernat
Kelly Kilen
Judy Kishel
Catherine Kit
Peggy Kjorstad-Kaatz
Elizabeth Kleber
Kelly Klein
Carolyn Klevgaard
Wendy Klocko
Rene Klumb
Anne Klus
Andrea Knox
Kathryn Koessel
Melissa Dilger Kolb
Jeryn Konezny
Katie Kraus
Gailen Krug
Aasha Desloge Kurr
Rafina Larsen
Lori Lauber
Debbie Lee
Linda Lee
Terri Lee
Terri Lehman
Christine Gerbig-Lema
Maria Lemcke
Paula Len
Amy Leonard
Margaret Leonard

Patty Lillefloren
Nancy Lindahl
Charisse Litteken
Judy Litzow
Harriet Ludwick
Mary Lynch
Julie Madison
Michele Marshall
Cecelia Martin
Tara Martin
Jena Marxer
Sharon Mattison
Landis Mayasich
Jeanette McCauley
Joy McGinnis
Laura McLain
Sara McLenighan
Ellie Meade
Tara Melsha
Ann Marie Metzger
Greig Metzger
Debbie Miller
Iris Miller
Mary Miller
Phyllis Miller
Rhonda Miller
Carole Millis
Charlotte Minor
Margarette Minor
Kris Mollison
Sue Morrison
Christi Movrich

Laura Mueller
Katy Mulheran
Kristyn Mullin
Julie Munderloh
Bess Munsterteiger
Joan Musumeci
Barbara Nanzig
Rose Nanzig
Sarah Nanzig
Jo Ann Neau
Ann Nelson
Jan Nelson
Karen Nelson
Kris Newcomer
Lori Norris
Cynthia North
Kris Nugent
Barb Olmscheid
Esti Olterman
Jane O'Neill
Sonia Palmer
Lesya Parekh
Dolly Parker
Annette Patient
Kristy Paulsen
Jayne Pemmaraju
Polly Perez
Paula Peterson
Margaret Pfohl
Martha Philpott
Terri Pieper
Jane Pirtle

Always Superb: Recipes for Every Occasion

Fiona Pradhan
Polly Prendergast
Kris Prochniak
Nora Ragatz
Ellie Rathe
Kim Reeves
Marcia Rehnberg
Terry Reine
Shannon Richter
Lori Ricke
Robyn Riddle
Sara Rieland
Jennifer Risdall
Eda Rivers
Julie Robicheau
Lisa Robinson
Katie Rottier
Jennifer Ryan
Janet Saint Germain
Jennifer Sall-Balcerzak
Susan Sampson
Stuart Sandler
Tina Scheid
Ashley Schmidt
Robin Schoenwetter
Dinah Swain Schuster
John Scribante
Tina Scribante
Susan Seiler
Mariana Shulstad
Sandy Shuster
David Sisk

Ellen Smith
Patty Smith
Bill Snedeker
Karen Snedeker
Karen Somers
Rachelle Stanko
Gabrielle Stanley
Mary Steele
Lisa Steveken
Cheryl Stever
Jan Storey
April-Lynn Stovern
Elizabeth Streeper
Elaine Swanson
Kari Sweeney
Mary Taylor
Rebecca Taylor
Stephanie Taylor
Tara Lee Teresi
Lauren Thunem
Rima Torgerson
Susan Trammell
Sandra Tranby
Jane Truckenbrod
Jolene Tucker
Mary Underwood
Jane Venell
Kate Vogl
Amy Vose
Tina Wagenbach
Traci Wahl
Betsy Waldo

Janet Waldo
Yolande Waldo
Susan Waldoch
Lisa Walker
Sue Walker
Cyndy Wallin
Sandy Warner
Lisa Warren
Cindy Werner
Barbara Westgard
Ardele Wheeler
Courtney White
Liesl Wiborg
Donna Wilcoxson
Connie Wilde
Lori Wilken
Lindsay Willbanks
Gaye Williams
Suzie Wilmot
Jennifer Winge
Stacy Winjum
Jan Witort
Steve Witort
Jean Wohlrabe
Susan Wolling
Marilyn Wooldridge
Amy Wooters
Sara Yaeger
Julie Young
Laura Zastrow

Index

Always Superb: Recipes for Every Occasion

The Junior Leagues of Minneapolis and Saint Paul have been active in our communities for many years. The purchase of this book will help us to continue our work. We have listed only a few of many projects, some of which you may recognize.

Junior League of Minneapolis

Adopt a Child Care Challenge
Breakfast Buddies*
Bright Beginnings
Bucket Brigade
Children's Protective Society
The Clothes Line*
Free Arts for Abused Children of Minnesota
Girls' Circles*
Greater Minneapolis Crisis Nursery
The Group Home of The City, Inc.
Helping Hands*
Jeremiah Program—Life Skills Education
John H. Stevens House
Leader Within*
LeagueAires*
MOTHEREAD/FATHEREAD-MN
Moving Ahead—
    After Your Breast Cancer Diagnosis
Project Breakthrough
SEEDS/Division of Indian Work*
SEEDS/Lifeskills*
Smart Cents*
Success By 6
Washburn Child Guidance Center

*Current Projects

Junior League of Saint Paul

Awareness, Advice, Advocacy—
    The Child Abuse Project
Bucket Brigade
Children's Hospital Association "Free Bed Fund"
Community Arts Survey
    (now Council of Arts and Sciences)
Community Chest (now Children's Service)
DreamSacks™
Eye and Ear Alert
Harriet Island Information Kiosk
Hands On*
Junior League Convalescent Home
Nature Center Project (now Lee and Rose
    Warner Nature Center)
Next-to-New Sale*
Project Breakthrough
Saint Paul Community Service
    (now Merriam Park Community Center)
Saint Paul Rehabilitation Center for Crippled
    Children and Adults (now Lifetrack Resources)
Science Museum of Minnesota volunteer program
Silent Witness: The Minnesota Effort*
Too Early Pregnancy "Too Far/Too Fast"
Women's Advocates, Inc. *

To Order More Books:

The Junior League of Minneapolis, Inc.	The Junior League of Saint Paul, Inc.
6250 Wayzata Boulevard	633 Snelling Avenue North
Minneapolis, MN 55416	Saint Paul, MN 55104
763-545-9423	651-291-7377
Cookbook @JLMinneapolis.org	*Cookbook @JLSP.org*